C000197618

DANTE'S
INVENTION

DANTE'S INVENTION

JAMES BURGE

The
History
Press

Front cover images: © iStockphoto

First published 2010
This paperback edition 2013

The History Press
The Mill, Brimscombe Port
Stroud, Gloucestershire, GL5 2QG
www.thehistorypress.co.uk

© James Burge, 2010

The right of James Burge to be identified as the Author
of this work has been asserted in accordance with the
Copyrights, Designs and Patents Act 1988.

All rights reserved. No part of this book may be reprinted
or reproduced or utilised in any form or by any electronic,
mechanical or other means, now known or hereafter invented,
including photocopying and recording, or in any information
storage or retrieval system, without the permission in writing
from the Publishers.

British Library Cataloguing in Publication Data.
A catalogue record for this book is available from the British Library.

ISBN 978 0 7524 9922 2

Typesetting and origination by The History Press
Printed in Great Britain

CONTENTS

For Gemma Donati

PREFACE TO THE PAPERBACK EDITION

Dante's *Inferno* has been in print ever since printing was invented and its influence has been felt in every corner of world literature for 700 years. It is a story which begins with a man lost in a dark wood who discovers that his way out is barred by three ferocious beasts. To escape he is obliged to descend through successive circles of Hell to the centre of the earth. Dante's journey, at first sight simple, is made complex by a succession of incidents and encounters.

Inferno has exercised the minds of readers from the start. Questions abound concerning the identity of spirits, the names of demons, the number of circles in Hell, the number of seconds from the beginning of time to the downfall of Satan (about twenty, as it turns out), not forgetting Dante's cord in which some have seen a reference to the Templars who were being massacred while Dante was writing. These puzzles – some solved, some still mysterious – are all part of Dante's purpose. He wanted his readers to understand something which he could not express in a straightforward way. Only a delicate web of allusion and symbolism had a chance of giving them an insight into the true nature of the universe.

As I write this preface, I am conscious that the most recent writer to fall under Dante's influence is the great storyteller, Dan Brown. There will be, no doubt, those who will find reason to quibble with his use of Dante in fiction. They should remember that, although entertainment was not the only purpose of Dante's work, it was important to him. The inferno was originally read out loud to an audience. Keeping their attention at all times was vital and, to achieve it, Dante adjusted the facts where necessary and delighted in adding creatures entirely of his own invention to the denizens of Hell.

That much is part of the craft of fiction, but not the only part. Above all Dante was able to master the mysterious interplay between symbols and narrative which gives fiction its ability to enchant and fascinate. He realised that, in the right hands, a story could even have the power to lead us out of the dark wood.

James Burge, Florence, March 2013

MAPS

Dante's Florence

Key

1. Church of Santa Trinità
2. Spini Palace
3. New Market
4. Orsanmichele
5. Cerchi Palace
6. Donati Palace
7. Dante's House (traditional location)
8. Via dei Cimatori
9. Badia Monastery
10. Palace of the Podestà (Bargello)
11. Palace of the Priors (Palazzo Vecchio)

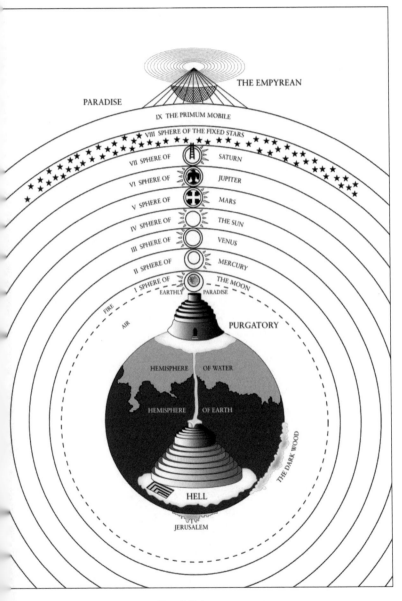

Dante's Universe

INTRODUCTION

This is a book about two stories. The first is the life of Dante Alighieri, a Florentine of the minor nobility who lived at the beginning of the fourteenth century, when the Middle Ages were coming to an end. He fell in love, became a poet and then got involved in sectarian politics which resulted in his exile under threat of death. He studied all the knowledge of his age about the world which, despite everything, he continued to find wonderful. The event which transformed him into something more than a footnote in the history of ideas was his decision to abandon the educational work of popular philosophy on which he had embarked and write fiction instead. The result was what we know as the *Divine Comedy*, the second story with which this book is concerned.

In three parts – Hell, Purgatory and Heaven – the *Comedy* recounts Dante's imagined epic journey to the centre of the earth and out again to the stars. In the course of the tale he presents a picture of the entire universe as it was understood in his age; he gives us a portrait of the human vices and human worth of which he was so acutely aware and he traces a unique view of the connection between his inner feelings of love and the whole of creation. In this book I have presented both these stories, juxtaposed in a way which works quite naturally. Along the way I have tried to show how Dante's supreme craftsmanship as a writer makes the *Comedy* work as fiction, as well as how his life, his ideas and his work all illuminate each other.

As befits the biography of a writer who invented a new form of fiction, this book is intended to be a readable narrative. I hope that the reader will continue to want to turn the page regardless of whether or not they have previous knowledge of Dante's life and work. On the other hand, it is not fiction. The story is constructed entirely from the known facts of Dante's life, of which there are enough to sketch a biography with some certainty.

I have tried always to indicate the evidence for assertions about Dante's life. The question 'how do we know' is one that I always find myself asking. Wherever possible, therefore, I have indicated sources of information in the body of the text. This job has been made easier by the fact that the two main witnesses to the events in his life are interesting characters in themselves, the veracity of whose opinions (and in one case obsession) are all part of the story. Where it is not easy to deduce the sources from what is written I have included endnotes. On the rare occasions where I speculate I have said so. I have also made it clear when I am reporting the speculation of others or, as is more often the case, reporting that centuries-long process of group speculation referred to by historians as 'tradition'.

1

VISION

One day in the year 1284 a young man stood on a street in Florence gazing into space with the distant, dreamy look of an 18-year-old poet. He gave the outward appearance of floating in a sea of his own thoughts yet at the same time he was aware of every person who came into his field of vision. He was hoping for a glimpse of Beatrice. He had first seen her nine years ago when she was 8 years old and he was 9. Since that day he had adored her with an intensity that had turned into an independent force, 'Her image, always in my mind, inspired Love to take control of me'.[1] A day had not passed without his hoping to catch sight of her. There must have been many times when the eagerness of his love played tricks with his vision and it turned out not to be her. But on this day there was no doubt. She was walking towards him along the road which borders the River Arno, in the company of two of her friends.

The spot where Dante Alighieri is traditionally said to have been standing when he caught sight of the three women can now be seen from anywhere. A webcam[2] keeps watch over that corner of the Ponte Santa Trinità. Its constantly updated image is relayed to the internet where it can be viewed from any point on the earth. The bridge provides the foreground for a classically beautiful view of the old city. In the background is the Ponte Vecchio, the more famous shop-laden bridge. Beyond that, on the hilltop, is the ancient Romanesque church of San Miniato al Monte, framed by Tuscan cypresses. There is no indication that the designers of the website had in mind this or any other event in Dante's life when they set up the camera. It was just a good view. But it is

pleasantly appropriate that the location of such a private moment should now be so universal. Appropriate because, although for now the young poet kept his intense feelings close within him as a well-guarded inner secret, one day they would provide the emotional mainspring of the three-part epic of fantasy fiction known as the *Divine Comedy*[a] – they would fuel the story of his journey to the far edge of the universe.

In 1883 the British artist Henry Holiday depicted the scene a little after Dante had seen the women.[3] Holiday was a follower of the Pre-Raphaelites, a group who prided themselves on their close observation of the natural world. But, to our eyes, his version of Dante's world is not naturalistic: it is a nineteenth-century view of medieval Florence. The streets and buildings are a little too clean; the women in the scene are too mannered. The positions of their bodies and the drapery of their dresses have been composed into something that is recognisable as art. Holiday was painting an event in the early life of a genius and he has made the entire work reflect the importance of the moment. To the observer at the time, however, the moment would have appeared perfectly ordinary. Anything extraordinary that was happening was going on entirely inside the poet's head. It would take a long time, during which Dante, his city and his world would have to go through cataclysmic changes, before the consequences of his inner thoughts would become visible to the rest of the world.

Holiday's depiction of Dante himself, on the other hand, does seem to have the ring of truth about it. The figure we see is awkward and intense. Everybody

---

a Dante himself refers to his work simply as the *Comedy* which is the term we shall use for the rest of this book. The 'Divine' was introduced as a, not wholly inappropriate, mark of respect about two centuries after his death.

who describes him says that he was a very serious man. 'Melancholy and pensive' is how his first biographer, the writer Giovanni Boccaccio, puts it. Accounts usually add that he was not unpleasant, quite likeable in fact, but we can well imagine that in his teens that seriousness combined with awkwardness gave a slightly disquieting effect. The figure in the painting is standing in a peculiar way, striking what he may well consider to be a poetic pose.

The women, in their behaviour if not in their dress, would have been much more like their modern successors (who knows, perhaps even their descendants) whom one sees on the streets of Florence today: a trio of girls in their teens, well dressed but not ostentatiously so, absorbed for the most part in their own excited chatter, giving only occasional regard to the citizens around them.

As the girls passed him, Beatrice – quite possibly egged on by her companions – did something provocative. She said hello. Dante describes the effect that this had on him: 'she greeted me so graciously that at that moment I seemed to experience absolute blessedness ... I was so overcome by her sweetness that I left the crowds like a drunkard and went to be alone in my room.'[4]

In other words, Dante had to go and lie down in a darkened room because the girl he loved had said hello to him. This reaction is arguably a little extreme, but among sensitive young poets it is certainly not unique. It is what he describes next which is exceptional. Dante remained in the darkened room and, while the real Beatrice was probably still with her friends discussing the encounter with the intense young man from the Alighieri family, in his imagination she was featuring in a vision.

Dante tells us that he fell into a gentle sleep. He was about to have what is known today as a hypnagogic vision, a vivid hallucination experienced as one drifts in and out of consciousness. Dante notices that the room is becoming suffused with an intense red colour. A huge figure then appears, mumbling words in Latin which Dante cannot make out, apart from the frequently repeated phrase, 'I am your lord'. He becomes aware that the visitor is carrying something: 'In his arms I saw a woman sleeping, naked apart from a blood-coloured cloth lightly wrapped around her. As I looked at her closely, I recognised the lady of the salutation, who had greeted me.'[5]

Dante had a precise visual imagination and we can be sure that in his mind the details of the scene were clear. He knows that Beatrice is naked beneath her diaphanous red covering because he can see the fabric following the curve of her thigh up to her waist and falling gently across her young breasts. He tells us that he then became aware that the Lord of Love was holding something else.

In one of his hands he held something that was all on fire, and he said, 'Behold your heart'.[6]

The fact that the phantom lord can hold Dante's flaming heart in one hand while still cradling the unconscious Beatrice in the crook of his other arm indicates (if, like Dante, we visualise the scene precisely) that the sleeping girl was in the arms of an immense giant. The action that follows would be the main talking point of any feature film which was to include the scene. It would be endlessly discussed until it became an icon of notoriety independent of the movie from which it came. Dante's description is brief: 'When he had stayed there for some time, he awoke the sleeping woman and forced her to eat the burning thing in his hand; and she ate it, with great misgivings.'[7]

Described in words, it can be passed over quickly: 'Beatrice eats the flaming heart of Dante.' There is something almost comical about the sentence. But as we try to visualise it the picture becomes more sinister. If we imagine, for a minute, the close-up: a real piece of glistening meat which the massive lord introduces into Beatrice's reluctant but ultimately acquiescent mouth while all the time angry flames lick around it, we see something grotesque and frightening. This is an image of sexual violation. There is nothing in the literature of the age up to then to match the shock of this vision. It is an image calculated to provoke both disgust and fascination in the reader.

This is Dante's first vision (he was to have many others) and there is more to it than just a startling, slightly nasty image. It has the hallmark skill which Dante would be so slow to deploy: the gift of constructing a detailed, consistent, imaginative world. The scene has a direct effect on its audience but at the same time invites a symbolic interpretation which remains ambiguous and subtle. It can even be read in different ways with completely opposite meanings. In one sense Beatrice is apparently graphically violated by being force-fed a heart but, on the other hand, it is Dante who has had his heart removed in the first place and Beatrice who eats it, so he has also been consumed. Have we witnessed the destruction of love or its consummation? The scene ends equally mysteriously: 'In a short time his joyfulness changed to the bitterest weeping; and so, lamenting, he clasped the lady in his arms and turned away with her up to Heaven.'[8]

Dante himself calls it a vision but we might prefer to say it was a product of his unconscious. Such things are believed nowadays to be messages from concealed areas of the mind. Whatever signal in this case may have been bubbling up from the depths of the young poet's soul, one message is clear: he had a gift for dramatic visual narrative. But, for the moment, Dante ignored his gift and did something very unusual for a man who in his later life would demonstrate scant familiarity with the concept of modesty: he asked for help from other writers.

He circulated a poem which begins with the line 'To every captive soul and noble heart' in which, having asked the reader for an opinion, he describes what he saw:

> Already the third hour was almost over,
> That time when all the stars were shining bright,
> When unexpectedly Love came in sight,
> Whose memory alone fills me with horror.

Yet Love seemed happy, holding in one hand
This heart of mine, while in his arms he had
My lady wrapped in cloth, and sleeping sound.

Then he awakened her, and reverently
Fed her my blazing heart. She was afraid.
I watched him weeping as he went away.[4]

(J.G. Nichols (trans.), *The New Life*, III)

The poem went to members of the group of Italian poets who are known to history as the *Fedeli d'Amore*, the Faithful Followers of Love. Many of them replied (also in verse) with various options for the symbolic meaning of monster, heart, robe etc. One of them was a man called Guido Cavalcanti, the unofficial leader of the group, who later became Dante's best friend. He says that the Lord of Love 'took your heart away when he saw that your lady's death might well be close at hand' and it was out of this fear that he fed her the heart. Fellow poet Cino da Pistoia offers a completely different analysis. He suggests that, in feeding the heart to Beatrice, Love was 'bringing your two hearts together'. As interpretations these are both, at the most, plausible but neither of them has quite got the point. Both poets seem to have moved, as did all[b] the *Fedeli* who replied to Dante's poem, straight from words on the page to symbols in the mind without pausing in between to notice the cinematic quality of the vision itself.

Their problem was that Dante's vision was a true original. It did not have footholds or reference points to anchor it within an existing intellectual framework. Those who search for such things will always have difficulties with it. It has even recently been dismissed by an eminent English Dante scholar as 'an adolescent fantasy'. But the opposite is the case. Dante was clever and knowledgeable but there is nothing unique about that. He had an outstanding

---

b All except one of them. Dante da Maiano (Dante, which means something like 'giver', was quite a common name at the time), a doctor by trade, at least grasped the carnal nature of the imagery. He chose to give a medical interpretation of the vision and replied that Dante was obviously getting a little overexcited. He wrote him a sonnet advising him to '*lavi la tua coglia largamente*', 'wash your testicles thoroughly' (one gets the feeling he is talking about cold water). He does not attempt to interpret the vision further. With this remark Dante da Maiano probably identifies himself as temperamentally unsuited to be a member of the Faithful Followers of Love, but to be able to raise a smile after 700 years is surely an achievement.

facility with words, which was an exceptional gift, but even that does not, in itself, amount to an invention to which every future novelist and film-maker must acknowledge a debt. To achieve that would require the originality inherent in that piece of imagined drama which, although unheeded and unrecognised at first, is at the heart of his greatness.

But at the time the intense young poet wanted more than anything to become one of the *Fedeli*. He was not yet ready to exploit his unique talent. He would only be in a position to do that after two hard decades of progressively painful misfortune had passed and he was in the middle of his journey through life.

2

FLORENCE

The history of Florence is visible from above. The narrow, canyon-like lanes which delight the visitor on the ground with surprise glimpses of Duomo and Palazzo show up, in an aerial view, as dark lines amid the jumble of red-tiled roofs. Buildings have come and gone for 2,000 years – replaced and improved in times of prosperity, allowed to decay in times of difficulty – but they have done so in a piecemeal fashion, always keeping to the line of the streets on which they stood. The result is that the street plan of the distant past has remained long after everything else has gone.

In an aerial photograph, the centre of the city is seen to comprise square blocks formed into a well-defined rectangle. This is the original Roman town, laid out to an imperial plan that owes its origins to the design of a legionary camp. Roman Florence was built in the time of the emperors as an overspill town for the nearby ancient hilltop settlement of Fiesole. Its military precision was chosen more out of tradition than necessity, but it set a stylistic tone which future ages perpetuated, usually because they had to. Warfare and violence would never be far from Florence in succeeding centuries.

Only the later upgrade of the church of Santa Reparata to a cathedral (which happened in Dante's lifetime) has occasioned a significant distortion of the imperial rectangle in the top right-hand (north-eastern) corner. Just to the west of its centre the open space of the forum is still visible. The Roman marketplace continued as a medieval and, later, a renaissance one. It was known from the time of Dante and before as the Old Market to distinguish it from the New Market, a medieval addition a few blocks to the south.

The Roman city prospered. Residential and commercial building soon expanded beyond the walls. Mass entertainment and spectacle were the inevitable companions of Roman prosperity and soon the appropriate venues were constructed nearby. Almost incredibly, the oval outline of an ancient amphitheatre is still preserved in the street plan to the south-east of the original city.

Florence is a natural survivor. It rode out the difficult period of European history which followed the fall of the Roman Empire, sometimes called the Dark Ages, and appeared alive and well in the Middle Ages at the centre of the lucrative international woollen garment trade. By the twelfth century it had expanded again to four times the size of its Roman ancestor and new walls were necessary. These were built in the 1180s, about a century before Dante's birth. This time they were aligned with the river bank, not with the points of the compass in the Roman style. They also enclosed a triangle of land on the other side of the Arno river to the south – the Oltrarno.

Most of the churches, museums and palaces that are visited by tourists today lie within these walls. The exceptions are the great churches that belong to the two mendicant orders of friars: the Dominicans and the Franciscans. These orders were founded after the walls were built. They were monasticism's response to the changes in society that took place at the beginning of the thirteenth century as final vestiges of the old feudal system gave way to a more urban, cash-based style of living. The Franciscans (in the church of Santa Croce to the east) and the Dominicans (in Santa Maria Novella to the west) practised a new form of monasticism which involved leaving the monastery to preach and teach among the people of the town. Around their churches, outside the walls, new residential and trade areas blossomed, mainly to accommodate the ever-growing number of people involved in the processing, dyeing, spinning and weaving of wool.

Prosperity is usually obtained and held through military might. In the case of Florence the access to the sea, which was vital for the wool trade, had to be defended. As a consequence Florence was almost constantly engaged in wars with her neighbouring city states. The city could not afford to have significant commercial areas left outside its fortifications and accordingly – at about the time that Dante was having his vision of Beatrice and the Lord of Love – work was begun on yet another set of walls. They increased the area of the city five fold, were 46ft high and 7ft thick, and took longer than his lifetime to build. These walls defined the defensible limits of the city for the entire period of the

Renaissance and after. Large sections of them survive to this day and almost every road out of town has one of their massive watchtowers situated on a traffic island at its starting point. They still represent the limit of the area which contains everything that makes Florence a unique city.

The building of the walls was a long and expensive project which in one way or another must have affected everybody in the city. But the lives of the citizens of Florence were touched by armed conflict in a much more direct way. The city of Dante was very different from the home of Italian high culture, art and fine shoes that we visit today. On the contrary, it would not be too much of an exaggeration to compare his Florence, not with today's living museum, but with Baghdad in the twenty-first century. Dante's city was rife with constant factional dispute, criss-crossed by invisible demarcation lines of hatred and vendetta. Rival gangs fought in the street; fragile alliances came and went; different systems of government were tried and failed; abduction and torture were commonplace.

Dante's family, the Alighieri, were part of the minor aristocracy. They owned small estates in the apron of countryside surrounding the city which was counted as part of the commune and whose produce was used exclusively to supply the town. In his later work Dante is very proud of his noble ancestors, one of whom is given a large role in the *Comedy*, but the family was not really part of the grand old aristocracy, known as the magnati. The Alighieri estates were not vast enough to provide sufficient income and therefore power which that name would imply. They made a living in part from the rents from their property but also from trade and commerce. In the patchy records of this period members of the family, including Dante and his brother, are recorded as being involved in the buying and selling of houses and operating the machinery of loans, interest and repayments which that involved.

The Alighieri were therefore part aristocrat and part merchant and, as such, they straddled one of the major fault lines of Florentine society: the conflict between the nobility and the guilds. These two groups interacted like a couple stuck in an unhappy and abusive relationship: constantly competing, bickering and squabbling yet bound to each other by mutual need.

The merchants had from time immemorial (some said from the time of the Romans) organised themselves into guilds: self-governing units based very loosely upon the type of trade in which their members were involved – wool merchants, silk merchants, doctors and apothecaries, dealers in fur, notaries, money-changers, etc. But guilds were, by this time, much more than trade associations. They had become a political entity which was effectively an arm of government, ruled by an elected committee (whose members were called priors); they even had their own armed enforcers presided over by a Captain of the Guard. The faction of the guilds is often referred to by chroniclers and historians as the Popolo (the People). This does not mean they were in some way the precursors of a popular democratic party. The broad mass of humanity referred to in later ages as 'the people' (as in 'People's Republic' or even 'We the People') did not have a voice and indeed they hardly feature at all in late medieval history. The guilds were an elite interest group. They were popular only in the sense that they were a little closer to the people than their rival elite group, the nobles.

The nobles were organised as a counterbalancing power base. Their political organisation was headed by an official known as the Podestà (the Power) and they had no difficulty in finding armed support if they needed it. The young men of each family were trained in warfare and the families were also responsible for raising an army in times of dispute with neighbour states.

The potential for conflict between these two groups is obvious: they were both struggling for control of the same city. The enmity between them was ingrained in their culture in a way which is almost universal: nobles regarded tradesmen as venal and vulgar while merchants regarded the nobility as arrogant and headstrong. On the other hand, neither could survive without the other. The merchants needed the military power of the aristocracy to protect the city and keep open its all-important lines of communication with the coastal ports. The nobility needed the merchants to ensure the continuing financial prosperity of the city. Aristocratic rule is by its nature capricious, depending as it does on the will of one man (it almost always was) who has been invested with an unhealthy amount of power to which he probably believes he has a God-given right. Such a system does not make for economic stability. Who will lend money to a despot who might at any minute engage in some ill-advised military adventure or who might simply refuse to pay his creditors and invite them to try to do something about it if they think they are hard enough?

Merchants, by contrast, have every reason to act together to produce a stable economic system where money can be lent securely at appropriate interest rates. Florentine merchants excelled at this. The city had a tradition of reliable banking practices, such as careful bookkeeping and meticulous record-taking. They were also natural diplomats, at home in foreign countries, always giving the impression of a safe pair of hands with whom one would be happy to do business. They had insinuated themselves into so many different areas outside their own city that Pope Boniface VIII once famously called them the fifth element.[a] It is thanks to the merchants, not the nobility, that the great buildings of Florence were built and that ultimately it was to become (about a hundred years after Dante) the powerhouse of the Italian Renaissance.

The attempt to reconcile these two competing arms of government is the major theme of the political history of Florence for the century before and

---

a   There is, of course, an unattractive side to this quality: deviousness and duplicity. To this day in French, to describe somebody as 'un Florentin' is not to imply their financial probity but to suggest that they are slick and smooth-talking to the point of dishonesty.

after the life of Dante. The Florentines made repeated attempts – all ultimately unsuccessful – to produce a fair, or at any rate workable, method of getting them to act together and avoid catastrophic conflict.[b]

The division between merchant and aristocratic classes was destructive enough but in Florence conflicts were never that simple. This division was overlaid by an even more deeply rooted one: that between individual families. The family was the social and legal unit of the city. Official documents note the family origins of citizens in the old Roman style, not with a surname as such but by specifying the clan from which they came: Bocca degli Abati, Farinata degli Uberti, etc. One member of a family could, in certain circumstances, be held legally responsible for the misdeeds of another, a principle of which the natural result was to induce Florentines to rate family ties above the rule of law.

The prominence of family divisions made it virtually impossible to find a suitable leader. Any candidate from one family would inevitably be unacceptable to several others. An ingenious and elegant solution to this problem was found. The podestà, who led the noble faction and had been, until the rise of the guilds, the sole ruler of Florence, was never allowed to be a Florentine. He would be brought in from another Italian town on a one-year contract. This visiting podestà would not be subject to the instant, unconsidered detestation of rival families and his rulings would therefore, in theory, be less prone to blind prejudice. There were strict controls on the foreign visitor, designed to shield him from the temptations of bribery. He was paid appropriately for his duties but his accounting was required to be transparent: he was audited on his first day in office and again on his last. Any profit over and above his agreed honorarium was summarily confiscated. The idea was not unique to Florence. It certainly worked quite well in a number of other Italian cities and records show that Florence in her time had taken a podestà from almost every other town in Italy. In our times there is no country that voluntarily imports foreign political leaders in this way, but a similar practice is followed by European football clubs where it is quite common for a manager to be brought in from another country if they have shown particular skill or if, for some reason, there is no qualified home-grown candidate who wants the job.

b This struggle continued for another 150 years until it was resolved, after a fashion, when total power was appropriated by a family of bankers with exceptional political acuity called the Medici.

Just as Florence from the air shows the history of its defences against outsiders, at street level its family-based social structure and the violence that went with it are still evident. Florence's buildings reveal it as a hard city. Its streets are not pretty. They are lined with large, forbidding fortified palaces, the lower part of whose outer walls are 'rusticated' or left rough-hewn so as not to show the marks of passing riots. The few exterior windows the buildings do have are protected by heavy-duty, permanent metal grilles. Typically, an entire extended family of aunts, grandparents and cousins lived within one palazzo. In the event of trouble on the street, they had only to close their vast iron-bound doors and wait for the disturbance to blow over.

In the thirteenth century those families that could afford it added a tall defensive tower to their palace. They could be up to 30m in height (that was the maximum, limited by city ordinance). Their purpose was partly to demonstrate the wealth and power of the family and also to afford ample views of any developing situation outside the palace. This gave the young men of the family the opportunity to join in the fray by loosing deadly bolts into the streets below from the latest hi-tech weapon, the crossbow. Families that could not afford a tower of their own would club together with their neighbours to build a joint one with access from each of their respective palazzi. In Florence today about a dozen towers survive in various states of decay, but contemporary accounts suggest that there were as many as 150 in Dante's day.

Its prosperity in the Middle Ages meant that Florence's street plan was fully formed well before the advent of the Renaissance, with its clear ideas about elegant urban planning. For this reason it does not have any of the stylish piazzas enjoyed by other Tuscan towns. The largest open space in central Florence was and still is quite close to the site of Dante's house, just to the south of the line of the old Roman walls. Rather than being a triumph of civilised town planning, this piazza exists as a monument to the destructive tidal flow of internecine conflict.

The area was once the site of a complex of houses and palaces belonging to an aristocratic family called the Uberti. In the decades before Dante's birth there had been two brief periods when the aristocratic faction gained an upper hand to such an extent that it was able to rule the city directly, excluding the merchant class from power. These periods were made possible because the aristocratic rule was being underwritten by military support from outside Florence. On each occasion, in the wake of victory the nobility confiscated the goods and destroyed the houses of their enemies. The New Market was constructed on one of the resulting vacant sites. In the euphoria of one victory, some noblemen even suggested that the beautiful and ancient baptistery be demolished because of its populist associations. Fortunately this view did not prevail. The anti-merchant putsches seem to have been led by the Uberti family whose arrogance was proverbial (in Dante's Hell one of their number pops up out of his grave to give a lengthy tirade. He is still insufferably disdainful). During these periods of uncontested rule, the detailed records of committees' decisions and debates that so characterise civic life in Florence all stop. There was no need for debate; the city was being ruled by decree.

But the fortunes of war take away just as they give and, in the year of Dante's birth, foreign backing was withdrawn resulting in the collapse of the aristocratic government. In true Florentine style the cycle of violence was perpetuated. This time it was the Uberti palaces that were razed to the ground. The Council of Priors decreed that they should never be rebuilt. The area which they occupied remained a rubble-strewn vacant lot for all of Dante's life. Today the site is bordered by an elegant Renaissance loggia, the world-famous Uffizzi art gallery, the iconic Palazzo Vecchio, which features on a million postcards, and a replica of Michelangelo's statue of David. It is the principal tourist venue of the city, called the Piazza dell Signoria, and it remains to this day – just as the commune of Florence intended – entirely empty of buildings.

3

THE GLORIOUS LADY OF MY MIND

ante grew up in the midst of these cycles of revenge and retribution. Even from childhood the conversation of adults around him, the stones in the streets that he walked, must have informed him that his home town was in a state of discord. He cannot have failed to be aware of it, but the first book that he wrote, about his early life, makes no mention of any of it. The *Vita Nuova* (New Life) is the work of a young man who defines himself first and foremost as a poet. He proudly tells us that he had 'learned by myself the art of speaking words in rhyme', that he was, in other words, a natural. And poets, according to the convention of his time (and even, to a certain extent, of our own), did not write about politics or violence in the street – they charted the progress of their own inner life. Dante's first book opens with the line: 'Early on in the book of my memory – almost before anything else can be read there – is a chapter heading which says: "The New Life Begins".'[1]

The event that signalled the beginning of his 'New Life' was a private one, decoupled entirely from the external world of greed, ambition and revenge. It happened when he was only 9 years old. Somewhere among the twisted lanes and the red roofs within the rectangle of old Roman Florence he caught sight of an 8-year-old girl, 'dressed in a very noble colour, a decorous and delicate crimson … she did not seem the daughter of a mortal man but of a god'. Her name, of course, was Beatrice.

The moment when he first saw Beatrice was so important to Dante that it wasn't enough for him simply to state that he was 9 years old. He had to place it in the context of the cosmic clock of the motion of the heavens. He tells us that 'since the time of my birth the Heaven of light had performed nine revolutions returning almost to the same point, when my eyes first lit upon the glorious lady of my mind'.[2] From this the attentive reader can work out that the Heaven of light (the sun) had made its annual journey around the sky nine times, so he was 9 years old.

Beatrice's age is given in an even more convoluted way: 'she had already been in this life so long that the starry Heaven had moved towards the orient one twelfth of a degree'.[3] This time it is not the movement of the sun that is being referred to but the apparent motion of the stars themselves. Dante is showing off his astronomical knowledge by citing an apparent fundamental shifting of the fabric of the universe that had been known since ancient times. With some arcane knowledge and a little calculation[a] this can be interpreted as meaning that she was just over 8 years old. Dante, in fact, confirms this figure in the next line, just in case it escapes his less mathematically inclined readers.

It is not uncommon for lovers to know the exact day, even the second, of their first meeting and even (slightly irritatingly) to calculate the time elapsed since that event. Dante has produced an intellectualised, late medieval version of this. To be fair, an interest in the positions of the heavens at a time of great import is not untypical of the age, but even so – even when one has filtered out the effects of cultural relativism – Dante's description demonstrates an obsessive love of technical details that some people might be tempted to describe as 'nerdy'. The intense young poet was destined to go through profound psychological changes as his life progressed. They would affect his style, his attitude and even his loves, but they would never make him lose that fascination with a detailed scientific explanations of things.

Later tradition, following his earliest biographer Boccaccio, places the first meeting at a children's party given by Beatrice's father, Folco Portinari.

---

a   These are not very taxing but technical enough to be consigned to a footnote: the main body of the stars in the sky, which were once thought to be fixed, had been known from late antiquity to shift around very slowly. We know now that this apparent effect is caused by the axis of the earth wobbling slightly, like a top. The rotation is so slow that it takes about 36,000 years to make a complete circuit, which works out conveniently at 100 years per degree. If Beatrice has been alive for a twelfth of a degree, therefore, this means that she is 100/12, or just over 8 years old.

The Portinari lived nearby but were much grander than Dante's family. Folco was very rich and a well-known philanthropist – there is a hospital in Florence that bears his name to this day. This might have increased Dante's nervousness while, by contrast, little Beatrice would have been confident and at ease. Dante gives very little description of her (ever) but he does emphasise that she displayed none of the brattishness of a spoilt rich child. She was 'lovely and quietly spoken, an angel child, dressed in a very noble colour, a decorous and delicate crimson, tied with a girdle and trimmed in a manner suited to her tender age'. The effect of this self-assured little girl wearing the very finest clothes might well have been devastating.

Dante does not give us any more information about the event itself. He moves quickly on to describe in detail the effect that seeing Beatrice has on his inner world. He gives an account of what it feels like to fall in love at first sight in terms of the basic mechanism of medieval psychology: Aristotle's theory of the soul. According to the ancient Greek philosopher all living things have souls. They come in three kinds: vegetable, animal and rational. Plant and animal souls have only the first one or the first two respectively. A human soul, however, has all three parts. Dante describes in turn how each of the parts of his soul was affected by the first sight of Beatrice.

Following medieval tradition, he personifies each one, imagining them each situated in its own room in his head, playing out the drama of his inner life. The most primitive form of soul is the vegetable one; it deals with feeding and nutrition. Because it is the lowest in the hierarchy Dante allows it a light-hearted approach: 'The natural spirit, that which lives in the part where our food is delivered, began to weep, and weeping said these words: "Oh misery, since I will often be troubled from now on!"' The spirit which guides digestion recognises that, after falling in love, Dante's stomach will frequently be upset. He was evidently one of those fortunate people for whom emotional turmoil produces a reduction in appetite rather than the opposite effect. Descriptions of him do indeed agree that he was thin.

Next up is the animal soul which is in control of perception. Not surprisingly, since the sight of Beatrice is what has moved Dante, this spirit is delighted by what has happened: 'The spirit of perception which lives in the high room to which all the spirits of the senses carry their messages was filled with amazement and made this pronouncement: "Now the source of your joy has been revealed."'

Finally in Aristotle's theory comes the rational soul. This is the part that makes human beings unique. It is the seat of intelligence, responsible for understanding. From its position in the 'innermost room' of Dante's mind the rational soul is able to recognise the importance of what has happened:

> At that moment (I am speaking all the truth) the spirit of life which lives in the most secret innermost room of the heart began to quiver so fiercely that its effect was dreadfully apparent in the least of my pulses; and, trembling, it said these words: 'Behold, a stronger god than I has come to govern me'.
>
> (*Vita Nuova* II)

In the *Vita Nuova*, Dante always speaks as if there really is a 'Thing Called Love', something like a force which has emanated from Beatrice and entered him. This 'Force of Love' is often represented by Dante and his poetry friends as a speaking, thinking being with a will of its own. The spirit at the very heart of Dante's mind has seen this force and recognised that it is outclassed: from now on this 'stronger god' will be in charge.

Dante goes on to explain that, although love had power over him, it was 'so noble that it never allowed love to guide me without the counsel of reason' – it would never lead him astray. Noble love is quite distinct from sexual desire (which does lead people astray). Theory said that the noble variety of love only occurred when it entered the body of someone with a refined soul (a *cor gentile*). Even then it only existed when the love went straight to the innermost room of the rational soul without, as it were, touching the sides. If it interacted on entry with the baser, irrational area of the body it could result in the obfuscating miasma of lustful desire.

As we shall see, Dante was not unfamiliar with this other kind of love but the New Life is not about that. He makes it plain with every word that he is talking about poets' love. The closest we ever come to a glimpse of Beatrice as an object of sexual desire is in the very next episode of the *Vita Nuova*, which is the startling vision of the Lord of Love where a nearly naked Beatrice devours Dante's heart.

It is possible to find the young Dante's celebration of a pure love a refreshing change in a sex-obsessed world. On the other hand, one might also object that, although the theoretical detail does give us a graphic metaphor for the power of love, it leaves Beatrice herself strangely out of the picture. All the action is happening inside Dante's head. She doesn't even get a speaking part.

4

THE ROAD TO
CAMPALDINO

After the vision of Beatrice and the flaming heart, Dante's love intensified to the point where he became ill: 'My soul was quite obsessed by the thought of that most noble lady – and I soon became so weak that many of my friends were troubled by my appearance.'¹ When his friends asked him what was wrong he admitted that he was in love. When they asked with whom – 'For whose sake has love destroyed you?' – he tells us that he answered only with a smile.

Dante was obsessively secretive about the identity of the woman he loved but it is not quite clear why. It is hard to imagine that Beatrice's reputation would in some way have been damaged had her name been known. She seems to have done very little to encourage him beyond a casual hello and there is certainly no doubt that the relationship, if that word is appropriate, was entirely chaste. But Dante even tells us that he sensed malice in those who asked her name. His extreme discomfort at having the inner chambers of his soul probed in casual conversation may well have given him the mistaken impression that he was being attacked.

He soon comes upon a solution which he explains in the following chapter. One day he finds himself sitting in the same church as Beatrice. He has placed himself in a position where he can see her but without being so close that his attentions seem obvious (in his opinion). A woman of noble birth (whose name Dante does not reveal[a]) is sitting between them, caught in the crossfire of his amorous gaze. The people behind him, mistaking the object of Dante's lovelorn looks, remark aloud that the young poet is plainly being torn apart by the love of this other lady. Far from being disconcerted by the mistaken identity, Dante is pleased by the rumour. It gives him an opportunity to use the lady (sometimes referred to by historians as the 'screen lady') as a kind of decoy. If people think that he is pining for the love of her they will not intrude on his true feelings with further questions. The ploy works: 'I hid behind this lady for several years and months', he tells us. Dante does not seem to have considered for a moment what possible consequences this mistaken identity might have had for the 'screen lady'.

The story continues with a puzzling episode which provides another insight into the mind of the young Dante. He tells us in the next chapter that 'it occurred to me to write a poem of praise of the sixty most beautiful ladies of the city'. This is something with which most readers will be familiar. Composing lists of people one finds attractive, placing them in a carefully considered order and then sharing it with one's friends is part of growing up. Sadly, the list-poem that Dante wrote is lost. He explains that he is obviously not going to include it in the *Vita Nuova* because it does not directly concern Beatrice. He then goes on: 'I would not have spoken about it at all except to mention a marvellous thing which happened when I was composing it – my lady's name refused to appear anywhere but at number nine among the names.' This is, at first sight, extraordinary. The 'Glorious Lady' who was so beautiful she seemed like a goddess has only made it to number nine.

The explanation can be found in Dante's inner world. Just as the position of heavenly bodies reinforces the significance of the first moment he saw her, for him certain numbers reveal and underline the importance of Beatrice. In particular, her unique place in his life is demonstrated whenever the number nine crops up. He tells us with satisfaction that he was 9 years old when he saw her; he is at pains to point out that the vision of the flaming heart happened at precisely the ninth hour of the day. Even the number and position of different types of poem in the *Vita Nuova* itself are believed by some to show a pattern involving the number nine. Dante is delighted, therefore, that Beatrice should, without any (conscious) effort on his part, appear ninth on the list of his

---

a   In the *Vita Nuova* Dante gives us no names at all: not his own, not that of the city where he lives, nor of any of the close friends and relatives whom he mentions. There is only one proper name in the entire *Vita Nuova* and that is 'Beatrice'.

favourite Florentine ladies. Presumably the women were not listed in order of attractiveness, though Dante does not make this altogether clear.

Few people live their lives without at some time seeing, or wanting to see, significance in apparently random details of their experience – the place where a book falls open, the number plate of a passing car, the number of words in a half-written chapter. In the condition of uncertainty and anxiety in which most of us find ourselves it is natural to seek meaning or the promise of good fortune in minutiae that fate seems to offer us like a series of upturned playing cards.

Dante does seem to have been particularly drawn to this mode of thinking. There is a moment in the *Vita Nuova*, for example, when he sees Beatrice walking in the street, preceded by a woman whose nickname we are told is Primavera, which means springtime. He muses that she was undoubtedly called so because she was destined to walk in front of Beatrice (in Italian *prima verrà* means 'comes first'). This is surely stretching credibility near to destruction. Are we supposed to believe that the Creator, in his infinite wisdom, has gone to the trouble of giving a woman a particular name simply for it to be apposite (and then only via a rather ungainly Italian pun) to a single incident in somebody else's life? In the *Vita Nuova* this sort of thing smacks of desperation, but in the *Comedy* he manages to make it work to great effect.

Dante continues the story. After some years of decoy work the screen lady is obliged to leave Florence for reasons which, as usual, Dante does not reveal. A little later 'something happened which meant that I myself had to depart from the city'. This time he does give us some scant details. He left the city, he tells us, riding a horse and in the company of many other people. The journey was unpleasant; he calls it 'the road of sighs'.

As the company sets out, Dante has another vision. Love appears to him in the shape of a young man dressed as a simple traveller. He is a little dejected and keeps his eyes cast down, apart from occasional glances towards the beautiful river whose course they are following. Love explains that he knows that the screen lady will not be returning to the city for a long time. He has therefore retrieved the heart which Dante had given her and is taking it to another lady who will be able to act as Dante's decoy in future. Love tells him her name and Dante is delighted to realise that it is somebody he already knows. Dante, of course, does not tell us the lady's name, nor does he tell us the reason for his own departure from Florence. But, as it happens, we have an idea of what the latter was: it is quite likely that Dante was on his way to fight at the battle of Campaldino.

On 2 June 1289 a Florentine army numbering 12,000 men (10,000 infantrymen and 2,000 mounted knights) left the city following the course of the River Arno to the east. Dante was certainly among them. We know from his own later references, as well as from the testimony of early biographies, that Dante not only did his military service as a cavalryman but that he took part in the campaign of which Campaldino was the major battle. Was this the occasion when he had the vision of Love in the guise of a young man? We can never be certain, of course, but the details he does grudgingly let slip – he is on a horse, in the company of others, following a river on a journey which he finds unpleasant – are all consistent with his being en route to the battle. Although they are far from conclusive for us, these references might perhaps have been all that was needed for the fellow poets, who were his intended audience, to recognise the road to war. Perhaps they were deliberately included as a sort of 'in' reference – enough information for the cognoscenti to recognise but not enough detail to spoil the featureless setting which Dante intended for the *Vita Nuova*.

The image of a medieval army is one which we are still able to conjure up in our minds today. At the head of the departing Florentine army the fleur-de-lys standard of the republic is drawn on a chariot pulled by white oxen. It is followed by 2,000 mounted knights. Their lances are topped by colourful flags and streamers; their shields are decorated with bright patterns. They are kitted out in light, state-of-the-art, flexible plate armour which is an Italian speciality. It sparkles dazzlingly in the June sunshine. Their horses too are decked out with colourful cloths, their heads covered by light protective armour. They are followed by the thousands of infantrymen who are not quite so finely armed but each one of them is helmeted, wearing a mail coat and carrying the vicious long pike which was used to dismount and neutralise an oncoming enemy horseman. If this is indeed the moment when he met Love in the guise of a traveller, perhaps it explains why Dante makes a point of describing the figure he saw as, by contrast, 'simply dressed'.

Campaldino was a decisive encounter in the long-term struggle for domination of Tuscany in the thirteenth century. Florence was the largest city in the area by a comfortable margin but it was not big enough to overcome a concerted attack by two neighbouring states in alliance. The pair of states that had historically ganged up on Florence most frequently were Pisa, to the west, and Arezzo, to the south-east.

Throughout the 1280s Arezzo had been making raids against Florence. They received support from various dissident Florentine families (including the Uberti, whose houses had been vengefully destroyed by the commune twenty-one years earlier), but their traditional ally, Pisa, had been weakened by another conflict. In 1284 its navy had been disastrously defeated by Genoa, its rival for control of the seas. This had left the city effectively under Genoese control. Pisa was disabled by conspiracy and betrayal as old and new factions struggled for power.

With Pisa preoccupied by domestic problems, Florence decided to take action over what she saw as Arezzo's aggression. Aristocrats and merchants united in this enterprise: they raised money through a special tax; they called on a loose coalition of more-or-less willing smaller city states to provide support and they hired elite mercenaries to back up their own highly trained but part-time army. The expeditionary force set off on the road to Arezzo. About halfway there they met the Aretines (as the inhabitants of Arezzo are known) coming the other way.

The usual tactic for such an encounter was to send in a force for a primary engagement while leaving a reserve for later deployment. Battles were often decided not in the first charge but in the more subtle endgame as reserve forces were brought into play. The Florentine reserves were commanded by Corso Donati, one of the city's best-known aristocrats. He was in many ways a good choice: a fearless, battle-hardened soldier, accustomed to command. He was also a skilled politician and had even been employed by neighbouring cities, in Bologna as podestà and then as Captain of the People in Pistoia. His one flaw was that he was not a team player. He tended impetuously to ignore orders and lead his men towards the thick of the battle even when overall strategy demanded restraint. This is a severe failing in a military commander and on this occasion he had been told on pain of death to remain in reserve until specifically ordered to attack by a named member of the Florentine command.

The two armies came together on the narrow floodplain of the Arno in the place known to local farmers as Campaldino. Despite being outnumbered by the Florentine coalition, the Aretines made a good initial showing. They were helped in this partly by the narrowness of the valley, which prevented the Florentines from deploying fully, but also by the leadership skills of their commander, Guglielmo degli Ubertini. Guglielmo's official job was bishop of Arezzo but, as the chronicler Dino Compagni remarks, he was in fact more familiar with the offices of war than those of the Church.

His Excellency the bishop had wide interests. He was a man of property, owning large sections in the countryside around Arezzo. When news of the Florentine expedition reached him he was concerned that the attack might cause a slump in property prices and (as two separate chronicles attest) he offered to sell or rent his land to the city of Florence in advance of any combat.

It seems that eventually even he came to realise that this was going a bit far and confessed what he had done to the ruling council of Arezzo. When the story became public one might have expected Guglielmo to suffer some dire punishment for his evident treachery, but, on the contrary, the Aretines still so valued his military skills that they put him in command of the army anyway.

As the battle got under way Corso Donati remained on the flank, watching Bishop Guglielmo pressing home his advantage. For some time he obediently awaited the order to attack but, unknown to him, the person whose job it was to give him the word had fallen early in the fighting. Eventually Corso's nature got the better of him. He made the remark which is frequently used to justify impetuous action, 'If I succeed I will be forgiven, if I fail it will scarcely matter', and led his men into the charge. Unfortunately for Arezzo, the commander of its reserves was not so impetuous. He failed to attack when he saw the battle going against Arezzo and as a result a Florentine victory was assured.

Techniques of metallurgy had improved greatly over the previous century, bringing with them refinements in the manufacture of both arms and armour, but warfare remained essentially what it had been for over a thousand years: people hacking at each others' bodies with metal implements. Injuries were inevitably horrific. As a member of the Florentine cavalry, Dante would have been in the midst of the adrenalin-fired frenzy of initial contact and then, as the attack progressed, locked into tight formations of soldiers during a brutal

period of blow and counterblow which gave way eventually to a shocked aftermath as men with severed limbs and other fatal wounds lay stunned and untreated on the ground. In an age when casualties numbering less than a hundred can sway the heart of a nation decisively away from the support of a war, it is worth remembering that, even according to modern estimates, between 3,000 and 4,000 people died at Campaldino in one day.[b]

Of course, it can never be proved that when he wrote about meeting Love in the guise of a young man, Dante had in mind the day when he left for the war, although the details he lets slip are quite persuasive.[c] What is certain, however, is that Dante did fight in the battle and that it happened during the period covered by the *Vita Nuova*. We cannot expect a poet's account of love to cover every detail of his life, but nonetheless we are left with a slight feeling of surprise. One cannot quite be rid of the thought that while Dante the citizen was fulfilling his duty of military service, Dante the poet was sleepwalking through a day of carnage under the impression it had nothing to do with him.

The *Vita Nuova* narrative continues. Dante returns to Florence and, as instructed, he starts to feign affection for the new lady whom Love has mentioned. He seems to have been a little over-enthusiastic, however, because his behaviour causes comment: 'too many people spoke of it beyond the bounds of courtesy.' There was 'excessive gossip which was defaming me out of malice'. It is not clear exactly what this means but one is tempted to speculate that Dante's amorous posturing had become not just a source of disapproval but also a bit of a joke in some circles. The malicious gossip, we are

---

b   Among the dead was Bishop Guglielmo himself. He was buried in the nearby church of Certomundo. His remains rested there until 11 June 2008 when, by popular request, they were brought home to the cathedral of Arezzo. Guglielmo's return as a local hero was celebrated with a special Mass, celebrated by the current bishop.

c   There is one more casual remark that Dante makes that is consistent with this being the day that is intended. He tells us two further things about his departure from Florence: he was travelling in the direction of the city to which the decoy lady had moved but stopped halfway there. In a work with very few background details it is always worth asking why a certain fact is included, especially if at first sight it seems to be irrelevant. What is the point of mentioning the direction in which he is travelling if he never got there? Suppose, however, that the lady was either from Arezzo or that her family sympathised with the Aretines. In the run up to Campaldino she and her family would naturally have been obliged to leave Florence, just as Dante describes. To those of his readership in the know it would have been a kind of black joke to say that he was on his way to the place where she now lived – Arezzo. The joke continues when he says he stopped halfway: Campaldino was situated at almost exactly the midpoint between the two cities.

told, reaches the ears of Beatrice who is so incensed by his reported behaviour that 'she denied me that sweet salutation in which all my bliss resided' – she cuts him dead.

Dante takes a moment to impress on us the importance of Beatrice's greeting. Whenever she said hello he says he went into such a daze that, had anyone asked him a question at that moment, all he would have been able to do by way of an answer would have been repeatedly to utter the word 'love' in a humble way. The effect of being denied this encounter with bliss shatters Dante. He 'bathes the earth with bitter tears', goes to lie down and so finds himself once again in his darkened room, ready for another vision.

5

THE FOLLOWERS OF LOVE

I t is probably clear by now that the *Vita Nuova* is an unusual autobiography. It ignores most of the events that normally would be considered significant. Not only does it fail to mention a war and several political crises, but it gives no account of certain things no modern writer would resist: the death of Dante's mother when he was 5 and of his father (probably) when he was 15. Even though the book is self-evidently about Beatrice, it gives no concrete facts even about her: we do not know the colour of her eyes or hair, where she lived or even one sentence that she uttered (apart from 'giving a greeting', which is vague). Even in terms of the book's avowed aim of documenting Dante's inner world it is frequently either frustratingly sketchy or downright opaque. The naivety of its expression coupled with the lack of detail and almost fetishistic refusal to mention names does give the narrative an eerie quality which some readers have found charming. As a resource for a biographer, however, it is not helpful.

This is partly due to young Dante's obstinate secretiveness, but another reason is simply that the purpose of the book is not to make life easy for posterity. Dante wrote it to impress the *Fedeli d'Amore*. All the poems in the *Vita Nuova* (thirty-one of them) had already been written; the point of collecting them in a book was to provide the *Fedeli* with a brief contextual background. In addition to the story, each poem is followed by a brief analysis which breaks it into sections and summarises what it says. To modern readers these explanations seem almost unbelievably simplistic. For example, the commentary on the poem in which he invites comments from the *Fedeli* on the vision of the flaming heart ('To every captive soul and noble heart') reads in its entirety: 'This sonnet is divided into two parts. In the first part I give a greeting and ask for a reply. In the second part I say what it is that needs a reply. The second part begins: "Already the third …"'

It is hard to see how this could help anyone to understand the poem better. Few people have ever had a good word to say for these passages. The nineteenth-century artist and devoted Dante scholar, Dante Gabriel Rossetti, was so disturbed by them that when he translated the *Vita Nuova*, it is said that he insisted that his brother work on those bits. The most recent English edition[1] puts them in italics so that (to quote) *'readers may easily skip them if they wish'*.

The poets of the *Fedeli* came from diverse (mostly rich) backgrounds and had varying poetical abilities. What united them was a shared mission. They wanted to develop a new kind of Italian poetry. You could almost say that they wanted to invent Italian poetry itself because, until just before their time, all poetry written in Italy was in Latin. They took as their starting point the work of the poets known as the troubadours who, about a century earlier, had begun to write in their own language, the old version of French from the south-west of France, known as Occitan. The troubadours had been very successful. Their fame spread and their work had been copied as far away as Flanders to the north and, more recently, Italy.

The troubadours wrote about a specific type of love, known as 'courtly love'. This was a kind of ritualised adoration from afar. The courtly lover suffered the agonies of unsatisfied desire and expressed it as poetry, while the object of his affection remained haughty, frequently uninterested and always unattainable. Their aristocratic audience was thrilled to hear about people of noble birth like themselves experiencing intense passion. To talk about emotions which were above the base level of carnality seemed daringly modern to them. Even the fact that the passion remained unconsummated added to its popularity: it meant that there was no risk of stray pregnancies which might disturb the all-important lines of inheritance on which nobility depends.

The *Fedeli* themselves were conscious of continuing the troubadour project but there were also important differences in their approach. A city is quite different from a feudal court and the idea of courtly love had to be modified slightly. To the *Fedeli*, love remained an exclusive pursuit but it was not restricted to people of noble birth. It was restricted instead to those who had a noble heart, a *cor gentile*. This was, for them, an essential prerequisite. Dante even begins one of his poems with the bald statement, 'Love and the noble heart are one and the same thing'.

The *Fedeli* also intellectualised more than the troubadours had done. They wanted to find a theory of love that was consistent with ideas such as Aristotle's notion of the soul. The style which they developed is now called the *Dolce Stil Novo* or 'New Sweet Style'.[a] It involved a more subtle use of symbol and metaphor and, at its least successful, reads like a combination of a medical textbook and a treatise on medieval philosophy. At its best, however, it produces images and insights that have fascinated poets and scholars for centuries.

The poem which Dante sent to the *Fedeli* following his vision of the flaming heart was by way of a calling card for the group. When he began with the line 'To every captive soul and noble heart' it was clear he was addressing them directly. And when he asked them to give an interpretation of the symbolism of the vision he was demonstrating that he shared their agenda.

When the *Fedeli* read the poem they may have missed the point of the vision, but they did not miss the point of Dante. They recognised both his intelligence and his talent as a poet. Soon he was one of them. In particular, he quickly established a rapport with Guido Cavalcanti, the de facto head of the group. Guido was seven years older than Dante and a glamorous, slightly larger-than-life character. History knows him not only from references in Dante but also from Boccaccio's *Decameron*, the collection of tales written about sixty years later. In one of the stories he makes a brief, swashbuckling appearance when he puts down a gang of threatening (but less gifted) Florentine noblemen with a subtle quip, before vaulting nimbly over a gravestone and making good his escape. He was highly intelligent. 'Courtly and bold but haughty and solitary and given to study' is how one chronicler describes him. Another gives a different description of what may be exactly the same combination of brains and volatility: 'He was a philosopher accomplished in many things, though he was too sensitive and irascible.' He was not only a respected poet but also a politician, a member of the ruling General Council of the commune. For Dante to receive a reply from him was an achievement.

---

a   This phrase, like *'Fedeli d'Amore'* itself, comes from the work of Dante. This may seem a little unfair since the *Fedeli* and their style existed before him and he came to them virtually begging for admission. But the right to name movements and styles is given to the victors in the race for fame.

Guido's poetry is delightful. Like Dante he has a gift for rhythms and the music of language. In his early poems he celebrates the pure pleasure of being in love with direct short-lined verse: 'Fresh new rose/Pleasant spring/By meadows and by field/Gaily singing' ... 'I see in my lady's eyes a radiance full of spirits of love, that brings fresh pleasure to my heart such that it awakens there vitality of joy'.[2]

Guido and Dante became very close. In the *Vita Nuova* Dante refers to him as 'my best friend'. Later on in the story he tells us that the whole book is dedicated to him. Dante obviously looked up to Guido as a mentor. In the *Vita Nuova* he uses him as a kind of touchstone to validate his opinions: 'my best friend and I know ...' or 'my best friend understands the reason for this ...'

The *Fedeli* communicated with each other through exchanges of poems. Some of them contain earnest philosophical observations but others are frivolous and jocular. In one which Dante wrote for Guido, for instance, we find him fantasising about a sort of floating poetry commune in which the two of them and fellow *Fedele*, Lapo Gianni, sail away together:

> Guido, I wish that you and Lapo and I
> Were seized by enchantment
> And set in a boat that at every wind
> Would sail on the sea at your wish and mine.

The poets would head for the magical isles of bliss and harmony:

> Then neither evil times nor stormy weather
> Would seem the slightest obstacle
> Our wills would turn into a single will
> With but one wish – to be like this for ever.

And, as in all the best fantasies, the three poets would be accompanied by their girlfriends: Vanna (short for Giovanna) for Guido, Lagia for Lapo, and a third lady whom Dante predictably refuses to name. Of course, there is absolutely no question as to what the young folk in the boat would be talking about.

> Love the sole topic of our conversation.
> The ladies would all three be very happy,
> And we the happiest men that could be found.

> (Lowry Nelson (trans.), *Lyric Poems*)

Guido sent a poem in reply which has also survived. In it, however, he declines the invitation to join the floating poets society. He is grateful to have been asked but he regrets that he cannot accept because he has been brought down by a thing called love: 'The swift archer has taken aim at my spirit and destroyed its strength.' He is in no state for enjoyment.

Such a reply is partly a move to continue the light-hearted poetical banter, but beneath the light tone can be seen the predominant theme of Guido's work: love is a pain. Time and again in his poems, the joyful celebration of 'the fresh pleasures that my heart feels' gives way to the 'torments that consume my body with grief'. He visits 'the cruel palace where love holds court' only to find that 'love is an archer fit only to kill people'. In his most reflective poetry the thought is elegant but the conclusion is the same: 'Love goes about making colours change and turning laughter into tears.'

This attitude is typical both of the *Fedeli* and of the troubadours before them. Love is a random event that causes unhappiness and, once the accident had happened, the victim has no satisfactory remedy. Carnal consummation was not an option to be considered by a poet with a *cor gentile* (and anyway, it is an unreliable cure for the pain of love). The idea of settling down and leading a long and happy life in partnership with the object of one's affection likewise did not feature in the *Fedeli*'s domain of discourse. A poet in love had no way out. He was stuck. All he could do was produce verse celebrating the exquisite agony of love forever, or at least until the next source of misery presented herself. It really does prompt the question, 'Why bother?'

6

'YOU, HOWEVER, ARE NOT'

As Dante lay in the dark, therefore, suffering the pain of Beatrice's refusal to greet him, he was in fact living out the poetic ideal of the *Fedeli d'Amore*. Inside his soul the emotion of love burned so brightly that nothing else mattered, but instead of filling his every move with goodwill and happiness it had turned to hopeless pain.

For the troubadours there had traditionally been no way out of this emotional dead end. Dante had made sure that he was now in exactly the same situation. He had insulated his love from the outside world, jealously guarded it from his family and friends and kept it scrupulously separate even from the great dramas of life and death in which he took part. He had hidden it even from Beatrice herself. Now that love had become misery there was nothing in his life that could relieve it, since it connected with nothing in his life.

And that is where he might well have stayed were it not for two timely interventions. The first was a hint from his old friend, his own unconscious: 'My son, it is time for us to put away our false images.'[1]

A vision has finally arrived and he opens with these words. It is the same figure who spoke to Dante on the way to fight the battle of Campaldino, 'Love in the shape of a young man'. He sits, serious and sad, looking at Dante without speaking. Plainly something has gone wrong. In the past Dante's unconscious has attempted to prompt him (the vision of the flaming heart was a nudge in the direction of creative narrative, for example), but now it seems to be trying to pull the young poet up short. Eventually it is Dante who breaks the silence and asks what is wrong. Love replies with a gnomic remark: 'I am like the centre of a circle, equidistant from all points on the circumference. You, however, are not.'[2]

What does that mean? The implication is that not being equidistant from all points of a circle is a bad thing, but why? Dante tells us in the *Vita Nuova* that, at the time, he did not know the answers to these questions either. But we can make a guess. Medieval ideas about circles go back, like almost all thought of the period, to the Greek philosopher Aristotle. For him, the circle and its three-dimensional analogue, the sphere, are the most perfect geometrical figures. His reason for saying this is that these figures have, in modern language, an infinite set of symmetries – they can be rotated and reflected in an infinite number of ways and still remain the same figure. It is because of this 'perfection' that Aristotle asserts that the whole universe is spherical and that it has a spherical earth at the centre of it.[a]

Circles and spheres were eventually to hold particular significance for Dante. To move ahead slightly in our story, in the *Comedy* the whole universe is composed of them. Hell consists of a series of concentric circles narrowing down to a point of maximum evil in the centre of the earth. Purgatory is a mountain of circular terraces ascending to the sky and Paradise broadens out from the earth with sphere nested inside sphere inside sphere, until it reaches the edge of the universe, beyond which there is nothing except God. If we wrote down the full cosmic address of Dante in his darkened room, in the way that fascinates every child at some time or another, it would end with every line being the name of a sphere which contained the previous one: 'Dante Alighieri Esquire, a darkened room, Dante's house, Florence, Italy, Christendom, the Earth, the atmosphere, the sphere of the Moon, the sphere of Mercury, the sphere of Venus, the sphere of the Sun, the sphere of Mars, the sphere of Jupiter, the sphere of Saturn, the sphere of the fixed stars, the Primum Mobile, the Empyrean.'

---

a It is worth pointing out here that, dating from a time long before Aristotle, nobody who thought about it for any time has ever believed that the earth was flat. There is readily available evidence that it is not: ships disappear over the horizon from the bottom up, the horizon itself appears curved, etc. The obvious roundness of the moon and the fact that the stars move around us in circles lend credibility to the notion of a round earth. The widespread belief that people in the past thought the earth was flat is just one more example of one group of human beings choosing to hold prejudiced views about another.

The circle is, in short, a symbol for the whole universe. Dante's unconscious is nudging him, trying to stop him writing poems about the inner space of his lovelorn soul and encouraging him to start taking account of the world outside. With benefit of hindsight we might wonder whether it is even suggesting that Dante write something which encompasses all aspects of human existence, good and bad, draws on the entire history of Florence, Italy and the world, deals with the ultimate significance of human life and yet has Beatrice and Dante's love for her as its central theme and motivation. But that would be going a bit far, and anyway, Dante was not nearly ready to take that hint at this stage.

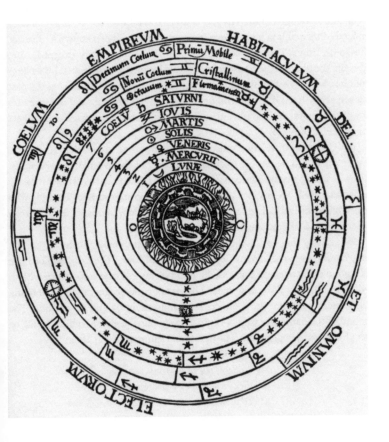

By his own admission, Dante does not understand Love's remark about the circle so he asks the young man to explain it. Love refuses any clarification and Dante returns to a question to which he really wants to know the answer: 'Why did Beatrice refuse to greet me?' This time the apparition is happy to give a full answer: 'Beatrice has gathered, from what certain people have been saying about you, that the lady whom I named to you on the road of sighs was being harmed by you.'[3]

Beatrice, of course, has a good point. It seems more than likely that Dante's dalliance with the emotions of the second decoy lady could have hurt her. Toying with another person's feelings for some clandestine strategy of one's own is evidently irresponsible and potentially very destructive.

It now also seems that Beatrice is aware of Dante's love for her (this has not been acknowledged in the *Vita Nuova* up to this point). The young man does indeed confirm this in his next remark: 'your secret has been known to Beatrice for some time.' This should come as a surprise to nobody except Dante. Despite the obsessive secretiveness, it would be hard to believe that his feelings had not been guessed by the lady in question at some time during the past eleven years. Even if his general demeanour in her presence did not give him away, she might well have heard a whisper from other, less discreet members of the circle of poets.

For Dante this revelation must have brought home to him the fact that his inner world was beginning to creak with contradictions and inconsistencies. He was facing a crisis. His conception of love had created as many problems as it had solved. The secrecy of his love had been compromised. The lady who ruled his emotions had criticised him and reduced him to misery. Even his own unconscious had now apparently turned against him.

He tells us that conflicting ideas circled around inside his head. On the one hand there are so many positive aspects of love: 'The Lordship of Love is a good thing because it draws the mind of his follower away from what is base.' But there is also a downside, 'Love is not good because the more faithful his subject is to him, the more crises he must endure', and then again, 'The sound of the name love is so sweet that it is impossible that his effect should be anything less than pleasant'. The next poem summarises his dilemma:

> My thoughts talk of love time and again.
> But they include such wild diversity
> That one submits to Love's authority,
> While one declares that loving is insane.

(J.G. Nichols (trans.), The New Life, XIII)

It is one thing to realise that you are in a perplexing and painful emotional impasse; it is quite another to find your own way out of it. It needed an unnamed woman whom he met at a party to give Dante a push in the right direction.

The *Vita Nuova* continues. A well-meaning friend has taken Dante to a wedding in the hope of cheering him up. Dante drops his guard long enough to give us some details. We are plainly in a large palazzo; it has frescoes on the wall and the main chamber is surrounded by a gallery. We are, of course, left to imagine the proud mothers and fathers, disreputable uncles, hearty friends and aunts who enjoy a drop, which are the essential elements of a wedding in the Western European tradition.

There are, as one might expect, a number of girls at the party and we gather that this is the reason why the friend has brought him there: to show him that there are plenty more fish in the sea, as it were. Unfortunately, as soon as two of them enter the building Dante feels a sharp pain in his left side. He staggers and is obliged to support himself by leaning against one of the frescoed walls. It transpires that Beatrice is in the house and, even though he has not yet seen her, the spirits that work in the rooms of his soul are reacting to her presence. When he looks up and actually catches sight of her in the gallery the spirits go into such disarray that his senses are all but put out of action. Dante nearly faints but he is also aware that his reaction has caused a stir among the guests. 'Many of the ladies were surprised to see my transfiguration and they spoke mockingly about me to my gracious lady.'

It must have been all too easy to mock and it is almost a relief for the reader of the *Vita Nuova* to be given, for a moment, a glimpse of the world outside the rooms of Dante's soul, a world where people meet for light conversation and groups of girls giggle at the antics of love-struck boys. But the mocking women are too much for Dante and he leaves, assisted by his friend. He retreats once again to his darkened room. But this time no vision appears.

A few days later he happens to meet the same girls again. They evidently were a group – 'certain ladies who enjoy each others' company' is how he describes them. One of them asks a very good question: 'Why do you love your lady if you cannot bear her presence?'

Dante replies that, for him, all possible bliss is associated with the greeting of Beatrice and that when it is denied he is naturally devastated. 'Well, if that were true your poems would surely be very different', comes the reply. And that is the remark that, according to Dante, saved him from the troubadours' dead end and changed his life.

The young woman's observation is absolutely right. You would think that since he loved her so much Dante's poems would be full of extravagant celebration of how blissful Beatrice is, but they are not. Of the nine poems in the *Vita Nuova* so far, seven complain, in one way or another, about the pain which Dante is feeling and the other two are straightforward descriptions of his visions (both of which involve tears). Perhaps it was the surprise that this mocking girl read poetry or perhaps she had just stumbled on something that Dante was on the point of realising for himself, but he took her comment instantly to heart:

> When I thought about it I was rather ashamed and I went away, asking myself: since there is so much bliss in words that praise my lady, why had I ever written otherwise? … I decided that ever after I would take as my theme the praise of my lady.

On the face of it, the decision to praise Beatrice in verse is not an over-whelmingly radical adjustment to his subject matter. Poems in praise of ladies were nothing new. But this turned out to be more than just a resolution to accentuate the positive. It was the seed of an idea which reached, as Dante was to put it, even beyond the widest circling sphere of the heavens. From this moment on, not only was Beatrice no longer a source of pain – no more 'Weep lovers, since you see that love is weeping'[4] – she now gave him access to bliss of a special kind. The joy of Beatrice is the joy of divine love.

Dante explains this in the next poem. It is addressed to the girls who asked the key question (the first line is 'Ladies who have intelligence of love …'). Beatrice is seen from the viewpoint of the heavenly host. We hear that 'God intends to make her a marvel'.

> An Angel cries within the Highest Mind,
> And says, 'Down in the world below us, lord,
> People can see a miracle proceed
> Out of a soul that shines out even here.
>
> (J.G. Nichols (trans.), *The New Life*, XIX)

From now on Dante begins to say something about his love which is entirely new: that it gave him an insight into the love of God.[b] This is not some quaint

---

b To speak of romantic love as a conduit to divine love was entirely novel. Theologically it was not really a heresy, perhaps more of an eccentricity. Nonetheless, some sixteenth-century editions of the *Vita Nuova* were so concerned about the idea that they altered the

religious metaphor. In medieval terms he is linking his love to the fundamental fabric of the universe. Now his love has the power to travel to the edge of space and time:

> Even beyond the widest circling sphere!
> There's where the sigh goes when it leaves my heart.
>
> (J.G. Nichols (trans.), *The New Life*, XLI)

'Beyond the widest circling sphere' is the final line of Dante's cosmic address, the outer edge of the universe, beyond which there is only God. It is His will that decides not only how things are but how they ought to be. Human beings can do what they want – they have been given free will – but whether what they do is right or wrong is measured in terms of God. Every single thing that exists or happens is connected to God's love, just as every leaf is ultimately connected to the roots of a tree. Whatever meaning and value any of it has is by virtue of its relation to the all-pervading cosmic presence of the divine will. And Beatrice is Dante's route to understanding all of it. She is now connected to everything, and through her, potentially, so is he.

---

text in order to make it less theological. The word *beatudine* (blessedness) was replaced with the less God-orientated *felicità* (happiness). And on one occasion even the word *Deo*, God, was replaced with *Deh*, which is a virtually meaningless exclamation.

7

THE NAME OF BEATRICE

I n addition to the *Vita Nuova*, there are two early biographies which give us information about the first phase of Dante's life. The earliest is entitled *A Short Essay in Praise of Dante*. It was written by Giovanni Boccaccio, the Florentine writer who is best known for his collection of frequently bawdy tales known as the *Decameron*.

Boccaccio was in awe of Dante. He says that he worshipped him as a god. This may seem a little surprising given that Boccaccio, in the *Decameron* at least, gives the impression of not being interested in any story that does not involve actual sexual penetration, whereas Dante reserves his passions, on paper at least, for more spiritual areas. But from the very earliest example, Boccaccio's writing is full of allusions and references to Dante. They never met. Dante died when Boccaccio was 8 years old and he did not start work on the biography until about 1357, towards the end of his own life, when the events of the *Vita Nuova* were nearly sixty years in the past.

Boccaccio did research his book as thoroughly as he could, scouring Florence to glean information from anyone who had known Dante or who had known people who had known him. This is presumably the method by which he arrived at the description of Dante in his later years, which is the only credible account we have of what he looked like. Because he is a fellow Florentine, Boccaccio refers to him as 'our poet':

Our poet was of medium height and in his later years he walked slightly bent over, with a grave and gentle gait. He always wore the most seemly attire, as befitted his ripe years. His face was long, his nose aquiline, and his eyes big rather than small. His jaw was large and his lower lip protruded. His complexion was dark, his hair and beard thick, black, and curly, and his expression ever melancholy and thoughtful.

(Boccaccio, Biography of Dante, VIII)

This does not read like a description of an overwhelmingly good-looking man, but we do see very clearly the sober and serious poet that Boccaccio's biography is eager to present to us. Nor can we fail to miss, either visually or verbally, the aquiline nose that, along with the intense, almost magisterial demeanour, characterises later visual representations. Over the centuries a specific face has become associated with him. This seems to derive from a picture that was probably painted in the year 1325, shortly after his death. It depicts a young man who is part of a group of Florentines painted on the wall of the chapel of the Bargello, the newly built palace of the podestà in Florence. The fresco was whitewashed over not long afterwards and only rediscovered in 1839.

When it re-emerged, a group of Florentine Dante aficionados campaigned vociferously for its complete restoration on the grounds that this was certainly the earliest and most authentic portrait of their poet. One worries that the resulting restoration might have been a little over-zealous, because it is noticeable that, whilst most of the surface of the fresco is pitted and scratched with much of the original painting irretrievably lost, the alleged face of Dante seems miraculously to have escaped all such ravages. Opinion has raged ever since about whether this picture, or rather its pre-restoration original, might be a very early example of the emerging tradition of lifelike portraits and whether, even more tantalisingly, it might be by the great early Renaissance painter Giotto.[a] The balance of scholarly opinion seems, at the moment, to give the

---

a   Giotto di Bondone (1267–1337), the undisputed innovative genius of early Renaissance painting, is another of the frustrations encountered by Dante biographers. He was a Florentine and an almost exact contemporary of Dante. Although he was from more humble origins, they both grew up in Florence at the same time and came to share many interests. It is hard to believe they did not know each other, yet we have no record of any contact between them beyond a rather fanciful conversation reported by commentator Benvenuto da Imola about eighty years after the event. Dante himself does mention Giotto once, when discussing the transience of fame in the *Comedy*, noting that he has replaced the older painter, Cimabue, as flavour of the month. But the remark hardly counts as evidence of a relationship.

answer 'no' on both counts but this image has nonetheless served as a model for all subsequent pictures of Dante, even down to the characteristic headgear. The beard which Boccaccio mentions does make some brief appearances in the fourteenth century, only to be dropped from all future depictions.

Boccaccio had the advantage of living close in time to the events he was describing. He was, in addition, an intelligent and highly educated man who knew Florence and the Florentines as well as anybody living. His biography is, therefore, an invaluable source of information for many of the details of Dante's life and we should be inclined to believe him in the absence of any other evidence.

On the other hand, Boccaccio was separated from his subject by at least one major barrier. Between the death of Dante and the writing of the biography Florence had, along with the rest of Europe and Asia, undergone the cataclysmic upheaval of the Black Death. Bubonic plague had carried off nearly three-quarters of the people of the city. Not only were many witnesses lost but, to those who had lived through the horror and the near social collapse, pre-plague Florence must have seemed a very distant world.

Boccaccio himself had undergone some sort of personality change as well. By the time he started the biography he had had an unhappy love affair and ill health seems to have turned him from an impish teller of rude tales into an embittered old misogynist. It is perhaps unsurprising that he finds it very difficult to come to terms with the idea that Dante's love for Beatrice was chaste (his knowing aside, 'no small marvel in today's world' has lost none of its freshness), but when he then continues with a lengthy and impassioned diatribe about the evils of marriage we wonder if his own feelings are not impinging a little too much on the work. He himself came to exactly that conclusion because he rather charmingly rounds off the outburst with a statement that the opinions expressed are his own and not necessarily those of Dante.

The other reason to exercise caution with Boccaccio's account is simply that he is a writer of fiction and therefore someone who makes untruths credible for a living. He is as likely to be drawn to a detail or event because of its appropriateness to the story as by its credentials as an objective fact. There is even some evidence that in his eagerness for poignant detail Boccaccio faked a document. A copy of a letter exists which purports to have been written by a monk who had just read the *Divine Comedy* and was now sending it on to his own patron with the highest recommendation. It contains one of those dramatic moments that are a little too good to be true. The monk says that he himself had met Dante and describes a moment when, after some serious discussion, he asked the poet what he wanted most of all. Dante simply smiled and said 'peace'. There are other reasons not to believe the authenticity of this document: it does not fit with other known facts about the early dating of the *Comedy*; in style it is all a bit too literary; and most suspicious of all, manuscripts of the letter have only ever been found in close association with copies of Boccaccio's own work.

The next biographer, Leonardo Bruni, would certainly not have countenanced dodgy evidence. He was a highly respected humanist historian whose twelve-volume Latin history of Florence is considered a key source for the emergence of the political conditions that created the Florentine renaissance. Although he was writing about a hundred years after Dante's death, Bruni too made efforts to research his life by speaking to Dante's descendants, many of whom by then lived in other cities. Like Boccaccio, Bruni was a champion of all things Dantean. When Dante's grandson visited Florence from his native Verona, for example, Bruni made a point of personally taking him on a 'heritage tour' of significant places in his eminent grandfather's life.

Bruni begins his book by explaining how he came to write it. He had finished work on a lengthy volume of the history of Florence in Latin and, as relaxation, felt the need to read something in Italian.[b] He picked up Boccaccio's biography. He enjoyed the book but he had one problem with it. Boccaccio, he feels, spends far too much time and emphasis on Dante's unfortunate attachment to 'that girl' (Bruni does not care to name her). He feels that more emphasis should have been put on Dante's fulfilment of his civic duties on the field of battle rather than his amorous excursions: 'I could wish that our Boccaccio had made mention of this valour rather than of his falling in love at nine years old and such like trifles, which he tells of so great a man.' Boccaccio might well reply (and with no small justification) that he was doing no more than following Dante's own emphasis about what was important in his life. But Bruni is convinced that the fault lies with Boccaccio. The eminent teller of rude tales has been unable to keep away from the salacious themes of his previous work: 'the tongue goes where the tooth aches', as he memorably puts it.

---

b   It is interesting to observe how the project of the *Fedeli* to make Italian a respectable language has made progress: a hundred years later Latin is still the tongue of choice for serious scholarship but it is acceptable even for an intellectual to read Italian for recreation.

No biographer of Dante since has gone quite so far as to try entirely to dismiss the importance of Beatrice in Dante's life. But there can be few who have not felt slightly frustrated about how little we know of her. Dante tells us virtually nothing about her which does not involve either the effect she had on him or her theological function as a conduit to the divine. He spends a great deal of time telling us what he saw through her but he never tells us anything at all about what he saw *in* her.

This absence of solid information has led some scholars seriously to suggest that Beatrice never existed, that she was no more than a theoretical construct introduced to allow Dante to dramatise his spiritual journey. This is hard to credit: the sheer human idiosyncrasy (and indeed battiness) of the *Vita Nuova* account seems to be overwhelmingly suggestive that Dante is talking about his real love for an actual person, albeit filtered through the organising mind of a late medieval intellectual.

Scholars have scoured the history of theology in search of an intellectual ancestor for his idea of a beloved woman as the route to divine revelation. Surprisingly, they have found one. The idea is apparently entirely new to Christianity but there is one previous example from the world of Islam. Muhyi ad-Din ibn Arabi was a Spanish poet, born a hundred years before Dante in the town of Murcia in the south-east. At that time Spain was the most sophisticated and creative centre of Islamic culture. Arabi, like Dante a serious and scholarly man, had, while on his travels in Mecca, lodged in the house of an eminent sage. He fell in love with the daughter of the house and started writing poetry.

Arabi's poems are every bit as analytical and as single-mindedly passionate as those in the *Vita Nuova*. He explains in detail that it is through his beloved that he sees the glory of divine wisdom: 'her virgin breasts are the nectar of its teachings; the smile on her lips its illuminations. Her eyes are the emblems of light and revelation. The mournful sighs of the lover represent the spiritual longings of the soul.'[1] The language leans rather more towards the sensuous than Dante's ever does, but intellectual kinship between the two poets is clear.

It is quite possible that Dante had heard of Arabi. The connections between Christian Europe and the Muslim world are well known. Islamic scholars had kept alive and interpreted the wisdom of the ancient Greeks; their learning had been filtering into the west for over a century and was continuing to do so in Dante's time. In particular, Brunetto Latini, a Florentine scholar who was to have a great influence on Dante, had served as ambassador to the court of King Alphonso X in the Spanish city of Toledo, which, by Dante's time, also owned Arabi's home town of Murcia. It was there that King Alphonso had set up an institute staffed by Christian, Muslim and Jewish scholars engaged on the translation of Greek, Hebrew and Arabic texts. Even closer to Florence, the island of Sicily had, until the eleventh century, also been a Muslim kingdom. Even when it later came under the control of the Holy Roman Empire, Islamic and Christian intellectuals again mixed freely at the imperial court. Given Florence's position as a centre of international trade, it is, in fact, very hard to imagine that at some time Dante had *not* met at least one Muslim visitor who had knowledge of Islamic literature and traditions.

If we are convinced that Beatrice was a real person the next question is obviously, 'Who was she?' Only Boccaccio has ever proffered an answer to this question. He says that she was the daughter of Folco Portinari, the head of a famous and wealthy Florentine family. Folco was a philanthropist; in 1288 he had founded the Santa Maria Nuova hospital which exists to this day as the major hospital for the city. Records confirm that Folco had a daughter who is referred to not as Beatrice but by the name's (to anglophone ears rather unattractive) diminutive, 'Bice'.

Records tell us that this Bice Portinari was married to one Simone di Bardi. The *Vita Nuova* does not mention that Dante's Beatrice was married. Perhaps we should not be surprised if Dante does not mention Beatrice's marriage – after all, he also fails to mention battles in which thousands of people were killed – but, even so, it is an odd omission since, unlike the battle of Campaldino, this is an event that involved Beatrice.

Scholars have tended, in the absence of any evidence to the contrary, to go along with Boccaccio's assertion that Beatrice was Ms Portinari. After all, runs the argument, Boccaccio was in Florence not long after the events and would have heard the truth from those who knew. But this is not quite so obvious: even if Boccaccio had, at the age of 10, started precociously taking an interest in the life and love of his fellow Florentine, it would have already been thirty years since the events in the *Vita Nuova*. By the time he was actually writing the biography it was sixty years later. Dante struggled to keep the identity of his beloved hidden from all but a few intimates. We can safely guess that, at the time, the vast majority of Florentines neither knew nor cared who some unknown teenager happened to be in love with. By the time Boccaccio was writing both parties were dead, and plague, war and political meltdown separated him from Dante's era. It is quite possible that the information on which he based his assertion about Beatrice's identity was no more than an amalgam of rumour, gossip and post hoc invention which, with the instinct of a fiction writer, he represented as fact. The Portinari family themselves would by this time have been happy to have their Great Aunt Bice associated with an emerging cultural icon.

If the woman whom Dante loved was not Bice Portinari, would there be any reason to believe that her real name was Beatrice? After all, the *Vita Nuova* avoids all proper names and nearly a third of its chapters revolve, in one way or another, around his attempts to conceal the woman's identity. Why would Dante break his golden rule and make it easy for anyone to identify her by revealing her real first name?

Dante makes one puzzling remark when he first uses the name Beatrice. He says, 'She was called Beatrice by many who did not know what the name meant'. The name Beatrice is derived from the Latin *beatus*, blessed, and this remark is usually taken to confirm that Beatrice was her real name which was therefore used by everybody, even those who had no understanding of its Latin derivation. Well, yes, if Beatrice was her real name that would be absolutely true but it would also be unremarkable. By definition someone's name is used by all and sundry, irrespective of educational level – that is hardly a surprise. The remark becomes much more interesting, however, if Beatrice is *not* her real name but a special, almost sacred one used by Dante alone. It is not so unusual to invent a pet name for another person in whom one is interested, even before one has met them. For Dante, having a special name for his beloved would have been part of the paraphernalia of concealment.

We know from the poems they exchanged that his friend Guido Cavalcanti and some of the other *Fedeli* knew the identity of Dante's beloved. It is quite possible that they had, in the way of young men, referred to her at some later time without due respect ('Saw your Beatrice in the market this morning, Dante, she certainly is a healthy looking girl, if you know what I mean!').[c] We can imagine the distress such a remark would have caused Dante and we might well expect there to be a bitter reference in the *Vita Nuova* to the effect that the name had been misused by those who did not really understand.

This is no more than speculation with little prospect of being anything more. But the possibility that we do not know Beatrice's real name seems almost to add to the poetic solidity of a woman who walks out of history having left no trace of herself and yet at the same time informs Dante's entire universe. It is

---

c In Dante's later work Guido is indeed admonished (and forgiven) for having at some time mocked Dante's feelings for Beatrice.

worth pointing out that, were a poet looking for a name for the woman they loved, Beatrice would be a good choice. Not only does it have the linguistic association with Latin blessedness, but pronounced out loud in the Italian way (Bay-ah-*tri*-chay) it has a sonorous complexity that can be modulated to give a rich diversity of tone and feeling. 'Say it loud and there's music playing; say it soft and it's almost like praying',[2] as Dante might have been quite proud to have written.

Of all the passages in all the works of Dante there is only one which brings us close to the woman whom he calls Beatrice. It does not supply details about her: we will never know the colour of her eyes or hair, let alone anything about the way she wore her hat or the way she sang off key. But in a single rather generous paragraph Dante celebrates the effect she had on those around her. The passage gives us a fleeting impression of what it might have been like to meet her. 'She came into such favour with people that when she walked down the street they ran to see her … there are many who can bear witness to this.' Dante makes it clear that it was her humility as much as her beauty that moved them: 'She went crowned and clothed in humility, displaying no pride in what she saw and heard … Those who saw her felt in themselves a delight so pure and sweet that they could not express it.'

The poem he includes in this section begins in Italian, *Tanto gentile e tanto onesta pare la donna mia quand'ella altrui saluta* – literally something like, 'My lady is so noble and so honest when she greets another person'. In Italy this is a popular archetype of poetry, roughly the equivalent of Shakespeare's 'Shall I compare thee to a summer's day?' Generations of unwilling Italian schoolchildren have been obliged to learn *Tanto gentile*; it is sung by earnest young women strumming guitars and spoken aloud with full expression by Italian cultural celebrities who really ought to know better. But it is a great poem for all that. It is also the closest we will ever get to a picture of a person who must have possessed, even allowing for exaggeration, an exceptional presence. There evidently really was something in the way the woman, whose name may or may not have been Beatrice Portinari, moved and smiled, something which went beyond sexual attractiveness. It affected not just Dante but all who met her, and it reminded them of the possibility of kindness in a world of selfishness, anger and greed.

> My lady shows such gentle dignity
> To everybody whom she deigns to greet
> That every tongue is stricken and falls mute,
> And no one's bold enough to look her way.

She walks along, hearing her praises swell,
Clothed in humility as in a gown.
She seems to be a creature coming down
From Heaven to earth to show a miracle.

She looks so beautiful as she goes by,
And she sends such a sweetness to the heart
As no one understands who does not feel.

And from her lips at times there seems to steal,
Gentle and full of love, a speaking spirit
Whose constant message to the soul is: 'Sigh!'

(J.G. Nichols (trans.), *The New Life*, XXVI)

8

LAMENTATIONS

As everyone can readily understand, there is nothing stable in this world, and if there is one thing that changes easily it is our life.

(Boccaccio, Biography of Dante)

Dante's Beatrice died on 8 June 1290, one year after the battle of Campaldino, when Dante was 25 years old. He records the event, about three-quarters of the way through the *Vita Nuova*, in a chapter headed with a quotation from the Book of Lamentations: 'How lonely sits the city that was full of people! How like a widow she has become, she that was great among the nations.'

He tells us that when he heard the news he was in the middle of writing a poem but gives us no further information about the circumstances of her death. He realises that we will want to know more but has made a conscious decision to say nothing: 'Perhaps at this point some account of her departure would be welcome but it is not my intention to give any.' Which is surely the most minimalist example of fine dramatic writing in the history of literature.

Anyone who has read the *Vita Nuova* up to this point can get an inkling of Dante's distress. Boccaccio is not able to provide any more information about the reason for her death but he does give us a description of Dante at the time, quite possibly based on eyewitness accounts handed down by friends and family: 'Weeping, pain in his heart, and neglect of himself had given on the appearance of a wild thing. He was lean, unshaven, and almost completely transformed from what he had been before.'[1]

Dante's tormented confusion continued until it seemed that his grief was on the point of completely overwhelming his personality. A poem survives from his friend Guido Cavalcanti which expresses his concern: 'I come to you during the day countless times and find you thinking too basely: I deeply grieve over your noble mind and your many virtues of which you are deprived.' Guido has no solution to offer beyond hoping that his poem will persuade the demon that possesses him to leave him alone.

The short chapters of the *Vita Nuova* which follow the death of Beatrice are like disjointed snapshots of a state of near breakdown. Following immediately on her death, Dante gives us a demonstration of how the number nine was once again involved with Beatrice, this time in the matter of the exact date of her demise. This is, at first sight, a difficult task because he has already told us that she died on the eighth day of the sixth month. But Dante is adamant: it is not apparent in our calendar, he says, but 'according to the Arabic calendar, her most noble soul departed in the first hour of the ninth day of the month and, according to the Syrian calendar, she departed in the ninth month of the year since, the first month in that calendar is Tixryn the First which is our October.'[a] There is surely a no more telling sign of his despair than this desperate invocation of arcane learning to force a reassuring pattern on to a universe that has just dealt him an unbearable, random blow.

In the next chapter he returns to the quotation from the Bible with which he prefaces the death of Beatrice and which is the only direct expression of sorrow which he allows himself. It is natural to project one's grief on to one's surroundings and so it is quite understandable that, to Dante, the city of Florence had become lonely and bereft like a widow, as the Book of Lamentations puts it. This impression, however, seems to have taken on a frightening solidity for him. He tells us that, in response to what had happened, he 'wrote to the princes of the land describing the state of the city'. Did he really write to the rulers of other cities and, if so, what did he say? Had he slipped temporarily into a disturbed world where metaphor was becoming so real that he believed that Beatrice's death had affected the civic well-being of

a In fact, most modern authorities count Tixryn, or *tišrnu al-awwal*, which is indeed the equivalent of our October, as the tenth month. Perhaps whatever friendly Muslim visitor he asked about it bent the facts a little, just to be kind.

Florence to such an extent that neighbouring cities needed to be advised of the situation? That is certainly how it reads in the *Vita Nuova*.

The next incident is equally more strange. Exactly a year after Beatrice's death he tells us that he was 'sitting thinking of her and drawing an angel'. The absence of context is disconcerting. We do not hear why Dante was drawing an angel. There is no record before or since of his taking any interest in drawing but he says it as if this was an everyday activity.

The story continues in a way which is totally unexceptional. Dante looks round and sees 'certain men to whom respect was due', possibly members of the governing council. He says that he was told later that they had been watching him for some time. When Dante notices the onlookers he greets them, tells them 'someone was on my mind and I was lost in thought'. He then proceeds to go back to drawing. The angel apparently had nothing to do with it.

There must be something missing from this non-story, some embarrassing element that Dante is failing to mention. Was he so absorbed that he ignored the passing dignitaries to the point of rudeness? Was he still so deranged by grief that he was drawing the angel in some unacceptable place? Was drawing an angel in itself so bizarre that it needed justification? What the *Vita Nuova* has recorded must be Dante's answer to a story that had already circulated showing him in a bad light. His version of it is unexceptional because he is trying to persuade his readers that the incident was perfectly ordinary, despite what they may have heard. The original cause is lost, only the reply and the embarrassment remain.

Still in a state of desperate grief, Dante finds himself in 'a place which brought past times to mind' (Florence must surely have been full of them). Lost in misery, he looks up to see 'a noble lady, young and beautiful' looking down from a window. She is visibly full of pity. As Dante says, 'when unhappy people see others having compassion for them they are more easily moved to weep', and so he breaks down in tears.

This encounter is the beginning of the episode of the *Donna Gentile*, the kindly lady. At first Dante went to her whenever he found he could no longer weep or give vent to his sadness. From his description, their early relationship seems to have been based entirely on her ability to facilitate his mourning for Beatrice. That is probably not the healthiest basis for a relationship but it is a basis and, probably inevitably, we are told further on that he has 'started to take too much pleasure in the lady'. A new relationship has a special appeal and he soon says that he is fascinated with 'this strange new loving little spirit placing all its desires in front of me'. We are not surprised at all when he confesses that 'the sight of this lady has such a strange effect on me that I often thought that I liked her too much'.

The *Donna Gentile* has her own place in the story of Dante's life but her appearance at this point raises the more general question of whether Dante had relationships (and of what kind) with women other than Beatrice. We know by now that just because Dante chooses not to mention something does not mean that it did not happen. Boccaccio gives us no help in this matter, other than to assure us that Dante did have strong lustful appetites. There are in existence a number of love poems by Dante, not in the *Vita Nuova*, which are addressed to women other than Beatrice. Some of his most beautiful love poetry, in fact, is written for someone he calls *la Donna Petrosa*, the Stone Lady. Others mention a *pargoletta*, a young girl. Neither of these women have found a place in any of the available biographical material. The existence of these poems is not, of course, conclusive evidence of a physical liaison. The convention of courtly love, to which Dante and his fellow poets were heirs, was to write poems to people with whom one had *not* had carnal relations.

There is one conclusion about Dante and women which is easier to draw from a reading of his work. He seems genuinely to have liked them. We have seen that he had written poems listing his sixty favourite women, and also that he let himself be persuaded by a group of them to write a different kind of love poetry. He would hardly have done that if he did not rather enjoy sparring with them verbally. In the *Comedy*, as well as the principal female characters, women with names like Gentucca[b] and Matilda also make mysterious, brief appearances.

The more interesting question is not, 'Did Dante have physical relationships with other women?' – Boccaccio finds it impossible to believe that he didn't and most modern readers will probably agree – but rather, 'Was Beatrice, at all times in his life, the most important feature of his emotional landscape?' Was she, in the words of the song, always on his mind? The answer to this question is, surprisingly, no.

The man whose name will forever be associated with Beatrice actually turned his back on her about a year after her death. The *Donna Gentile*, who

b   Early writers on Dante doubted whether Gentucca was real and tried to give her an entirely symbolic existence. Modern scholarship favours her reality. The great English Dante scholar Barbara Reynolds, whilst accepting that she is a real person, rather uncharitably suggests that she is only in the *Comedy* because her name rhymes with Lucca.

had started by helping to put back together the pieces of his shattered soul, finished by replacing Beatrice in his affections. It seems that he became so obsessed that he stalked her, hanging round her house at night: 'I was full of desire for her and even for all those close to her, acquaintances or kin. How many were the nights when my eyes gazed intently on my love's dwelling-place, when those of others were closed in sleep.'[2]

But this was much more than an obsessive infatuation. The rebuilding of Dante's soul had turned into a reinvention of himself. He came out of the experience with new ideas and a new attitude to love. And the *Donna Gentile* was an essential part of that transformation.

It is estimated that one in twenty-three people has a psychological condition called synaesthesia, a quirk of the mind which causes them to link radically different sensations. Some of them associate colours with days of the week, for example; others see shapes when they hear musical notes or even taste a particular flavour when they hear a sound. Dante seems to have had a variant of this which made him associate intellectual standpoints with particular women. Beatrice had become so mixed in Dante's mind with theological concepts of love and redemption that she became those things for him: they could not exist without her. The *Donna Gentile* in her turn also became part woman, part philosophical tenet. He called her the 'Lady Philosophy', the personification not of love-based religion this time, but of rational, analytical thought, 'The lady whose eyes are her demonstrations and whose smile her persuasiveness'.

After the death of Beatrice the study of philosophy (which at the time included what we now call science) became a passion for Dante. Like others before him he found consolation in the contemplation of how things are at a deep level: what matter is, how it moves, what existence is, how truth can be sorted out from error. He read the great philosophical texts of the age with such enthusiasm, he tells us, that his eyes went funny – when he went out at night the stars seemed covered by a white haze. After a little rest in a cool (and presumably dark) room he tells us he recovered enough to resume his studies.

Dante was so moved by philosophy and so convinced of its potential to make the world better that he would later begin work on a lengthy book which he intended to be an explanation of all philosophy for the general reader. It was called the *Convivio*, the Banquet, the idea being that it would provide a nourishing feast of ideas for its readers. The book (of which only four out of fifteen planned volumes were ever completed) was to be constructed around a series of his poems in praise of the Lady Philosophy. The chapters would at the same time act as explanations of the poem (much more meaty than the ones in the *Vita Nuova*) and as primers in philosophy and science. It is, or rather would have been, a milestone in the history of popular education. It is also in this book that he lets slip many of the pieces of information that give us clues as to his relationship with the *Donna Gentile*. Her main function is allegorical and as usual he gives us no indication as to the physical nature of the relationship unless one counts some exquisitely ambiguous passages. Here, for example, is his description of his fumbling first encounter with that notoriously exacting discipline of philosophy: 'Philosophy seemed proud to me, at first, as regards her body (that is to say, wisdom) for she did not smile at me, for as yet I failed to understand her proofs. The fault in all this was mine.'[3]

It is hard not to suspect that somehow he is deliberately teasing his readers with a paragraph that is equally a description of first steps in philosophy and also an account of the uncertainty of a first date.

By the time he was writing the *Convivio*, Beatrice and the *Donna Gentile* had come to stand for two opposing attitudes. To oversimplify grossly, they represented the conflict between the world of the senses and the world of reason. On the one hand is the power of love which, he has explained to us, entered his mind in a blinding flash through his senses. Dante never doubts the power of love, but in the *Convivio* it is outranked by the strength of rational thought personified by the Lady Philosophy. Dante's mission is to spread the word among his readers (he is confident that he has a following inherited from the readership of the *Vita Nuova*). His passionate belief in the power of philosophy to do good is evident throughout. To ignore philosophy and choose the other path is to court disaster by putting oneself in the thrall of one's senses: 'He who forgoes his reason and merely utilises his senses lives as a beast and not a man.' This really is a new Dante with a completely new attitude. He is certain also that the old view cannot coexist with the new: 'Just as this thought, mentioned above, used to be my life, so another appears which makes that one cease to exist.' To put it another way, Dante has left Beatrice for the *Donna Gentile*.

There is one woman in Dante's life whom he never mentions. Gemma Donati was a distant relative of Corso Donati, the impetuous hero of the battle of Campaldino. She was also Dante's wife. There is ample documentary evidence that she and Dante were married: both early biographers mention her by name and there is an extant copy of Gemma's mother's will in which Dante is mentioned. Their betrothal is recorded in the city archive as having taken place on 9 January 1277 when Dante was 10 years old.[c]

Nowadays it would be called an arranged marriage, as most were among even the minor nobility. The young couple would have grown up knowing each other and would have had the right, should either of them have really objected, to veto the marriage. Boccaccio says that the union was hastily brought forward as an attempt by Dante's family to help him get over his grief. We could guess how effective that would have been even had Boccaccio not confirmed that it was to no avail. Some historians, however, believe that the wedding had already happened before Beatrice died. If that is so the marriage is just one more thing to add to the list of events that Dante does not mention in the *Vita Nuova*. But, whatever the exact date, married they were and Gemma was to bear him at least three children: Pietro, Jacopo and a daughter, Antonia.

Not only does he never mention her in any poem or any other writing, but he does not ever allude to the fact that he is married. No scholar who has searched his work has come up even with one arcane, gnomic or coded reference to Gemma. The mother of his children was invisible to Dante the poet. And yet it is possible that they had a perfectly amicable relationship. His failure to mention her is not necessarily a sign that he did not care. His silence may be no more than a consequence of his single-minded interest only in the rarefied love of the troubadours – that hallmark of the noble heart. Whatever affection he and Gemma shared did not fit into the schema of Aristotle's theory of the soul. Yet through the simple facts of proximity, shared humour and common hope, Gemma must have made some impression on Dante. When, in the *Comedy*, he describes his characters it is hard not to believe that at least once, in a phrase, a look or a gesture, there is an echo – too faint to be detected by even the finest scholars – of Dante and Gemma.

As to what Gemma thought about 'the Beatrice thing' there is no indication, apart possibly from one incident. In the last years of Dante's life, when he was living in Ravenna, his daughter Antonia became a nun in a convent in the city. Following the custom of the time this was quite possibly as much of a retirement plan as an unwelcome incarceration. There are only sketchy records of Antonia's life as a nun but we do know that, as nuns always do, she took a new name at the time she took her vows. The name she chose was Sister Beatrice. Doubtless the choice was intended principally to please her father, but surely we can be certain that she would not have

c In fact, the record seems to have been lost at the beginning of the last century but its
   existence is well attested.

done it if the name was a source of pain for her mother, who was still alive at the time, possibly even with Dante in Ravenna. Either Gemma had managed eventually to overcome any hostile feelings towards Beatrice or she had just never been overly concerned about a rival who was ethereal, theological and dead.

9

ORDINANCES OF JUSTICE

One evening, at about the time Dante was finishing the *Vita Nuova*, a man stood on the steps of the church of the Santa Trinità in Florence. He spoke to a disgruntled crowd, urging them to action. He told them that they did not have to put up with their current circumstances, that change was possible. 'The situation is not beyond righting', the chronicler gives a verbatim account of his words, 'the time is now'. The man, whose name was Giano della Bella, was playing the role of a popular rabble-rouser, appealing to the class of tradesmen and merchants, known as the Popolani, and perhaps even to some of their employees and servants who were so far down the social scale that they do not show on the radar with which historians scan the thirteenth century.

The situation to which Giano was referring was a growing imbalance in the finely tuned stand-off between Florence's two major power groups: the merchant Popolani and their counterbalancing class, the landowning old aristocracy, the Magnati. The event that had upset the previously workable coexistence was Florence's victory over Arezzo at the battle of Campaldino. Warfare was the business of the magnati and, having delivered such a spectacular victory, they seem to have experienced a burst of euphoric self-confidence which had led to a resurgence of the high-handed bullying behaviour which is the default position of the European aristocrat. The magnati began to take what they wanted, ignoring the rights of merchant citizens. The rule of law, which had never had a particularly firm grip on them, was either ignored or reduced to impotence through intimidation and corruption. The merchant classes felt that they were suffering the indignity of a regression to the feudal state out of which they had dragged themselves through hard work and aggressive business practices more than a century earlier.

Giano della Bella was demanding that action be taken to redress the balance. Interestingly, he was himself a nobleman, a veteran of Campaldino who was famous for having fought bravely even when the enemy cut out his horse from under him. The story goes that he became disillusioned with the magnati way of doing things when one of his own class had threatened to cut off his nose. This particular form of mutilation seems to have been favoured by the Florentine nobility, presumably because it had a relatively low risk of death and an associated murder charge and yet had the advantage of a highly visible result. Giano was an honest man who, the chroniclers tell us, had the gift of speaking out about things which others ignored. Beyond his relief that the threat had remained only a threat, he evidently saw the nose incident as a symptom of a deeper malaise.

When Giano was elected to the Council of Priors in 1293 he had decided to act. Now he was seeking support for what was effectively a package of constitutional reforms which would severely curb the power of the magnati. The new package was indeed adopted soon after Giano's speech. It was known as the Ordinances of Justice. Far-reaching and radical, the Ordinances were designed greatly to increase the power of the Council of Priors and to make sure that in future it represented the interests of the merchants alone. Priors would from then on be selected only from members of the guilds. This move by itself would have had the effect of excluding the magnati from the process of government but, as a back-up, a number of families – 150 were eventually put on the list – were specifically banned by name from becoming priors, effectively stripping them of citizenship. In order to enforce the decisions of the newly purged council a new post was created with the grand title of the 'Standard Bearer of Justice'. This person was the council's enforcer. He had a body of a thousand armed men, drawn from the popolani, at his disposal (for use only within the city limits). This seems like a very large force but it was quite possibly the minimum needed if the popolani were to have a chance of matching the assembled band of retainers, hired thugs and violent members of the young generation that the magnati could call on at short notice.

The Ordinances were very popular with a large section of the popolani, less so with the magnati. The final act of legislative aggression was a new law to the effect that if any member of a noble family was found guilty of a crime (a 'public report' attested by two witnesses was all that was needed to secure a conviction and the accused could be tried *in absentia*), then if they defaulted on their fines, punitive damages could be imposed on the rest of the family. This, in practice, seems to have invariably involved the traditional Florentine method of retribution: knocking the family's house down.

'The damned lawyers objected' is how one translator renders the remark of the chronicler Dino Compagni as he reports opposition to the Ordinances. Dino speaks with some authority because he was actually a member of the Council of Priors when the Ordinances were adopted. He went on to become the second Standard Bearer of Justice in the new regime and (at the beginning) he was a keen supporter. He was a contemporary of Dante and knew him. About twenty years later, Dino was to judge that political circumstances in Florence were such that no harm would come to him and he wrote a brief account of events in Florence during the period of the Ordinances. It was just as well that the book was brief because by the time he had finished it the political climate in Florence had changed yet again and his remarks would have brought him into conflict with the authorities. He hid the book in a safe place where it remained for 400 years until it was discovered again in 1726. Only one copy has ever been found.

Dino writes in a clear, no-nonsense style. He had the great gift of a chronicler of describing the salient features of a situation that would be needed for the understanding of a reader from the future. He had a ringside seat on the first test case of the Ordinances. A member of the Galli family, travelling in France, had been involved in a brawl with a member of another Florentine family. A death resulted. The young man remained abroad for the trial and was found guilty in his absence. In accordance with the new laws, because he was not available for punishment, Dino, as Standard Bearer, was eventually obliged to oversee the destruction not only of the alleged murderer's house but also those of his relatives. It is not difficult to see that a policy of destroying somebody's house because one of their relatives has allegedly done something wrong is unlikely to promote peace. But the popolani had been wounded by magnati excesses. Public displays of vengeance made them feel better and they encouraged the work. Dino records that even the priors, who had been picked in the first place because they were supporters of the Ordinances, were frequently unwilling to exercise their discretion and stop the destruction because 'The Popolo called them cowards if they did not destroy the houses utterly'. The magnati were predictably outraged, as Dino quotes one of them: 'If a horse runs and its tail hits the face of a popolano; or someone bumps into someone else in a crowd, meaning no malice; or a bunch of little children start to quarrel. Must they be destroyed for such things?'[1] Eventually the Council of Priors would find itself in the ridiculous position of destroying a house because of popular enthusiasm for vengeance but then compensating the owner for what they themselves saw as an injustice.

The Ordinances had gone far beyond any democratic idea of social justice and strayed into the realm of vengeful partisanship. Far from damping the cycle of tit-for-tat retribution which was such a feature of Florentine politics, they had raised the stakes of the conflict. Under such circumstances the only option left to the opposing side was to react with equal and apposite extremism.

Surprisingly, during this period Florence remained prosperous and even continued to expand. After all, the battle of Campaldino may have caused a certain amount of instability within the city but it had also given Florence the military ascendancy necessary to maintain its river links to the sea which were so essential for a landlocked city state that relied on international trade.

With a confidence in the future that would not at first sight seem to have been justified by day-to-day events, the Florentines invested much of their wealth in public construction projects. Of all the buildings that make up the familiar skyline of the Renaissance city none was completed during Dante's life, but almost all of them were started. A majority are the product of initiatives taken during the period of the Ordinances of Justice. The celebrated architect and sculptor Arnolfo di Cambio, as well as working on the new walls of the expanded city, designed both the first stage of the cathedral and the Franciscan church of Santa Croce. The priors, whose role had become increasingly important under the new regime, were given a new headquarters. It was built in the dour, stone, riot-proof style of Florentine palaces, designed to mirror and yet outdo in size the palace of the podestà, captain of the opposing magnati, which stood about 300m away (and is now known as the Bargello museum). The palace of the priors with its distinctive tower has been through several changes of use and is now known as the Palazzo Vecchio. Second to the Duomo, it is the most famous building in Florence. It stands overlooking the open space where the houses of the Uberti had been razed to the ground following a previous violent swing of the political pendulum, which, thirty years earlier in 1266, had also brought the merchant classes into ascendancy.

The building of the new cathedral was funded through a typically Florentine financial innovation. A kind of supernumerary guild was created called the Opera del Duomo, the 'Cathedral Works'. This was something rather akin

to a holding company, set up to manage and channel finance in the shape of donations and loans from wealthy citizens. In order to build the cathedral of Santa Maria Del Fiore, the church of Santa Reparata was expanded and the neighbouring church of Santa Michele was demolished along with a section of Roman wall.[a] The city would have to wait over a hundred years until that genius of the Renaissance, the architect Filippo Brunelleschi, was able finally to work out a way of raising the great cupola over the octagonal eastern end

---

a Visitors to the Piazza del Duomo today can see 'Dante's seat' from which the young poet is said to have observed progress on the site.

of the building; but it was the signoria of Dante's time that had the optimism to build the foundations and supporting walls for what was to be the world's largest dome, and then sit back and wait for engineering know-how to catch up with their vision.

States which possess wealth usually attract the interest of other, greater powers. Sometimes that interest is expressed as aggression, other times as friendship. In March 1294 Florence was visited by Charles Martel, a member of the European extended family that included the French royal family and a selection of other hereditary rulers. His full titles included 'Charles, first born of the illustrious King of Jerusalem and Sicily, king by the grace of God of Hungary, Dalmatia, Croatia, Serbia and Bulgaria', although he was never able to take up his role as king of Hungary etc. because the kingdom had been seized by his cousin Andrew.

Charles was on his way to visit his father, also Charles, who was king of Sicily. Any member of his family was particularly welcomed by the merchant classes of Florence because it was the military intervention of his uncle Charles of Anjou that had enabled them in 1266 to overcome the magnati and go on to recover from the brief period of aristocratic absolutism. As a gesture of gratitude, the city had taken as its emblem the Anjou symbol of the fleur-de-lys which can be seen to this day on Florentine documents, civic vehicles and tourist memorabilia.

The official visit of Charles Martel lasted three weeks, during which the grateful rulers of the city laid on festivals, fairs, parades and cultural events. Dante had the honour of being chosen to read one of his poems as part of a display of cultural excellence. Afterwards he met and talked to the celebrity visitor. The poem he chose is the one which opens the second part of his instructional book, the *Convivio*. In it he addresses the angels who reside in Heaven and move the sphere of the planet Venus; 'You whose intelligence moves the third sphere', it begins.[2]

The poem is about the contorted emotional balancing act between his grief for Beatrice and the power of the Lady Philosophy. Dante believes that only the angels in the sphere of Venus will understand what he is going through, 'And so I beg that you will listen to me. I shall tell of the strangeness in my heart, how here inside my sad soul weeps, and how against her speaks a spirit that comes descending on rays from your star.'

It is a subtle, philosophical poem, a beautifully constructed pattern of sound which carries a complex discussion of abstract concepts. It is really only possible to understand it if one has either a knowledge of Dante's mental state at the time or the benefit of the didactic explanations of his *Convivio*.

Dante himself admits in the final stanza that he thinks very few people will get the point. It is hard to imagine that such a poem would work well on a first hearing, yet Charles Martel liked it. In fact, it impressed him so much that he could quote it six years later when he met Dante again. By that time he had died tragically young of cholera, but the meeting takes place, nonetheless, in Paradiso of the *Divine Comedy*. Charles' immortal spirit has entered Heaven and risen, by more than coincidence, to the very celestial sphere of Venus mentioned in the poem he heard. As Dante's ascent takes him into this sphere, the third from the earth, he finds himself surrounded by lights. They are, he says, like the sparks in a fire, swirling together yet remaining separate. The lights turn out to be the souls who are blessed enough to inhabit this relatively elevated sphere. Out of the multitude one of them comes forward to talk to Dante. As he approaches he quotes the first line of the poem: 'You whose intellect moves the third sphere', but even then it takes Dante a moment to recognise him because he is glowing so much with heavenly bliss. When Dante does realise who it is they have a conversation. He is now writing the dialogue himself, of course, and it is quite obvious that Dante believes that the two of them had got on extremely well at their previous meetings. Charles Martel quickly expresses his regret that their friendship did not have the chance to develop further: 'Had I not died so soon, you would have seen more than the first leaves of my love for you.'[3]

They do seem to be very close after what can, at most, have only been one or two brief meetings in the midst of a busy official schedule. They were both young men – probably younger than most of those around them – and it is quite possible to discover an instant rapport with someone on a first meeting. It is also possible, however, to overestimate how well one has got on with a celebrity. Perhaps the very fact that Charles spoke to him at all went a long way towards giving Dante the feeling that they were friends. Whatever the reality of their meeting, it is clear that we are no longer seeing the introspective Dante who was capable of writing embarrassing letters to neighbouring princes or absent-mindedly ignoring local dignitaries because he was absorbed in drawing an angel. This time he had not failed to notice Charles' imposing presence, regal bearing or the smart retinue of 200 knights in scarlet and green who accompanied him. The new Dante wanted to be part of the world of Charles Martel.

Charles did indeed have the potential to be a peacemaker: his family connections would have put him in a unique position, had he lived, to succeed his father as king of Naples and Apulia, and to reconcile conflicting factions across Italy. It would not have been ridiculous to imagine that one day

Florence and its neighbouring city states might together enter a new era of peace and reconciliation presided over by Charles Martel. It would certainly not have been beyond Dante's powers of imagination to see himself as having a role in this bright future. He could be an assistant to his new friend Charles, working perhaps in a capacity for which he was qualified, possibly as some sort of historical and poetic adviser.

Charles himself says that he is sad that this was not to be and regrets in particular that he was not around long enough to avert the disaster: 'The time I spent on earth was very brief; if my life had been longer, much evil that will be would not have been.' The contemplation of what might have been is, in its most positive interpretation, an important way of understanding the course of one's life. Charles' words reflect Dante's own perception in retrospect that the visit occurred just at the moment when a chain of events was starting that would not only cause evil in a general way but would end by precipitating Dante himself into chaos and downfall.

Chronicler Dino Compagni does not mention Charles Martel's visit to Florence. He is too busy chronicling the measures taken by the magnati to get rid of the class traitor Giano della Bella. The first thought to enter the collective head of the party of the nobility had been to use violence. To this end, one Vieri dei Cerchi hired in a mercenary called Jean de Châlons from the independent dukedom of Champagne, together with a force of 500 battle-hardened soldiers. This was probably about the level of military strength needed to tip the balance in favour of the magnati if it came to a pitched battle, with the thousand home-grown fighters under the command of the opposing captain of the popolani.

Dino records that, at one of the meetings of the disgruntled magnati, a nobleman who was too eager to wait for the hired help to arrive, stood up and said, 'Why don't we all just go into the piazza now and kill as many of the popolani as we can find?' Despite murmurs of approval it was eventually realised that this suggestion had brought to light one of the principal weaknesses of a full-on physical attack: the risk of a violent backlash. 'The advice of this knight is good – except that if our plan fell short we should all be killed',[4] is how one speaker put it. Plans to overthrow Giano by force were abandoned in favour of other measures.

The magnati then determined to undermine Giano's popularity. In a modern democracy they would probably have been able to achieve this by manipulating a supine press into publishing nothing but negative half-truths and lies about him. As this option was not available, they resorted to what nowadays might be termed a 'viral campaign'. Twelve of their number – two for each of the *sesti*[b] – were sent out into the streets to spread discontent and mistrust in Giano della Bella and his Ordinances.

The problem with such a campaign was that, without the aid of opinion polls, it was difficult to determine whether or not it had been successful. But after a few months, a way of telling presented itself in the shape of a disastrously unpopular legal decision. Corso Donati, the hero of the battle of Campaldino, had been involved in a dispute with another member of his clan. Corso had sent some of his men round to teach the man a lesson. Unfortunately things had got out of hand and the man was killed. The popolani were in no doubt that Corso was entirely at fault. He typified everything that the popolani disliked about the magnati: he was a foul-mouthed and aggressive man who frequently resorted to violence – he liked his followers to call him *Il Barone*.

Because the dispute involved nobles the trial was held in front of the podestà, the aristocratic ruler who was traditionally brought in from another city. At this time it was Gian di Lucino, from near Lake Como in Lombardy. Somehow (Dino strongly hints at corruption) Gian di Lucino was persuaded that the murder victim had been in the wrong and therefore acquitted Corso. The popolani saw this as a typical example of the nobility flouting justice and looking after their own. They turned out on to the street, chanting 'death to the podestà!' and headed for his palace. Florentine defensive architecture stood the podestà in good stead and the iron-bound doors and window grilles withstood the attack. But the rioters were locals: they knew that every defensive measure has a counter-measure. They lit a bonfire against the palace door.

When he heard about the mounting trouble, Giano della Bella, confident of the people's support in a way that is essential for a rabble-rousing politician, announced that he would restore order. He mounted his horse, rode alone into the piazza and started to address the crowd. They may have listened to him for an instant, stunned perhaps by the audacious courage of such an act. But the viral campaign had been successful: they no longer saw him as their trusted representative and they turned on him. He was obliged to run for it. When news reached them that Giano had fled, the rest of the Council of Priors, thinking that they could succeed where he had failed, went into the square

b   Many towns have quarters; Florence had, from early times, divided itself into sixths or
    sesti.

themselves, proudly displaying the banner of the popolani. But by this time the door of the podestà's palace had succumbed to the flames and nobody was interested in them. The mob entered the palace by the charred remains of the front door as the podestà and his retinue left by the back.

The podestà's possessions were looted and legal records were trashed. Anybody who had a case pending against them made sure that it disappeared that day from the historical record. Once the mob had become aware of its own power it went on to destroy whatever magnati property was accessible – 'as long as we have begun let's burn the rest', Dino quotes them as saying. The rule of law had broken down. 'Many people did strange things in that furore', he adds darkly, before reassuring us that the podestà's wife at least managed to make a safe escape. Giano della Bella was now equally a target for the mob as for his own class. His followers advised him to leave town and he did so that very evening. He did not stop until he had reached France, never to return.

The next day, when the force of the riot was spent, whatever of the podestà's personal belongings that could be retrieved from the outraged citizens was returned to him. He was paid in full and left for his native Lombardy directly. It was to be some time before a replacement could be found. The city was slow to recover: the Council of Priors was discredited and the magnati needed time to regroup. Those followers of Giano della Bella who had unwisely remained were arrested one by one and put on trial on a broad selection of charges.

Just a few weeks later, with the aftermath of these events still hanging over the city, Dante chose to embark on a career in politics. A few months on we find a record of him speaking to the council of the major guilds which advised the captain of the popolo. The following summer we find him speaking to the Council of One Hundred, Florence's finance committee, opposing a motion to give financial aid to a military campaign of Charles of Anjou, Charles Martel's father. His intention to enter the world of Florentine politics can also be seen from the record of his membership of the Guild of Doctors and Apothecaries. He did not join them because he wished to become a doctor or an apothecary (he is actually described in the register as 'Florentine poet'), but because, according to the Ordinances of Justice which were still in force, only a guild member could be considered for public office.

The new Dante had embarked on a new career. He had the makings of a successful politician. He had always been highly intelligent, knowledgeable and, according to early accounts, not without a certain straight-laced charm. Now, with the Lady Philosophy by his side (as a metaphor at least), his behaviour was governed by rational analysis and logic. Now he could, as they say, walk the walk and talk the talk. It seems that he did both: by December he was a member of the Council of the Heads of the Arts, the ruling body of the guilds. Records show him speaking on such subjects as electoral procedures and the funding of new roads.

In the image employed by the vision of Love, he had put himself in touch with a further segment of the circle of experience which he had previously ignored. He had in fact become what we might nowadays call an activist. Behind the move into politics is a facet of Dante's character which is both one of the most constant and sympathetic. While he was focused only on the content of his innermost room, it did not show itself. From the moment he started to pay attention to the outside world, however, he was gripped by an overwhelming desire to bring about peace by helping other people to understand the true nature of things.

He believed that, if people really understood how things were, they would no longer be greedy or violent and justice would prevail. The so-called Ordinances of Justice had failed because they were mired in vengeance and self-interest from the start. They were finally pulled apart by people acting out of anger and greed. All these things – vengefulness, dishonesty, anger, greed – are sins which (as Dante will enthusiastically document in the *Comedy*) God will surely punish in the end. But Dante is in reality less concerned with punishment than with preventing the sin in the first place. The city of Florence had been severely damaged by sin. Now only understanding could put it on the path to peace. It was, therefore, time for a man of understanding to enter political life.

Dante repeatedly expresses his despair at humanity's headlong rush towards self-inflicted misery. His factual book about philosophy, the *Convivio*, is not simply a work of entertainment, or even education. Its purpose is to save its readers from the errors that will lead them into misery. His passionate urgency is evident as he addresses those who are ignorant of philosophical thought: 'In what blindness do you live, if you raise not your eyes to these things, but drown them rather in the mire of ignorance!' Ignorant people are like sheep who, if one of them jumps into a well, will all blindly follow the leader to perdition. He says he has actually witnessed this phenomenon: 'I have seen many sheep vanish into a well after one leapt in, thinking perhaps that they were leaping a wall, even though the shepherd, weeping and shouting, tried to check them with his arms and his body.'[5] Dante's purpose in going into politics, just as with his writing, was to promote justice by stopping the human sheep from jumping into the well.

All young politicians who start out with hope are destined to end up disappointed. Dante was to meet disappointment and an end to his political career in the most extreme manner. He would see very little evidence of justice for the rest of his life. But through it all he was never to lose that desire to see the world set on the right path. Only the method of expression would change. The aspiring young politician can best hope to effect change by diligent committee work. The factual writer might do the same through a project of popular education. The imaginative poet has another option. Later, once again in the company of Beatrice, he finds himself in the sphere of Jupiter, the most distant planet, closest to the edge of the universe. The souls of great rulers of the past express the same sentiment through a different medium. In their millions they fly up before Dante like flocks of lakeside birds at evening. They form up so that their glowing spirits produce something that is familiar to us but which had, at that time, never been seen before: a vast illuminated sign spelling out a single message. They flash it out letter by letter: D-I-L-I-G … a cry from Heaven which has the same insistent urgency as Dante's pleadings in the *Convivio*. The souls spell out the Latin words which begin the Biblical Book of Wisdom: … I-T-E-J-U-S-T-I-T-I-A-M … *LOVE JUSTICE* … Q-U-I-J-U-D-I-C-A-T-I-S-T-E-R-R-A-M[6] … *ALL YOU WHO RULE THE WORLD*.

10

TWO SUNS

In February 1300 Dante visited Rome. There he had the chance to contemplate the two great political entities that shaped the large-scale political structure of his world: Church and Empire. His new concern for the rational organisation of society would lead him soon to believe that justice itself depended on striking a balance between these two. Peace and harmony could only be achieved if secular and spiritual were kept separate yet constructively interlinked, each one in its natural, divinely ordained place. He thought that in the early days of Christianity the imperial city of Rome had got the balance right: 'Rome, that made the civilised world, used to have two suns that made the two roads visible: that of the world, and that of God.'[1] But he was soon to be convinced that, by the time of his visit, the squalid realities of thirteenth-century politics had dragged the eternal city very far from God's plan for a just universe and that neither of the two suns were shining anymore.

In Rome, Pope Boniface VIII had declared 1300 to be a 'Holy Year', marking the beginning of the new century.[a] Quite possibly, as an ambitious young politician, Dante was in Rome in an official capacity as part of the Florentine delegation to what would later be called, using the Pope's own coinage, a 'jubilee'.

---

a   Happily there seems to be no contemporary record of any airing of the tired and sterile debate about whether 1300 or 1301 is actually the first year of the new century, which is surprising for the Middle Ages.

For a six-week period the city was given over to celebration and festivity. But, above all, what occupied the 20,000 or so visitors as they thronged to every church in the city were the rituals of pilgrimage. Rome was overflowing with pilgrims praying, singing and venerating relics. Special one-way pedestrian systems had to be introduced on the bridges over the Tiber to cope with the crowds. This is how we know for certain that Dante was there: he mentions it when he recounts his visit to Hell. In the overcrowded eighth circle, well down in the depths, similar crowd-control measures are employed by the demons to keep the hordes of flatterers and pimps separate from the massed seducers.

Some of the reasons that people came to the Jubilee are the ones we associate with recreational travel today: sightseeing, eating, drinking and making new friends. But the Jubilee had a unique selling point that would be beyond even the wildest imaginings of any modern tour operator. Those who visited Rome at this time believed that they had the opportunity to ameliorate the fate of their souls after they died. This benefit was offered by the Church to any pilgrim who performed a prescribed fifteen-day cycle of prayers and observances in front of the appropriate relics in a succession of churches. Pilgrims who completed the course would automatically be granted the exceptional boon of a plenary indulgence.

Indulgences were, from the time of Dante and after, much prone to misuse. They eventually became part of a culture of corruption in the Church which was certainly a major contributory factor in persuading nearly half the population of Europe 200 years later to abandon the Roman Catholic Church and become Protestants in the Reformation. But these were abuses; the original concept of an indulgence was well-defined and, although undoubtedly one of their by-products was to reinforce the authority of the Church, indulgences were in themselves neither ill-intentioned nor absurd within the context of medieval Christianity.

An indulgence was definitely not the forgiveness of sin; much less was it a guarantee of impunity against future sins, although those who sold indulgences in the street often claimed exactly this. Only God can forgive sins. An indulgence had a much lesser, but not insignificant, purpose: it reduced the amount of time a soul had to spend in Purgatory after death.

All people who are neither so spectacularly evil that they will go straight to Hell nor so saintly that they will go straight to Heaven (and that is most people) are, according to the Christian doctrine of Dante's time, destined to spend some time in Purgatory. It is a sort of holding position where the departed soul undergoes a process of purification to remove the stain (or pay off the debt, as some theologians express it) of sins which have already been forgiven. Only when this process has been completed can the soul move on to Heaven. An indulgence is granted by the Church when a person is deemed to have reduced the debt of previously committed sin by some worthy activity in life. This activity can range from something as simple as studying the Bible to something as difficult as defeating armed forces of unbelievers in the Middle East or, as in the present case, performing the appropriate rituals at the Jubilee. Even run-of-the-mill sinners could expect to spend periods of centuries in Purgatory, so any means of reducing the time was worth the effort.

The plenary indulgence, as opposed to the various other kinds available, was the platinum card of indulgences. It removed the need to spend any time at all in Purgatory. Something this special, a ticket for instant admission to Heaven, could only be granted by the Pope in person. Until Boniface VIII's first Jubilee, popes had only given plenary indulgences to those who had risked their lives fighting in the Crusades. The radical broadening of its scope to include all comers is witness not so much to Boniface's good-hearted generosity as to his talent for public relations.

We know that Dante, along with almost everybody else at the time, believed in the efficacy of indulgences. In his account of his own visit to Purgatory he meets an old friend called Casella[b] whose soul, after his untimely death, had been obliged to wait for several months where the River Tiber flows out to the sea. This is the collecting point for the souls of Italians who have passed on. Casella remarks to Dante that for the past three months (exactly the time since the Jubilee had started), large numbers of newly arrived souls have been ushered past the queue and swept off directly to Heaven. These are, of course, fast-tracked souls who have just been granted a plenary indulgence. Casella, having died before the institution of the Jubilee, was not eligible for this. He evinces no bitterness, however; he is simply happy that as someone on his way through Purgatory he will eventually get to Paradise.

b Dante greets Casella enthusiastically. He tries to hug him but since he is an incorporeal spirit, the poet's arms pass straight through him. He then asks Casella to sing – evidently he had set some of Dante's poems to music. An entry in the Vatican archives suggests that Casella was indeed a professional musician. He makes one more appearance in the archives, this time in Siena, where he is recorded as being fined for 'loitering on the streets late at night'. Nobody knows what this was about or whether it is significant that the record is dated only very shortly before his death.

No matter what festival may be taking place or how much theology is being discussed, it is impossible to stand in the streets of Rome without being aware of the ancient brooding presence which literally underlies the entire city. The Roman Empire has still not, even today, altogether left Rome and to Dante, with a newly discovered sensitivity to history, the ancient empire and its physical remains exercised an intense symbolic power: 'The stones themselves demand reverence', he tells his readers in the *Convivio*.

To a visitor of Dante's time, Rome's ancient ruins were even more impressive than they are today. For one thing they were in much better condition. The wholesale looting of the fabric of classical buildings in order to construct the great edifices of the Renaissance, such as St Peter's Basilica, had not yet reduced most of them to misshapen piles of brick. For another thing, the grandiose white marble architecture of the ancient city stood out in sharp contrast to the medieval one. Ruins apart, the Rome of Dante's time was a small city. It was the home of the Pope and all the associated machinery of the Church but it had not flourished economically in the early centuries of the Middle Ages. It had certainly not found the same prosperity as Florence and, as a consequence, it was about a fifth of the size. Dante would not have seen anything to match the physical remains of the empire in Florence simply because there the expanding city had long ago demolished its classical heritage and built over it.

In Rome at the same time was another Florentine, a man called Giovanni Villani. He was about fifteen years younger than Dante but they came from similar backgrounds and it is hard to imagine that they did not know each other. They had similar attitudes to Rome as well. The spirit of the Roman Empire that he found among the stones so impressed Villani that his life was changed. On finding himself 'on that blessed pilgrimage in the holy city of Rome, beholding the great and ancient things therein, and reading the stories and the great doings of the Romans', he decided to become a chronicler in order to leave a record of his own times just as the Romans had done of theirs. 'I took up their style and design, although as a disciple I was not worthy of their work.' Villani did indeed go on to write an absorbing history of Florence which he called the *New Chronicle*. It is one of the essential primary sources for this period of Dante's life. Like Dante himself, Villani always mixes a taste for accuracy and an almost scientific regard for statistics together with a highly developed sense of divine justice.

The influence of ancient Roman civilisation on the Middle Ages cannot be overstated. Even though it had been over for the best part of a thousand years, one still sometimes gets the impression that the main business of medieval thinkers was to react to the Roman Empire. Roman writers – Cicero, Virgil,

Livy and Ovid were probably the most celebrated – informed all thought and writing. This was so fundamentally ingrained that they themselves did not see it as a restriction but rather as an honour. Roman writers were just acknowledged to be better, and therefore it was natural that their works would be the model for how to write a book and a paradigm for all thinking. The Romans were the primary authority that could not be contradicted: if Cicero had said something one way, it would be hard for a fourteenth-century writer, even so long after his death, to say something different.

The effect of seeing the ruins was to reinforce in the mind of the medieval visitor the feeling given by their authors: that there was something about the Romans. Their solid and confident buildings with sharply delineated columns and pediments were more stylish (perhaps even in some paradoxical way more modern) than the medieval buildings around them. The ancient Romans had been pagans, it was true, and therefore lacked the benefit of the true religion. None of them would be allowed to enter Heaven, for example. But for all that, their world was a natural paradigm for anyone with aspirations to 'civilisation'.

This same feeling has, in one way or another, informed Western culture ever since. There have been no European empires, good, bad or unspeakable, that have been able entirely to resist the temptation to ape the Romans. Charlemagne, Charles V, Napoleon, Francis I of Austria, Mussolini and Hitler all employed Roman insignia on their buildings and in their ceremonies of state. And a walk round the central area of Washington DC, with its tall fluted columns, triangular pediments, laurel wreaths and eagles,[c] will confirm that the West's special relationship with ancient Rome is not yet over.

Medieval Europe, of course, had at the time its own empire which claimed, on the basis of very tenuous connections, to be a direct successor to the original Roman one. It was known in Dante's day simply as 'the Empire'. Later, however, it would dub itself the 'Holy Roman Empire' and as such it clung on to a sort of existence until 1806, when the last emperor, Francis II, dissolved it after his defeat by Napoleon at the battle of Austerlitz. In the eighteenth century it was still an important enough player on the political stage for Voltaire famously and accurately to dismiss it as 'neither holy, Roman nor an empire'.

---

c Eagles, to the Romans a symbol of the sky god Jupiter and used as a talisman of military power, have been particularly popular with empires. Of all the empires that Europeans have started since, there is only one which has *not* used the eagle as its symbol.

Although he was talking about the situation in 1756, Voltaire's remark holds equally true for the empire of the late Middle Ages. It certainly wasn't Roman: emperors in Dante's time were almost exclusively from German families. The closest the empire got to being Roman was the patchwork of Italian possessions and affiliated states that made up about a third of its territory. These did not include Rome or the many Italian states that were more or less independent or owed allegiance to the Pope.

Neither are its claims to being a real empire entirely justifiable. Although it was headed by an emperor, the political structure which supported him was quite different from that of classical Roman emperors such as Augustus or Nero. The power of the emperor was not transmitted down through a well-defined pyramid of command and control. The empire was not in fact a single administrative unit. It could perhaps better be described as an agglomeration of small to very small states, each of which was ruled over by an assortment of despots, all of whom professed an allegiance to the emperor and practised it to a greater or lesser degree. Geographically, the totality of these states made up a patchy axis which stretched from Germany in the north, to the toe of Italy in the south.

To a modern historian, as to Voltaire, its imperial claims conceal an ad hoc structure and an element of wishful thinking that makes it different from all subsequent, or indeed previous, empires. To Dante, however, it was always 'the Empire'. As he studied history and contemplated the way things ought to be, he became increasingly convinced that an empire which would carry on the work of the Roman one was a logically necessary part of the divine scheme of things. In spite of everything that was to happen, he never lost the hope that one day an emperor would emerge whose nobility would revitalise and cleanse the empire so that once again it would shine as one of the two suns illuminating a just world.

As to Voltaire's third claim that the Holy Roman Empire was not holy, one might respond that empires are not, by definition, holy. Not one of them has yet survived the scrutiny of history with a reputation for self-denial and spiritual contemplation. Dante, with his own (slightly awkward) image of the two suns, presumably would not have been concerned that the empire wasn't holy: that was the business of its co-sun, the Church.

In fact, entirely predictably, Church and Empire seldom if ever combined to provide joint light and heat for the people of Italy. They were, like the aristocrats and the merchants of Florence, yet another duo locked in fierce conflict but held together by mutual dependence. As they struggled with each other, threats, counter-threats, excommunications and military raids frequently escalated into open warfare between states supporting different factions.

In Italy the political factions that supported these two sides adopted names which have remained some of the best-known words in the history of political partisanship: Guelfs and Ghibellines. The nomenclature dates back a century before Dante to a vicious struggle for the imperial crown between Otto IV, whose family was called Welf, and Friedrich of Hohenstauffen, who owned, among other things, a castle in a small town near Stuttgart called Waiblingen. After several years of fighting Otto lost the contest. Friedrich became emperor and duly had Otto killed. After the defeat of their candidate, Otto's supporters let their allegiance drift away from the empire to settle naturally on the side that opposed it, the Church. Now, as the party that defended the interest of the Church and the Pope, they took Otto's family name, Welf, and Italianised it to Guelf. Their opposition, still staunch supporters of their emperor, took the name of the triumphant Friedrich's castle (and occasional war cry), Waiblingen, or, in Italian, Ghibelline.[d]

In the hundred years since the names had been coined, the Guelf-Ghibelline divide had spread into almost every aspect of Italian life. In theory, of course, different classes or social groups were naturally drawn to support one party rather than the other. A Florentine merchant, for example, would, other things being equal, naturally support the Guelfs, who championed independence from imperial authority; whereas a nobleman would be more likely to have Ghibelline leanings, this being the party which underwrote inherited wealth and despotic authority. But the logic of class interest was quickly overridden by the forces of family loyalties and feuds. Eventually allegiance to one party rather than another became more a matter of taste, habit or family tradition. There were distinct Guelf and Ghibelline attitudes and ways of thinking in areas which were not at first sight even political. It is not obvious, for instance, why heresy should have been seen as a particularly Ghibelline sin, but it was. There was a Guelf and a Ghibelline line on every contemporary issue – there were even Guelf and Ghibelline styles of dress and architecture.

The most famous family feud in history is a Guelf/Ghibelline one. In his account of his visit to Purgatory, Dante breaks off the narrative to deliver an

d Rather than having to remember details of the squabble between Friedrich and Otto, there is a simple mnemonic which helps historians remember which party has which allegiance: Guelf is a short word like pope, while Ghibelline is, like empire, a comparatively longer word.

anguished diatribe against the pointless, destructive effects of sectarianism in Italy: 'The garden of the Empire is laid waste', he says. He mentions *en passant* two families from Verona among those who have been ruined by the dispute: the Montecchi and the Cappelletti. They were such icons of sectarian fanaticism that the same names reappear 300 years later as the Montagues and the Capulets in Shakespeare's *Romeo and Juliet*. In the *Divine Comedy* Dante does not go on to mention the story of the star-crossed lovers, even though it would have been a perfect example of the tragic consequences of conflict, because their story seems to date only from a century later when Guelfs and Ghibellines were part of history but the family feud was still alive.

Cities also identified themselves as either Guelf or Ghibelline. Florence was, for all but a short period of her existence, a Guelf city. Her neighbours, Pisa and Arezzo, were Ghibelline. So the military campaign between them which culminated in the battle of Campaldino, in which the young Dante took part, would have been more naturally characterised by observers at the time as a war between Guelfs and Ghibellines. When party strife turned into full-scale war those in the city whose loyalties lay with the minority party found themselves in a difficult position. Young Villani, in his *New Chronicle*, confirms that at Campaldino disaffected Florentine Ghibellines fought on the side of Arezzo and vice versa. The resentment caused by these overlays of conflicted loyalties did much to fuel even more the fires of discord within the city. Likewise, the brief period just after Dante's birth, when the despotic aristocrats of Florence gained an upper hand over the merchants, would have been described by Dante's contemporaries as a Ghibelline coup. The restoration of Guelf authority in Florence in 1266 occasioned not only the destruction of the houses of Florence's foremost Ghibelline family, the Uberti, but also (again according to Villani) the arrest of 2,000 Ghibelline hard-liners and the foundation of an official Guelf party office to deal with their confiscated wealth. The real cause of this abrupt change of fortunes for the Ghibellines lay outside Florence. In the south of Italy the empire had suffered a crushing military defeat; Emperor Manfred had been routed by a Guelf army[e] at the battle of Benevento.

The immediate consequence of the defeat of Benevento was for the empire to lose its hold on the kingdom of Sicily, which reverted to the status of a papal fief. But beyond that it was as if the shock of Benevento had made the empire slowly begin to lose interest in Italy. Subsequent emperors paid almost no attention to the territories that they owned there and the Ghibelline party

e Led by Charles of Anjou, the father of Charles Martel who had so impressed Dante on his visit to Florence.

everywhere lost power through lack of funds and military backup. Like most imperial declines it was a gradual process, but by 1300, when Dante was in Rome, although the terms Guelf and Ghibelline were still in use, people were aware that at the very least the empire in Italy was in temporary eclipse and the conflict between Empire and Church was less of a live issue than it once had been. So when Boniface VIII invited the world to his Jubilee he was looking at an Italy (and indeed a Europe) that had lost a strong overall authority. There was a power vacuum and Boniface was the perfect pope to fill the gap.

Nothing is known of the early life of Benedict Caetani, the man who was to become Pope Boniface VIII, beyond the fact that he came from a noble Italian family. He makes his first mark on the historical record in 1260 when he is listed as a canon of the cathedral of Todi, where his uncle happened to be bishop. He was in his early twenties at the time so it is clear that his progress had already been rapid. From his later writing we can tell that he had had a good education: he writes with deft concision on a broad range of topics. For the next forty years he worked his way up the ecclesiastical ladder, studying law as well as doctrinal texts, eventually becoming a cardinal then a legate, the highest ranking representative of the Pope.

He had the advantage of becoming famous and powerful at the time when portraiture was just beginning to develop so we have a number of likenesses of him, mostly sculptures. It is hard, however, to read very much from the face that looks at us from a distance of 700 years. But perhaps that is as it should be for a career diplomat.

Before becoming pope he had travelled Europe on papal business first in France and then later on a mission to England, which in those days had the semi-dependent status of a 'papal fief'. While he was there he had the memorable experience of being besieged in the Tower of London. His delegation had been sent in support of King Henry III (and therefore of the Pope's feudal rights over England) against a party of rebel barons led by Simon de Montfort.[f] They found that strife had left England in a bad way: 'few or none were the places in which there was safety, and the land was filled with robbers of the dead.'[2] They lodged in the Tower while they continued their diplomatic business but in 1267 London was overrun by the rebels. They sacked Westminster and headed east

---

f This conflict was the second of two open fights between an autocratic king and rebel barons, the first having led to the signing of Magna Carta in 1215. This time Montfort, in 1264, was to set up a rival, breakaway legislative assembly which is frequently claimed to be the first English parliament.

to lay siege to the Tower. The young King Henry III lost no time in turning his full might against the insurgent barons in order to rescue his important allies. The event made such an impression on the young Boniface that he mentions it years later in a letter: 'We remember how, when we were besieged in the tower, this king came to deliver us ... we set our affections on him with a particular love, judging that he would become the best prince in the world.'[3]

Boniface remained friends with the king of England and a committed Anglophile for the rest of his life. Historians have suggested that this may have some bearing on his less than cordial relations with France in later years.

Boniface was elected Pope in December 1294, just two months before Dante made his decision to go into politics. As he ascended to the throne of St Peter, the new Pope was no doubt aware that circumstances had given him two advantages that would contribute to a memorable papacy. Firstly, as we have seen, the empire had withdrawn from Italy, giving him a convenient power vacuum to fill. Secondly, his predecessor, Celestine V, was, of all the popes there had ever been, the easiest act to follow.

The appointment of Celestine is probably best described as a radical experiment that went wrong. His election followed two and a half years of deadlock in the College of Cardinals during which time no pope was appointed. Peter of Murrone, soon to be Celestine V, was eventually proposed as a compromise candidate with a difference. He was an unsophisticated, charismatic religious leader – 'muscular, simple-minded, barely literate', says one English historian. He had spent much of his early life meditating in a cave near the Gran Sasso Mountain in Abruzzo, in central Italy. Later he had founded a monastic house, the hermits of the Holy Spirit of Maiella, which, thanks to his naive enthusiasm, was very successful, spawning thirty-six sub-houses in a decade. By the time of his election, however, he had left the monastery and returned to his cave in an act of self-denial.

It seemed to the cardinals that this unusual choice was the only way out of the impasse which had deprived the Church of a leader. It is possible also that the very wildness of the idea of a 'hippy pope' had a certain appeal in an age which was becoming justifiably concerned about increasing materialism in the rapidly growing economies of Europe. Celestine was certainly untainted by any of that. On the other hand, he had had no experience at all of the business of Church management. Perhaps that is why, when they came to his cave to tell him the good news, Peter resisted vigorously. But the delegation insisted.

It would be nice to be able to say that Celestine's simplicity refreshed the papacy and that his innocence shone through as an example in the wicked, cynical world of Rome. In fact, he was useless. His inexperience manifested itself as a complete lack of judgement and his simplicity made him easy prey for every silver-tongued con-artist inside the Church and out. The only decisive thing he ever did was to promote members of his own order way beyond their abilities. He hated the meetings that are part of the day-to-day business of a pope and he would hide himself away, signing anything that was put in front of him rather than discussing it with advisers. It was said that, by the end, blank papal bulls were being circulated, ready-signed with only the content needing to be filled in by the purchaser.

Just five months into the Celestine papacy the cardinals decided they had had enough. They delegated the future Boniface VIII to have a word with the Holy Father. Not long after, Celestine decided that he wanted to resign and the rest was easy. The greatest problem for the soon-to-be Boniface VIII was to establish the legal procedure by which a pope could resign. He made sure that the act was legally watertight by ensuring that Celestine himself, while still pope, issued a declaration that it was possible for a pope to resign. There could be no contradiction of this edict. Celestine then resigned.[g]

There were some voices raised in protest. He was missed in Naples, for example, where he was regarded as a saint. In fact, Boniface himself refers to him as a saint[h] in the papers he issued nullifying all his predecessor's decrees (except the one legalising resignation), made, as he put it, 'in the fullness of his simplicity'. By and large, however, the new Pope was welcomed. Boniface was patently the complete opposite of Celestine and the general feeling was that things could only get better.

Most modern historians do indeed give Boniface VIII credit for his sure-footedness in difficult times. By a combination of iron will, erudition and political skill he set a new benchmark for papal authority. The long-term effect of his rule was to strengthen the papacy when it needed it most, thereby consolidating the centuries-long process of putting the Pope indisputably at the head of the Western European Church. That this should be so was beyond

---

g Nowadays, when modern medicine combines with the grace of God to extend a Supreme Pontiff's life to the extent that those about him begin regretfully to talk of the possibility of his stepping down, it is Celestine V who is quoted as the one and only clear proof that, rare though it is, it is possible for a pope to resign.

h That did not stop Boniface making sure Celestine did not become a focus of dissent by having him imprisoned in a small cell until his death from natural causes eighteen months later at the age of 80. Celestine actually was canonised twenty years after that, in 1313.

question in the lifetime of Boniface, but it had not been at all obvious in the early days of European Christianity.

Dante held a quite different view. By the time he was writing the *Divine Comedy* he believed that Boniface had sunk so deeply into the mire of corruption that he was a touchstone of papal criminality. So far had he departed from the natural and just path that only one fate could await his immortal soul: he would spend eternity in one of the deepest circles of Hell.

When Dante visits Hell Boniface is still alive so he does not have the opportunity of witnessing the Pope's punishment for himself. But he does get the chance to see what will happen to him when he visits the place where Boniface is scheduled soon to be forced headfirst down a fiery hole while searing flames lick around his upturned feet. While he is there he startles the current occupant of the hole, Pope Nicholas III, who imagines Boniface has been sent down to join him ahead of schedule. Nicholas has good reason to care about the arrival of Boniface because when it does happen it will be time for him to be forced further down into the fiery hole as the next sinful pope is shoved in on top of him.

Dante says that Boniface's avarice 'grieves the world, trampling on the good and raising up the wicked'.[4] But it is in Paradise that final judgement is passed. Dante does not voice his disgust himself. He lets the highest appropriate authority speak: in the outermost reaches of Heaven, among the fixed stars, St Peter himself, the first Pope and Apostle of Christ, whose remains lie at the centre of the church in St Peter's Basilica in Rome, becomes literally incandescent; he glows red with rage as he speaks of what Boniface has done and how it will please the Devil:

He who has taken over my place has turned my burial ground into a sewer of blood and filth, at which the Evil One who fell from here takes great delight down there.

(*Paradiso*, 27:25–7)

11

INVENTION

ante's desire that there should be features of the outer world which reflected events in his inner life never left him. Few people are entirely immune from this need. It is also typical of the Middle Ages and essential to Dante's world view. His insistence on these reassuring connections in the *Vita Nuova* – the occurrences of the number nine in the life and death of Beatrice being the most frequent – may well be a result of insecurity or uncertainty in his early life. A case could certainly be made for that, bearing in mind the early death of his mother followed not long afterwards by the death of his father. One does get the impression that these connections made him feel good; they have kept Dante scholars occupied for centuries. But they do not quite grip the modern mind in the same way that they gripped the medieval one. They are just a little bit too arbitrary. When it comes to the most significant event in his life, however, Dante does much better. For one thing, that event had the advantage of having happened in 1300, the year that began the century, giving it an instant significance. To this promising beginning Dante adds three more things to give it the resonance he is looking for.

Firstly, he tells us that the event happened at the time of the spring equinox: that day when the short, dark days of winter have lengthened sufficiently to be of equal length to the nights. This is the time when the world moves into summer and a new cycle of life begins. It is a time of hope and rebirth, but it can, of course, also be the beginning of conflict, struggle and death (for this reason April has been described as the cruellest month).

Secondly, Dante says that it was Easter, the day before Good Friday to be precise. In a Christian culture this could hardly be more significant. Easter commemorates another cycle of death and rebirth when God, through Christ, dies and is resurrected. This sacrifice is the ultimate symbol of God's love and of mankind's special place in the universe He created. If we add to this the observation that Easter was also believed to be the anniversary of the moment when God created the universe we can see how well Dante has chosen the moment.

Thirdly, just as it was the midpoint between deepest winter and the height of summer, he says that it was also the midpoint of his own life. The Bible[1] says that a man's natural lifespan is three score years and ten. Someone who is half-way through a life of seventy years would therefore be 35 years old. If we put all the information[2] together we find that the day indicated is Thursday 7 April 1300, less than two months after the Jubilee.[a]

These markers in the great flow of time do not feel nearly so arbitrary as Dante's earlier ones. They are not, for example, in the same class as ridiculous observations that because a girl called Primavera has a name which sounds like 'comes first' in Italian, she was destined to walk in front of Beatrice. They have their origins in the same need for significance but now Dante's quirk of mind seems to have come of age. This time the precise definition of the moment does not seem like the nervy obsessiveness of an introspective mind. The indicators come together to intrigue the reader; one wants to know what it was that happened on such a special day. It feels like the beginning of a story.

Of course it didn't really happen exactly as Dante says. Profound changes to one's life seldom occur in an instant on a particular day. Mental frames of reference cannot be so lightly swung around, not even by a genius – that is the stuff of stories. In reality there must be a process of realisation of a problem, followed by a period of doubt building up to the acceptance that something new must happen. Only then can it happen in a flash.

Every day during the Jubilee period (in the run-up to that special day) Pope Boniface VIII presented himself to the people. He appeared every morning,

---

a   Give or take a certain amount of informed debate, most of which revolves around the fact that Easter and the spring equinox were not at the same time in the year 1300. Dante is so keen to have the maximum significance for his moment that he fudges the issue and puts Easter at the equinox. By doing so he creates a kind of 'ideal year' where the position of the heavens is not exactly as it is in real life but their symbolic significance is enhanced. Dante has already entered the world of fiction.

seated on his throne, wearing the three-layered, beehive-shaped papal tiara (of which Boniface himself was responsible for introducing the third layer), together with the red slippers that had signified high Roman office since the time of the emperors. He was attended by his cardinals who were, then as now, the political facilitators of the Catholic Church. Being so close to the pontiff would have made Dante contemplate more closely the ideas about the role of the papacy which he had already formed. It would have been obvious that the whole daily ritual was, despite the religious paraphernalia, an unsubtle but theatrically effective display intended, as was the whole Jubilee, not only to make money but also to underscore the Pope's worldly power.

It was evident to Dante that by now, four years into his papacy, Boniface had already taken several large strides down the road towards sin that would one day gladden the heart of the Devil and make St Peter glow with fury. He had already, for example, caused the destruction of a whole city.

The eradication of the ancient city of Palestrina, just 30km to the south of Rome, was the climax of a violent feud between powerful families. As soon as Boniface had become pope, the other members of his family, the Caetani, had

celebrated the elevation of their relative by building up their military strength in the area surrounding their home town of Gaeta. They began buying up castles and strengthening the fortifications of the existing ones. Boniface always denied that he had diverted papal funds to the project but others (including Dante) were not convinced. Even if Boniface wasn't actually paying for the work it was a matter of public record that he was using his influence – calling in favours and issuing threats – to make various small towns hand over management of their fortifications to the Caetani.

It was inevitable that these actions would upset the other powerful family in the area, the Colonna. Like the Caetani, their activities ranged over a broad spectrum from the accumulation and maintenance of wealth by violence through to taking a hand in the running of the Church. Unlike the Caetani they did not have a pope in the family but they did have two cardinals. In fact, it was the intransigence of the Colonna cardinals which had caused the deadlock that had denied the world of a pope for two years and resulted in the election of the disastrous compromise candidate, Celestine. Records show that both Colonna cardinals had voted for Boniface at the time of his election but, as Caetani power increased, they began to have second thoughts.

Relations between the two families worsened until matters were brought to a head by some amateur swashbuckling on the part of some of the young Colonna. On 3 May 1297 two of them hijacked a shipment of Caetani money as it passed close to their property. It turned out to be a magnificent haul of 200,000 florins[b], intended for the purchase of three strategically important castles by Boniface's nephew, Peter.[3]

It seems quite possible that the escapade was a prank, that the kids were just lucky to hit the jackpot and that there was no intention to keep the money. There certainly seems to have been no attempt to maintain any secrecy about who had done it. Boniface, however, chose to construe the incident in the most serious light. For a man with a reputation as a diplomat, Boniface did have a terrible temper: in solemn conclave he is known to have grabbed at least one bishop by the beard in order to emphasise a point and to have thrown Lenten ashes in the face of another. He summoned the head of the Colonna to Rome and demanded not only the return of the money but that the family should

---

b   It is a measure of the Florentine economic solidity which Boniface found so alluring that the city actually had a coin of international currency named after it. The name of the coin, of course, remained in the English language until the 1970s when the two-shilling piece, or florin, became ten new pence.

forfeit three of their finest castles (to add to the ones Boniface would be able to purchase with the returned money).

After a sharp exchange of letters, the Colonna did return the money but they had no intention of handing over any castles. They found a very effective method of countering Boniface's attack. A rumour had been hanging in the air since his election; whispers persisted that Celestine had, after all, been coerced into authorising the resignation of popes and that therefore his own resignation was not legal. If this was the case Boniface's own election was invalid. The Colonna issued a manifesto, an open letter to Boniface, which they posted on various significant church doors in the region. The document managed to get straight to the heart of the legal issue: 'We do not believe that you are pope', it said. It went on to explain that, for this reason, all of Boniface's edicts were without authority, the implication being the Colonna were not obliged to comply with any of the so-called pope's edicts about forfeiting castles. To continue in the swashbuckling style which had started the affair, somebody even sneaked into St Peter's in Rome and left a copy of the letter on the high altar.

Boniface reacted using both his diplomatic training and his filthy temper. Firstly he marshalled support from loyal cardinals and other learned churchmen comprehensively to refute any suggestion of his own illegitimacy. He made a very effective case: there was no evidence for coercion and a number of eminent intellectuals pitched in with arguments supporting the right of popes to resign. The Colonna, however, would not back down and Boniface the diplomat was supplanted by Boniface the warrior.

He dismissed the two Colonna cardinals and followed that up with the excommunication of the entire Colonna family. Then he exerted all the influence at his disposal to persuade loyal towns and cities to join in a coalition to wage war against the Colonna on the grounds that they were now enemies of the Church. One way or another, Boniface was to persuade a number of cities to come to his assistance. Florence, for example, responded to the Pope's call by providing 600 footsoldiers and 200 cavalrymen (Dante was not among them). Many people would have considered that this was already an inappropriate use of papal power but there was more to come. When the Colonna refused to cave in, Boniface conferred the status of a crusade on his personal campaign. This meant that anyone who took part was eligible for a 'gold card' plenary indulgence. It also allowed the Pope to access funds which had already been collected for the more conventional crusades in Palestine and to request further financial aid from the institutions that had traditionally funded crusades. On this basis, the great abbeys of Citeaux and Cluny both contributed, as did the fighting monastic orders: the Knights Hospitaller, the Teutonic Knights and the Knights Templar.

Boniface was offering a spiritual reward in return for material benefit. This is a sin which was particularly offensive to Dante. It has a special name: simony. It is derived from Simon Magus, a popular magician of the first century, who is described in the Acts of the Apostles as attempting to obtain the power of the Holy Spirit from two of the disciples in return for a cash payment. Saint Peter rounds on him with the words: 'Thy money perish with thee for thou hast thought that the gift of God may be purchased with money ... thy heart is not right in the sight of God.'[4] Peter advises him to pray for forgiveness but the account ends there so we do not know the fate of the immortal soul of Simon Magus after his death. Dante, by the year 1300, was already forming a clear idea of the ultimate fate of those guilty of the sin of simony if they remained unforgiven.

Perhaps he even let the scene run through once or twice inside his head as he looked at Boniface during those days in Rome. If he had done so he would have been taking the traditional comfort of the helpless candidate at a job interview or the carpeted junior employee: imagining his superior in some terrible, humiliating plight. Dante had just the imagination for it. In his mind the upturned red slippers would have been kicking the air in desperate fury as the soles of the papal feet were burnt but never consumed. The joints and sinews would be twitching until, as he says, they were in danger of snapping like willow branches, while all the time the head and torso of the Holy Father would remain wedged into a fiery hole in the ground as the melting fat dripped off him like roasting meat. Pope Boniface VIII is now better known as the person for whom Dante imagined that scene than for any of his own actions, good or bad.

After two years Boniface had all but won his war against the Colonna. They were exhausted and sued for peace. Only one town remained in their hands: the ancient city of Palestrina. Dante believed a story current at the time that Boniface had offered reasonable terms in order to persuade them to surrender and then reneged on the deal. Modern historians doubt this but nobody denies the arrogant brutality of Boniface's actions. The senior members of the rebel family came before him. Pietro Colonna, the head of the family, publicly agreed that all their fortresses now belonged to the Caetani. He then knelt and kissed the red slippers. Boniface later announced that he would have the town of Palestrina destroyed. This he did, dismantling it stone by stone, ancient Roman remains, elegant palace and all. He was clearly not expecting the town to make a comeback because, soon afterwards, he went to the trouble of founding a new city nearby, intended to replace Palestrina. He called it Città Papale, 'Popeville'.

Dante would also have been aware of another example of Boniface's unusual combination of theological learning and temper. The row with King Philip IV, which was to develop into a lifetime feud, had its origins with a dispute over money. It was undoubtedly Philip who started it. Short of cash for the continuation of a war against England, he had broken with long established tradition and tried to impose taxes on the clergy resident in France. This was a direct drain on the Pope's financial resources as well as, more importantly, a direct challenge to his authority.

Boniface's response was to issue a papal bull which seethed with fury. Issued on 25 February 1296, it is known – in accordance with the Catholic tradition which continues to this day – by the first couple of words on the Latin text. In this case the words are *Clericis Laicos*, the beginning of a sentence which in English runs something like: 'Lay persons have traditionally been hostile to the clergy …' The feud was to continue as Boniface fired off a succession of bulls, the most famous of which is *Unam Sanctam* (One God, One Faith, One Spiritual Authority). Eventually relations between the two men worsened so much that Boniface sent Philip a personal letter, the Latin name of which, appropriately enough, has all the ill-restrained violence of a line from a seventies police drama: *Ascolta Filii!* – Listen Son! At all times Boniface made it clear that there was no room for discussion in his decision; he would accept only absolute compliance with his will. If 'the supreme spiritual power' (Boniface) is in error, 'it can only be judged by God'.[5] In other words, King Philip of France's opinion about the matter was not relevant.[c] Later he comes out with the unequivocal line: 'it is necessary to salvation that every human creature be subject to the Roman pontiff.'[6]

As it happens, Philip did have the power to counter the bluster of *Clericis Laicos* quite effectively. He came back with what would nowadays be called an act of economic warfare: he banned the export of gold, silver, precious stones, weapons or food from the kingdom of France. The papacy derived a great

c That may possibly sound appropriate for a pope, but in 1300 there was no doctrine of papal infallibility. Boniface does indeed frequently seem to anticipate this idea, which dates from 1869 when Pius IX (ill-advisedly, according to many) declared that in certain circumstances and even then only when talking of faith and morals, the Pope cannot be wrong. Boniface, by contrast, habitually spoke as if he were infallible in all matters at all times. Philip had his answer to this though: the *Etats généraux* of 1302, in which the Third Estate declared that the king had no superior on earth.

deal of revenue from France and, since he was in the middle of the Colonna war, Boniface decided he could not stand the loss. The diplomatic side of his personality kicked in and he issued a 'clarification', explaining that he had never meant to ban 'voluntary contributions' on the part of clergy to the French coffers. The royal ordinance was eventually withdrawn, and the painful incident seemed closed, but this rift would never heal – even death would not put an end to it.

Dante was well aware of Boniface's attitude to power. If he needed any confirmation he needed only to look at a recent letter in which his full absolutist fury had been turned on the young politician's own home town: 'Every man must yield to the highest priest of the Church. [i.e. the Pope] … The Bishop of Rome [the Pope again] enjoys absolute supremacy over the Commune of Florence, over Tuscany, over all kings and men on earth.'[7]

The reason for Boniface's interest in Florence was once again money. The papacy did not traditionally derive much revenue from Florence, the wealthiest city in Italy, but the withdrawal of imperial power from the Italian peninsula had provided a good opportunity to adjust that. Boniface had therefore been setting up a Florentine operation more or less from the moment he was elected. He engaged a Florentine family, the Spini, to be his bankers. They sent representatives to live in Rome and made good profits by attending to Boniface's business affairs. It is probably not a coincidence that records show that the large and sumptuous Spini palace, part of which survives to this day at the end of the Ponte Santa Trinità (near where Dante had been greeted by Beatrice just sixteen years earlier), dates exactly from the first year of Boniface's reign.

The Pope began to exert his influence on Florence through a combination of patronage and punishment. He bought the loyal support of Corso Donati, for example, by arranging his appointment as podestà of Orvieto. Giano della Bella, on the other hand, was the subject of vilification, mainly because he planned to sequester the funds of the Guelf party, which was one of the few pots of Florentine money that the Pope had access to. When Giano was driven out of Florence Boniface stepped in by threatening that, should they ever be tempted to reinstate Giano, excommunications would follow. It is hard to determine the reason for this statement – there was certainly no suggestion that Giano was coming back – Boniface just seems to have felt the need to assert himself.

In the beginning of the year 1300 a scandal developed which highlighted the issue of interference by the Pope. A maverick Florentine lawyer called Lapo Salterelli brought a civil action against three of his fellow citizens, Noffo di Quintavalle, Simone di Gerardo and Cambio da Sesto, who were living in Rome and working for the Spini bank on behalf of Boniface. The gist of the charge was that since they were working for a foreign power they were guilty of treason. Refusing to return to Florence, the three were tried *in absentia* and found guilty. Again Boniface overreacted; instead of just denying the charges he wrote to the bishop of Florence instructing him to annul the verdict, something which the bishop had no authority to do. He went on to threaten with excommunication anyone who harmed his friends in Rome. He followed this up with a letter to the ruling council in the finest 'Listen son!' tradition of Bonifacian promulgations. Instead of addressing any legal issues he concentrates on a personal attack on Salterelli, the lawyer who had started it:

> Salterelli is the very cornerstone of scandal, who wishes to attack the fullness of the power given us by God! We must silence all such barking dogs because they depart from the truth and is who take the place of Him who is the Truth and the Life.
>
> (Pope Boniface VIII, Letter to the Florentine Signoria, 1299)

There cannot have been many people in Florence who did not think that the Pope was meddling in local affairs that were well outside his jurisdiction. But Boniface put a different spin on the story. In a subsequent letter to the council he employed a self-justifying lie of the kind which seems to issue all too easily from the mouths of interfering bullies. Pontificating about himself in the third person, he told them that despite what people say, he was only interested in preserving the freedom of Florence and its people:

> children of iniquity, in order to turn the people from their submission to the Keys of St Peter, were spreading the rumour that he sought to deprive the city of its power of jurisdiction and diminish its independence, whereas, on the contrary he wishes to enlarge its liberty.
>
> (Boase, Boni Letter to Florentine Signoria, 15 May 1301)

The effect of this pressure on the political community of Florence was entirely predictable: it split into two factions. Each side then heaped up the resentment and hatred from previous disputes to lend vehemence to the latest conflict. The de facto leader of the pro-papal faction was, of course, Corso Donati, lately returned from his lucrative sojourn in Orvieto. He and his supporters fanned the flames of conflict. As tension mounted violence erupted on to the street. The chronicler Dino Compagni (who was there) tells how Corso even tried to have one of the opponents of the Pope murdered while he was away on a pilgrimage. The man survived and on his return repaid the compliment by attempting to stab Corso with a dart at a public gathering. Dante would certainly have known all about these events because the person in question was his best friend and fellow poet Guido Cavalcanti.

So, as Dante stood on those cold, grey February mornings in Rome, looking up at Boniface VIII surrounded by his cardinals, he knew he was looking at someone whose power ranged almost over the entire known world. The Pope could affect events anywhere in Europe; he could order the destruction of cities and he could, indirectly at least, threaten the life of Dante's best friend. Boniface was not just brutal and corrupt. He was going against the natural order of things. Providence had raised him to the throne of St Peter in order that he administer and protect one of the pair of suns that were intended to illuminate the world. Instead he was using his position to increase his own wealth and power. He had selfishly decided to go against the self-evident will of God. This was not just behaviour which would inevitably lead to evil; it was the definition of evil itself.

And there was nothing that Dante could do about it. No amount of sitting on the Council of One Hundred, discussing electoral procedure or approving the construction of new roads would ever affect the vast power blocs that ground together like tectonic plates to shape the political world beyond Florence. The arena in which Boniface operated would remain forever out of range for a young politician from the minor aristocracy.

Through his book, the *Convivio*, Dante hoped if not to change the world then certainly to prevent evil by stopping humanity's headlong flight to ruin. But this hope was utterly in vain in the case of Boniface. He was not an ignorant sheep jumping into a well out of a misguided belief that it was in his interest. The Pope was a highly educated man; he had read the same books as Dante. Boniface had, in Dante's terms, actually been introduced to the Lady Philosophy and had then turned his back on her. He had deliberately chosen to do the wrong thing.

As Dante approached his thirty-fifth birthday the realisation was building up inside him that he had made a mistake. The process of reinvention that he had undergone since the death of Beatrice – the dedication of himself to the Lady Philosophy – was a wrong turning. He had somehow left the path that he should have been taking and had chosen one which was vain and ineffective. If he continued in this way his life would be wasted.

The consequence of a realisation of powerlessness is very often rage; it certainly was in Dante's case. In the face of His Holiness Boniface VIII, Dante began to feel an ire that would resound through the rest of his life. As fate continued to heap injustice upon injustice it would grow inside him. It would intrude into his writings in places where they might otherwise have been merely urbane, intelligent and dull. Dante's rage would grow until one day it would be powerful enough to make the whole of the heavens glow with a burning red as St Peter delivers his final condemnation.

But rage does not necessarily lead to despair. Dante's intelligence had enabled him to find his way out of dead ends before. He had, after all, found (with prompting from the apparition of Love as a young man) an alternative to the emotional impasse of love-inspired misery that the troubadours were offering. The disquiet he felt in Rome in those weeks started a process in Dante which would lead him to a different path.

He began to go back and undo his reinvention of himself. Mentally he retraced his steps, as one must do when one is lost, to the last place where he really knew where he was. He returned to the origin of his feelings, to the point where both love and fury begin, the quiet room inside the soul where, even before religion, there is an inner sense of the rightness of things. To some people it is a sense of the love of God, which Dante was so sure pervaded the universe. To the persecuted it is the sacred, concealed part of them which, if only their aggressor could truly see it, would make them stop the pain. To lovers it is the part inside each of them which joins with the other in those moments when, just for an instant, the whole world seems connected. To Dante it was Beatrice.

That special day in 1300, which he marks with such care against the great scale of the cosmos, is the day Dante went back to Beatrice. The real chronology of how it happened is probably more complicated but the purpose of the day which Dante pinpoints is to make the narrative work. It is the pivotal moment in the story which Dante told himself about his own life. When he had understood the story he told it again in a fictional form: that special day is also the day when the journey through Hell, Purgatory and Heaven of the *Comedy* begins.

It seems that one of the first things he did after this was to go back and rewrite the end of the *Vita Nuova*, the bulk of which had been finished several years before. The final four chapters of the book as we now have it are introduced by an abrupt change. Following a poem about the *Donna Gentile*, he describes, with no preamble, a new vision of Beatrice. He says that at the ninth hour of the day (naturally) she 'rose up against this adversary of reason',[8] by which he presumably means the Lady Philosophy. She appears in the very same red dress she was wearing when he first saw her. He describes his decision to return to her, his mind already tinged with the guilty shame that would from now on always be present when he thought of her:

> Then I began to think about her and, as I remembered her through the sequence of past time, my heart began to repent sorrowfully of the desire by which it had so basely let itself be possessed for some time, contrary to the constancy of reason. Once I had discarded this evil desire, all my thoughts turned back to their most gracious Beatrice.

(Vita Nuova, XXXIX)

Just as he was at the beginning of the *Vita Nuova*, Dante is now focused on Beatrice. His love for her and the divine grace that he sees through her are once again central to his life. The only difference is that this time he is aware of things outside his own inner room. He can now, as it were, look in two directions. On the one hand, through his love of Beatrice, he perceives the will of God. That gives him an inner sense of the essential rightness of Creation: how the world ought to be. On the other hand, he has the intelligent observer's realisation of how the world really is. The *Comedy* is a three-part fictional narrative about how those two things are connected.

Dante's irritating, frustrating and (just occasionally) beautiful book, the *Vita Nuova*, ends with another vision. He does not describe it, he just says that it has convinced him not to write any more about Beatrice, 'until I could do so more worthily'. From now on he prepares himself for the task, 'I am trying as hard as I can to reach this state ... I hope to write of her what has never been written on any woman'. He did that all right.

12

EXTERIOR. A DARK WOOD – DAY

Scene 1. EXTERIOR. A DARK WOOD – DAY
We see a man lost in the wood. He looks up to see a
hill with its distant summit bathed in sunlight. He
tries to walk up it but is prevented from doing so by
three wild beasts.

> DANTE (Voice-over)
> Nel mezzo del cammin di nostra vita
> Mi ritrovai per una selva oscura
> ché la diritta via era smarrita.

'In the middle of life's journey I found myself in a dark wood, for I had wandered from the true path ...' These first lines will forever remain among the most famous openings of any book. The quotation is so well known in Dante's home country that no Italian will ever be impressed that you know it. They all know it: it is their 'To be or not to be'. Even to those outside Italy who may never have heard it before, the appeal of the line is immediate. It just sounds like the beginning of a story. As soon as we hear it there is some inquisitive but child-like part of our mind which cannot resist asking that most natural of questions, 'And then what happened?'

Dante had a gift for first lines. He begins the *Vita Nuova* by telling us that the first line of his private, inner 'Book of Memory' is about Beatrice; his short book about the importance of the Italian language, *De Vulgari Eloquentia*, opens forthrightly with a statement that since nobody else has written on the subject Dante realises that he will have to do it himself; and his projected great work of the popularisation of philosophy, the *Convivio*, opens with a resounding quote from 'the Philosopher', Aristotle, to the effect that all people desire to know things. But in all the works of Dante, poetry or prose, there is nothing else like the opening of the *Comedy*. It is one of few works which, in the first three lines, deposits its reader in the middle of an adventure. Its beginning can be written as a film script.

As he had planned in the final paragraph of the *Vita Nuova*, Dante's change of heart and return to Beatrice in 1300 had allowed him to find a radical new writing style. From somewhere inside him, the gift which had only previously shown itself as a hidden talent for bizarre, visually striking episodes emerged as a fully formed ability to write fiction. Story-telling was a new departure for Dante but the style of narrative he chose to use was an innovation for the time: the *Comedy* was fiction written in the first person. There had been first-person accounts before, of course, but they had been (or at least they claimed to be) true. And there had been fiction before but it consisted of tales about other people, usually saints, who were not the people writing the story. Never before had readers of the late Middle Ages read an account in which the author talked about his own experiences and feelings in detail whilst (tacitly) admitting that the events he was describing were not true. There is no attempt to deceive in the *Comedy* – Dante does not wish his readers to believe that he really had gone to Hell, Purgatory and Heaven, yet he wants us to feel the events as if they were real. The *Comedy* is new because it is less like a myth or a folktale and more like a personal account, informed by the consciousness of its author. Throughout the *Comedy* we feel the voice and the mind of Dante.

Dante's change of style from the factual *Convivio* to the fictional *Comedy* did not mean that he had abandoned his desire to transmit knowledge. The image of sheep rushing blindly into a well was still in his mind and he was still convinced that the way to stop human beings from doing the same thing was through knowledge and the intellect. In everyday life we tend necessarily to make a sharp distinction between fact and fiction, but in fact the differences between them are less clear cut. Fictional narratives are seldom merely free-form patterns of untruth; they may be lies but they are meaningful lies.

Stories, true or false, are the most ancient and effective way of propagating facts. The fundamental doctrines of Christianity, for example, are not laid out in a theological textbook but in the Gospels, a set of four collections of stories. Few people in the Middle Ages would have characterised the Gospels as fiction (although there were some who did) but, on the other hand, to have claimed that they were literally true would have been seen as ignorant and misguided. For one thing there were known contradictions between the different Gospel accounts of events, and if two Gospels told conflicting stories they couldn't both be true. That would have been a serious problem for Christianity if it had been thought to rely on the literal truth of the Bible. But it was not: the meaning of the Gospels lay in their significance as stories – they were a mystery to be puzzled over and thought about, not a straightforward concatenation of facts.

Even in our secular age, stories, untrue or part-true, continue to be the medium through which our ideas about ourselves are transmitted. Nations and peoples express their origins and identity not with dry historical facts but with myths about their creation. Even our current scientific understanding of the universe is mediated by the narrative of the big bang and the time scale of life on earth is told not through raw data but through a tale of mass extinctions and evolutionary metamorphoses. People remember stories; they enter their souls and affect their actions in a way that disjointed facts do not. The Middle Ages had the advantage of believing that at the heart of existence there was a mystical truth that was inexpressible to the extent that it could only be approached through a story. While Dante was in Rome contemplating the misdeeds of Boniface VIII he had surely realised that if he ever wanted to be able to touch the mind of the crowd and beat the power of corruption and military might, he too would have to tell a story.

By the time he started work on the *Comedy* Dante's programme of self-education was effectively complete. It had been so successful that, to this day, it is sometimes said that he was the last man in history who was able to hold in his head all the knowledge of his age. That is probably an exaggeration but he certainly did know a lot of things and, more importantly, he felt a passionate need to pass on what he had learnt. For this reason the *Comedy* is a compendium of late medieval knowledge, brimming with philosophical, historical and political allusions all held together by a web of symbolism, numerology and allegory. These are vital elements of the poem – it would be pointless without them – but no reader should ever forget that, at its foundation, the *Comedy* is a story.

Dante had invented a style of story which was able to carry the weight of factual information and at the same time convey the urgency of passionate belief. It is this element of fiction-as-opinion which makes the *Comedy* the ancestor of all subsequent first-person[a] fictional narratives. Any writer since who has used that form – and that is anyone from Marcel Proust to P.G. Wodehouse – owes Dante a debt for the idea. It really is not too much of an exaggeration to say that the introspective, obsessive poet from Florence had grown up to invent the novel.

The language that Dante uses to tell his tale is direct, even simple, and his sentence structure is (for the most part) straightforward. If you know a little French or some Latin it should often be possible to get the gist of Dante's Italian (especially with an English translation to hand). Even for someone who does not know a single word of Italian it is worth listening to the *Comedy* being read aloud at least once. The rhythmic pattern of consonant and vowel ripples like intricate music. The short, eleven-syllable[b] lines of the *Comedy* rhyme, following a pattern called *terza rima* which Dante devised for the purpose: interlocking triplets (the magic number three again) following the pattern 'aba bcb cdc ded, etc.' keep his verse rolling on and hold the listener's attention as the story unfolds over 14,000 lines. Dante's language is perfectly crafted for the task. He gives the poem a powerful but unobtrusive voice, personal yet perfectly suited for a vision of the entire universe.

The language of the *Comedy* may be uncomplicated but the use Dante makes of it – the descriptions and the similes which support them – is stupendous: spirits who fade away before his eyes 'like a stone falling down into deep water'; the telling detail of a man condemned to gnaw forever at the

a The *Comedy* was in fact not the first first-person fictional narrative in history: the Romans had got there first. There are at least two first-person fictional books that have survived from the ancient world (*Satyricon* by Petronius and the *Golden Ass* by Apuleius) and that is enough to indicate that originally there were more. Dante was certainly not aware of either of these and, in any case, the Roman examples, whilst they can achieve a high level of narrative panache, do not have the same feel of 'author-as-voice' that we find in the *Comedy*.

b That is an average. The number can vary slightly from line to line because the structure of Dante's verse is held together by a pattern of stress rather than counting of syllables. Nonetheless, it is interesting to compare Dante's verse with Shakespeare's ten-syllable iambic pentameters. In both cases the effect is to produce a comforting world of rhythm (you miss it when it stops) which unifies the poetry. The main difference between the two is that Dante's verse rhymes. The rhymes, however, do not overwhelm the sound of the verse. In English rhymes are comparatively rare and therefore stand out more when used in verse – it takes only a small misjudgement to choose a rhyme which is a little too unusual and end with a comic effect. In Italian so many words rhyme that it is hardly a surprise to hear them.

living brain within the skull of another who, before speaking, pauses genteelly to wipe his mouth on his victim's hair; the jaw-dropping spectacle of 100,000 angels who spontaneously ascend past Dante rising 'like glowing snowflakes falling upwards'; a detailed, scale-by-scale description of a man turning into a snake. These, and a thousand other examples, demonstrate Dante's innate ability (that first showed itself with the vision of Beatrice and the flaming heart) to imagine scenes of utter strangeness with meticulous precision.

Quite frequently in the *Comedy* he confesses how difficult it is to describe what he saw: 'if only I had words to describe the horrid hole of Hell'[1] ... 'Even if I called on genius art and skill, I could not make this live before your eyes.'[2] On one occasion he even tells his readers that he does not blame them if they do not believe what he is describing because he himself has difficulty with it and he actually witnessed it.[3] This is usually taken as a literary device, designed to heighten the realism, which of course it does, but the detail of what he does describe makes it seem quite possible that it is literally true. Dante seems to have had an inner cinema which was equipped with an ability to render scenes with an authenticity that outstrips the most modern computer-generated images. He really does seem to have written by constructing the scenes of the *Comedy* complete in his mind and then sitting down to work on describing them. Sometimes the act of description was a little frustrating for him; it is never disappointing for the reader.

The story moves on. Dante is lost in the wood but, beyond the gloom, he catches sight of the summit of a hill, bathed in the light of the sun (which Dante calls on this occasion 'the planet that leads all men on the straight road'). He is overwhelmed with relief. He feels like someone who has nearly drowned in the ocean and makes it to the shore at last where he lies for a while, exhausted, looking back at the sea which almost claimed him. As he, in his turn, looks back into the wood he gives us an extra piece of information. He calls it the valley 'from which no person has ever yet emerged alive' – this was no ordinary forest. Dante's relief is all the more for that thought and his disappointment is all the more sharp when his hopes are dashed. When he tries to make his way towards the hill he is stopped by a trio of wild beasts: a leopard, a lion and a wolf. One after another they drive him back into the darkness.

The symbolic meaning of all this is both clear and unclear. As we have seen, the dark wood is the tangle of wrong-headed ideas into which Dante has wandered with the addition of (perhaps) a dash of infidelity to Beatrice, physical or not. The light on the hilltop is undoubtedly the bliss of divine love that Dante realises he can only obtain through Beatrice (light will become an increasingly important image as the *Comedy* progresses). The beasts, however, are not so obvious. They plainly represent three things which prevent human beings from achieving that goal of divine bliss. Several candidates have been suggested: Lust, Pride and Avarice are a likely trio, as are Anger, Violence and Fraud which have the advantage of echoing the hierarchy of sins on which Dante's Hell is organised. None of them is a conclusive interpretation and, although it is quite interesting to speculate about what the three most savage impediments that prevent each of us from achieving our true goal are, it does not really matter to the reader at this stage. The point is that the main character wants something but is prevented from getting it so, in order to obtain it, he has to go the long way round. He has been forced into an adventure: the game is on. What we need now is some dialogue:

> As I fled downwards my eyes made out a figure. He looked faint, as if from a long silence.
>
> 'Help me,' I cried out in that deserted place, 'whoever you may be, whether a ghost or a man.'
>
> 'I am no longer living man, though once I was,' he replied. 'I was born in the time of Julius and lived in Rome in the reign of good Augustus in the age of false gods. I was a poet and I sang of the just son of Anchises who came from Troy.'
>
> (*Inferno*, 1:62–75)

One of the great double acts of literature has been born. The faint and ghostly figure whom Dante has just met has already said enough to identify himself as Virgil, the Roman poet who lived from 70 to 19 BC. His best-known work is the *Aeneid*, the story of Aeneas (the 'just son of Anchises' of Virgil's introduction of himself), a refugee from defeat in the Trojan War who went on to found the city of Rome. Virgil intended his own epic poem to be the defining myth of the Roman Empire and to a large extent he succeeded. Along the way he established Latin as a language suitable for poetry. Previously Greek had been seen, even in Rome, as the language which was most suitable for artistic projects. Virgil in the *Aeneid* even described a journey to Hell, albeit to the pre-Christian underworld of Hades. Most important of all, though, he is there because he is Dante's favourite poet. Dante would like to be Virgil; he scatters the *Comedy* with illusions, references and homages to his style. In the *Comedy* he calls him 'the spring from which the river of style rises … You are my master, the source of noble style'.[4] He even calls him father as the story goes on. Virgil's approval must have been of enormous importance to Dante as a writer setting out on the daunting journey of a lengthy, new (and totally uncommissioned) work in an untried style.

Virgil performs a vital dramatic function in the *Comedy*. Without his presence we would be entirely reliant on Dante's own inner voice for information about his feelings. It is, of course, quite possible to write a fictional journey which is described entirely through the lone voice of the traveller, but in order to give a well-rounded impression of Dante's reactions, especially the occasional moments when fear or despair overtake him, it is much more satisfying to dramatise them through his conversation with Virgil. Indeed, it seems that most fictional travellers need companions: Don Quixote had Sancho Panza; Phileas Fogg had Passepartout on his eighty-day journey round the world; Doctor Who has his succession of assistants; and Virgil gave Aeneas a faithful companion called Achates who accompanies him to Hell, although it has to be said that he does not get much of a speaking part. Compared with all of these, Virgil himself is given a much more authoritative role: he is the expert on Hell. The only area where Dante has superior knowledge is concerning the specifically Christian aspects of the universe.

Fulfilling his role as guide, Virgil confirms to Dante that there is no way past the three beasts. He offers to lead him out of the dark wood by another route. He is not specific but it is not difficult to guess what it is: 'Now I say for your own good, I think it best if you follow me. I'll lead you out of here through an eternal place where you will hear grisly screaming. You'll see ancient ghosts in tears howling over their second death.'[5]

Virgil's warning that the best he can offer is abject terror frightens Dante, the traveller, but for the reader it holds the exciting promise of thrills to come.

Dante's precisely imagined version of Hell gives details which previous writers had not specified. The starting point, in the Christian tradition, is that Hell is the dwelling place of those souls who are unforgiven, denied entry into Heaven and obliged instead to be tormented there. The physical geography of Hell had been discussed before but there was no orthodox, accepted view. Dante's imagination therefore had wide scope. He specified that Hell is a deep conical indentation into the earth, the lowest point of which is the exact centre of the globe. The tormented souls are distributed on a series of nine vast circular steps or terraces which descend, each one of decreasing size, down to the centre of the earth. The central axis of the cone runs directly through Jerusalem, a city whose significance for anyone writing about the history of the universe in 1300 cannot have been greater. It was the location of the crucifixion and resurrection of Christ, the dramatic symbol of God's redemptive power. Going further back it was also the traditional location for

Abraham's near sacrifice of Isaac, one of the defining stories in the explanation of man's relationship with God. Thirdly, it was the take-off point for the Night Journey, the episode mentioned in the Koran but elaborated by later writers in which the Prophet Muhammad ascended (as Dante was to do) through the celestial spheres to Heaven itself.

Assuming that the dark wood in which Dante found himself and from which he enters Hell was in Italy,^c this enables us to map the edge of Hell – the points where the cone meets the surface of the earth – on a terrestrial globe. It is a circle of a radius of about 1,500 miles which runs through Egypt and Afghanistan, but whether other ways into the underworld can be found along its length we are not told. We do know that the journey of the travellers is a long one. Estimates of the size of the earth were quite accurate in Dante's day, and had been so for the best part of a thousand years. The circumference of the earth was known to be about 24,000 miles. Elementary geometry would indicate that the bottom of Hell, at the centre of the earth, would have to be approximately 4,000 miles down.

The first chapter of the *Inferno* ends with the simple line, 'Virgil moved off and I followed on behind'.[6] It is evening on the day before Good Friday, the day when Christians remember the death and descent into Hell of Christ. The journey has begun and the mechanism of the story has been set in motion: a frustrated desire, a perilous journey needed in order to fulfil it, but there is one element still missing. This is not just a story of two men clambering down to the centre of the earth, it is also about great questions and the relationship between man and God. It is time now for Virgil to reveal the bigger picture and explain how it was that he came to be there when Dante found himself in the dark wood. He tells Dante the story. He was in his allotted place in the underworld when, one day, the spirit of a woman visited him: 'Her eyes were brighter than the stars ... She was so blessed and beautiful that I longed for her to command me.'[7]

It is Beatrice. She has descended from Heaven to give Virgil a message. 'With the voice of an angel' she tells him that her friend Dante is so 'impeded in his journey'[8] that he is in desperate need of help. As the travellers make their way towards the gate of Hell, Virgil recounts her words. It turns out to be quite a long story, the gist of which is that the Virgin Mary herself, the mother of Christ, was deeply concerned about Dante's plight, both his

---

c If it was it would be in keeping with the account given by Dante's new friend Virgil in the *Aeneid*. He locates the entrance to Hell in a volcanic crater called Avernus, near Naples.

departure from the direct pathway and the sorrow that he was caused. It is on her authority that Virgil is now empowered to act. When Dante hears about this and realises that Virgil has met Beatrice (and that he himself may once again do so) he is overjoyed. His trepidation at the thought of entering Hell lifts: 'My strength began to blossom within me like flowers which have been closed and bowed by the chill night open when the sun comes out and rise up on their stem.'[9]

Now he has even more confidence in Virgil: '"You are my guide my lord and teacher." Those were my words to him as I travelled down that deep and savage way.'[10]

And so the second chapter of *Inferno* closes. The *Comedy* comprises a hundred chapters, divided, of course, into three parts:[d] Hell, Purgatory and Heaven (*Inferno*, *Purgatorio* and *Paradiso*). A chapter in the *Comedy* is normally referred to by its Italian name, *canto*, a word which can also mean either poem or song. The choice of this word reflects not only the musical nature of Dante's poetry but also the fact that, when the *Comedy* was given its first airing, each canto was probably performed by being read aloud to a group rather than being read quietly by an individual.[11] This presents an exacting test for an author. A lone reader can always flip back and read again if the sense is unclear or if the mind has wandered. In a performance there is no safety net: once the attention of the audience is lost it is very hard to recapture it. One can see the effect of this in the *Comedy*. Cantos usually have their own thematic unity – they work as little stories in themselves. They often end with a cliffhanger, designed to keep the listeners' interest and make them want to come back for the next one. Sometimes Dante also uses the canto breaks to move the action on. He can finish with a telling phrase, avoid too much description and let the next canto open in an attention-grabbing way. This is exactly what happens at the end of Canto 2. It finishes with a simple statement of the travellers' departure and Canto 3 kicks off immediately with the sonorous words of the ancient inscription above the gates of Hell:

> THROUGH ME IS THE WAY TO THE CITY OF WOE,
> THROUGH ME IS THE WAY TO EVERLASTING PAIN,
> THROUGH ME IS THE WAY AMONG THE LOST PEOPLE.
>
> JUSTICE MOVED MY MAKER ON HIGH.
> DIVINE POWER MADE ME,
> WISDOM SUPREME, AND PRIMAL LOVE.
>
> BEFORE ME NOTHING WAS BUT THINGS ETERNAL,
> AND ETERNAL I ENDURE.
> ABANDON ALL HOPE, YOU WHO ENTER HERE.

(*Inferno*, 3:1–9)

---

d The parts comprise thirty-three chapters each. Dante wanted his three-part work to have 100 cantos. It is one of those arithmetical annoyances that plague the numerologist that the neat and significant century cannot be divided by the even more significant number three so there is a canto left over. He added this to *Inferno* as Canto 1, where, by convention, it is considered to be an introduction.

The final line of this is the most famous in the *Comedy*, '*Lasciate ogne speranza voi ch'entrate*', often rendered, slightly inaccurately, as 'Abandon hope all ye who enter here'.

The entire inscription is intended as the mission statement for Hell. It contains ideas that must be borne in mind during the journey to the centre of the earth. The first three lines (the inscription breaks naturally into three sets of triplets in Dante's *terza rima*) advertise once again the horrors to come. The final three lines emphasise the hopelessness of human souls in the face of an implacable eternity. The middle triplet is most interesting: it emphasises that God is the Creator and ultimate ruler of Hell. It is important to remember that the Inferno is not the headquarters of the 'official opposition to God', staffed by creatures who lurk in the darkness hiding from the Creator as they try to foil his plan. Hell is part of God's plan and, since He created the universe out of love, it follows (as the inscription makes explicit) that Hell and the torments of all the souls who remain there are all consequences of God's love. This is the tough love of divine justice (a word which in this inscription makes the first of seventy-one appearances in the *Comedy*). Everything which Dante sees in Hell, Purgatory and Heaven will be an example of God's justice and the natural rightness of the world which is guaranteed by God's love. The only things in the universe which deviate from the loving justice of the Creator are human beings. They have been given free will and are capable of going against the rightness of the universe. In most cases God's love is such that they are forgiven for any transgressions. Dante is about to see what happens to those who are not.

Many people have found the concept of a loving God who ordains cruel punishment difficult. Dante was one of them. As he continues his journey downwards, Dante the traveller shows a variety of reactions to the tormented souls he meets on the way. With some he views their plight with detached academic interest; with others, particularly when he knew the soul personally, he is even delighted and cheers the tormentors on; but there are other times when he is sincerely moved to pity by what he sees. Dante, as a student of theology, is committed to the view that God's justice is good by definition. But to maintain that view requires an inflexible moral certainty which makes for bad storytelling. A good narrative needs to reflect the complexity of experience, moral and otherwise. In a good novel the boundaries of good and evil are almost imperceptibly blurred – a totally evil character is hard to believe in. Even though he had only just invented the genre, Dante was aware of this and, as we descend with him into the depths, there are moments when the late medieval intellectual loses the battle with the novelist and a rogue element of sympathy appears in his descriptions. Dante knows that he is not *meant* to feel pity for souls in Hell. He notes the emotion but does not ever use it as a reason to question the authority of the divine justice. But neither does he ever say that he regrets having felt it. It would be nice to think that one of the unintended consequences of the invention of the novel was to make it slightly easier for us to empathise with the suffering of our fellow human beings.

13

THE BLACK, THE WHITE
AND THE NEUTRAL

Now moans, loud howls and lamentation echoed through the starless air, so that
I also began to cry. Many languages, strange accents, words of pain, cries of rage,
voices loud and faint, the sound of slapping hands – all these whirled together in
that black and timeless air, as sand is swirled in a tornado.

(Inferno 3:22–30)

The mixture of wailing and lamentation that Dante is hearing
has become the traditional soundtrack of Hell – most of us can
conjure up in our mind's ear the sound of souls in torment. To
this sound Dante adds the further element of a howling wind
that sweeps around the noises themselves together with the
souls that make them like grains of sand in a sandstorm. Quite naturally, Dante
asks Virgil what these particular souls have done to deserve such torment. The
answer is surprising: they have done nothing; they were morally neutral. They
are here because they stood on the sidelines: they did not speak out; they did not
choose to get involved. 'Loath to impair its beauty, Heaven casts them out, and
the depth of Hell does not receive them.' This is not even in Hell proper. It is a
featureless vestibule of the Inferno at the outer edge of the pit. Their destiny is
to be forever neutral, to live without hope of death. They swirl in their masses
back and forth following a big red banner which moves swiftly from place to

place like the latest shallow trend or modish fancy. There are, as one might expect, an awful lot of these souls. This is the moment when Dante makes his much-quoted remark that he is surprised to see that death has taken so many.[1] Dante the writer is determined that they will not go unpunished for their failure to look at the dimension of right or wrong in the world about them: 'These wretches who never really lived were naked and attacked by swarms of flies and wasps which made their faces flow with blood.'[2]

Dante tells us that he thinks he recognises a few of the blood-streaked faces as they fly past him in the wind. He does not name them. Unlike the *Vita Nuova*, the *Comedy* is full of proper names, but Dante also gives himself more possibilities by referring to people by means of brief allusions. In some cases these are rather formal intellectual references which display more than a hint of showing off. You are just meant to know enough classical mythology, for example, to realise that 'Latona's Daughter' is the moon.[a] On other occasions they are more topical references which one can imagine were a delight to their first audience. Some of these are still easy to decode, while scholars puzzle over others in vain. This is not surprising: one of the first things time erodes is the pithy up-to-the-minute comment and the irreverent in-joke. What, for example, would readers in 500 years' time make of a book which referred to 'the man who loved his duck house more than justice' or 'he who made the 45 minute claim'. Much less will anybody be able to explain that in the 1980s there were popular comic references so strong and precise that it was possible for the Royal Mail to deliver a letter addressed simply to The Teeth, London.

There is just one oblique reference here. As he observes the wind-blown neutral souls, Dante says that he thinks he caught a glimpse of 'the one who, out of cowardice, made the great refusal'. It seems more than likely that this is Celestine V, the simple hermit who was made pope against his will and then resigned in order to allow Boniface VIII to succeed him. Celestine does not appear anywhere else in the *Comedy* and, since Dante believed that the accession of Boniface was the start of most of the ills that were to beset him and his city, it would be strange if Celestine did not get a mention. We can tell from this remark that Dante does not give any credence to the claim, put about by the Colonna family, that Celestine was a simple dupe who was forced into abdicating by the ambitious Boniface. Dante must have believed that he

---

a Latona was the mother of the gods Diana and Apollo, so 'Latona's Son' is the sun and 'Latona's Children' refers to both.

acted (or rather did not act) out of cowardice not coercion. He could have resisted and hung on as pope but he walked away and let another take over, and in doing so was responsible for all the awful consequences that followed. As Edmund Burke was later to put it, all that is necessary for the triumph of evil is that good men do nothing.

The travellers walk on as far as the banks of the Acheron, the first of Hell's rivers where newly arrived souls mass on the banks waiting to cross. Here they meet the famous boatman from classical mythology, Charon, a character borrowed from Virgil. It is obvious to him, as it is to all the ghostly characters we meet in the *Comedy*, that Dante is a still living being. He has more solidity and, when there is light available, he casts a shadow. Charon comes over as a very ill-tempered jobsworth. He refuses to take him on board but Virgil is ready for this. He explains that Dante's journey is ordained at the highest level. When he hears this Charon is silent. The souls of the damned are not:

> They cursed God, their parents, the human race, the place, the time, the seed that made them and their birth. Weeping bitterly, they gathered together on the evil shore that awaits all those who fear not God.
>
> (*Inferno*, 3:103–8)

At that moment an earth tremor rocks the ground and Dante, perhaps for the first time realising the full implications of where he is, faints. He tells us, for additional realism, that even to this day he still sweats with fear when he thinks about it.

He wakes up in the next canto to find himself looking down into Hell proper, 'that profound pit of pain filled with the howl of endless woe'. He strains his eyes to see into the depths. He can make nothing out, but the audience need not be worried: there are plenty of horrors to come. Dante still has thirty cantos to go in which to build to a climax.

Virgil tells him not to dawdle. 'We must go down into the blind world … for the long road calls us on.' Dante cannot help noticing that despite his apparent eagerness Virgil has gone pale with fright. This worries him. How can he be expected to descend into the pit if even his teacher is frightened? But Virgil reassures him that the emotion he is showing is not fear but the pain of sympathy for the predicament of the anguished souls who are down there.

Again he chivvies Dante and finally they descend to a place where there are no screams, only sighs that hold 'an eternal tremor in the air'. Dante sees a crowd of souls: men, women and little children. Even before he can ask, Virgil explains who they are. These are the souls of those who died without having been given the redemption of God's grace. They are not being tormented here but, as Virgil explains, they sigh because, just like the neutrals, 'they live in longing without hope'.

This place is called Limbo. In Dante's time it was generally held to be part of Hell even though it is not mentioned in the Bible. Successive generations of theologians had thought about it until eventually it seemed to them to be logically necessary that Limbo should exist. This comes about as a result of Christianity's claim (in common with almost all other religions) to be a unique route to salvation and eternal bliss. As Christ Himself put it, 'I am the way, the truth and the life: no man cometh unto the Father but by me',[b] which Saint Paul later backed up with the rather authoritarian remark, 'One Lord, one Faith, one Baptism'.

It follows from this that any child who dies before being baptised is also fated to spend eternity in Limbo. To modern readers this seems a little extreme and, to be fair, medieval theologians had also been concerned by the conclusion that innocent children should end up in Hell, albeit the outer circle. Many of them, even hard-liners like St Bernard of Clairvaux, had at various times expressed surprise and even regret at its logical necessity. Discussion about the nature of Limbo continued for centuries until, in 2005, it was removed from official Catholic doctrine on the grounds that it had never been anything more than a 'theological hypothesis'.

The souls whom Dante sees here also include all those adults who died before the birth of Christ when baptism was available to no one. Virgil is, of course, himself one of these unfortunate souls, having died in 19 BC. This is the reason why he went pale as he approached Limbo and why he was so eager for Dante to know the status of the souls he saw there. This place is his home forever. It must be emphasised that Virgil has not done anything wrong. Far from it, he was seen in the Middle Ages as the only Roman poet who came close to predicting the coming of Christ.[c] But, despite his good character, he must

---

b It is not beyond the wit of theologians to find a different interpretation. Nowadays, many would turn the sense around and say that whoever finds God, by whatever means, has (whether they know it or not) arrived through Christ. This idea was not current in the Middle Ages.

c On the grounds of some rather obscure references (in a minor work) to the coming of a miraculous child and also his famous line from the *Aeneid* which was held to prefigure the Christian message: *'Omnia vincit amor'*, 'Love conquers all things'.

spend eternity excluded forever from the light which Dante longs so much to reach. At this point Dante, slightly hesitantly, asks a question: 'Master, tell me, Sir, did anyone ever – either through his own merit or through somebody else's – did they ever get out of here and make it to bliss?'[3]

Some people have suggested that Dante the traveller has asked this question with deliberate reference to Virgil. Is he perhaps looking for a way to spring his new friend from Limbo? It would be quite in character for him to wonder about this. He idolises Virgil and rightly feels sympathy for anyone stuck in this dreadful place.

There is, of course, no way to resolve this speculation because it has no connection with reality. It is an artefact of the hall of mirrors of truth and falsehood that is created by Dante's invention. Having devised the genre of first-person fiction, Dante seems to have enjoyed playing with the strange patterns that it creates. One immediate effect of the invention, for example, is to fictionalise the writer. As in this case, we find ourselves speculating about the undeclared thoughts of a made-up version of Dante in a situation which has never happened. Even when Dante speaks as the author of the *Comedy* we do not settle comfortably back into reality. He continues the game by telling us about the lingering horror which still stays with him. In fact, whenever the word or the idea of truth is mentioned in the *Comedy* it is worth asking if it is pointing to some new layer of ontological complexity. It is this 'hall-of-mirrors effect' which obliges scholars and biographers alike to tie themselves in knots as they distinguish between a variety of characters such as 'Dante the writer', 'Dante the protagonist', 'Dante the scholar', etc. The possibilities are endless.

With regard to the possibility of escape from Limbo, Virgil the character knows (as does Dante the writer) that divine justice is immutable. For him there is no way out. Instead of responding to Dante's suggestion of an escape (if that is what it is), Virgil gives a straight, if surprising, answer to the question. Yes, he says, it is funny that Dante should mention it because not long after he died (remember he died in 19 BC, only fifty-one years before the death of Christ) Virgil did see someone do exactly that. A man 'crowned with the sign of victory' arrived in Purgatory. He selected some of the souls and sent them on to paradise. Virgil says that among them were Adam 'the first parent', Abel his son (although obviously not his brother Cain, who murdered him), Noah, Moses, Abraham, King David and Jacob.

It is not clear quite how much of this Virgil himself understands but what he is describing is an event known in the Middle Ages as the 'Harrowing of Hell', which had its basis in Christian scriptural authority.[4] It was believed that, directly after the crucifixion, Christ had descended into Hell and released, by personal intervention, Adam, Eve (whom Dante does not mention) and some others from the Old Testament A-list.[d] But this was a one-off event, a special act of will on the part of Christ. It does not apply to Virgil who does not feature in the Bible and will therefore remain in the place of sighs forever.

Given that Virgil led a productive life and did no serious wrong, this may appear very unfair. Dante seems to have thought so too because, in Heaven, as he ascends successive spheres and meets a series of religious sages and luminaries, the question he asks most frequently is about the people who were known in the Middle Ages as the 'good pagans'. In *Paradiso* the problem is posed in a more general form:

> Suppose a man is born on the banks of the Indus, and there is no one to tell him about Christ but he is without sin in deed or word, so far as humans can tell. He then dies without baptism or faith. Where is the justice in his condemnation?
>
> *(Inferno, 19:70–8)*

It is a good question to which Dante deserves an answer. He will have to travel a long way before he gets it.

Virgil and Dante pick their way onwards through the dense forest of spirits. They are making for a specific group of souls. Dante sees a blaze of light emanating from them. These are the famous names from the pre-Christian world. Among them he sees historical figures: Caesar, Cicero, Seneca and even Saladin, the renowned Kurdish leader who resisted the second Crusade (he is standing by himself). There are also figures that we would consider mythological, such as Electra, who appears in Greek tragedy; Hector, a key figure in the *Iliad*; and Aeneas, about whom Virgil himself wrote. Aeneas does not acknowledge Virgil, even though it could be argued that he owes him everything.

Scientists and thinkers from the ancient world include, of course, Aristotle who was referred to simply as 'The Philosopher'. Dante just calls him 'the master of those who know' and does not feel the need to name him as this description is specific enough. He sees other philosophers: Democritus who invented atoms, Diogenes the Cynic, Empedocles who first spoke of the four elements of which all matter was believed to be composed, Averroes and

d They are able to enter Heaven because they are known to have had direct experience of God which for these purposes is as good as baptism.

Avicenna, two of the great names from Islamic science, and Anaxagoras who was driven out of his home for saying that the sun was nothing more than a hot rock. Dante says he cannot list them all. He has to get on with the story and anyway, 'descriptions often fall short of the fact'.

Then they hear a shout, 'Honour to the most glorious poet!' Doubtless both travellers turn round but it transpires that it is Virgil who is being hailed. This is the dramatic highlight of the visit to Limbo: the great poets. Four figures approach. Three are Roman poets: Horace who wrote a book called the *Art of Poetry* which was a big influence on Dante; Lucan whose work provided him with important details of the history of the Roman Empire; and Ovid whose book about changes and transformations, *Metamorphoses*, gave him something to try to outdo when it came to the more bizarre episodes lower down in Hell. The fourth figure is Homer, the great narrator whose stories of Ulysses and the Trojan War have provided models for the epic poem ever since they were written. Virgil is, of course, already a member of this exclusive poets' society which is why Homer had hailed him in such extravagant terms.

After some brief introductions ('Dante, I don't think you've met Homer and this is Ovid ... Horace, Dante. Dante, Horace'), the poets welcome Dante as the newest member of their group. This is, of course, pure self-indulgence on the part of the writer. He hasn't even written the *Divine Comedy* yet, so they must have based their decision on a few lyric poems coupled with their assessment of his innate worth. All artists would like to be judged by this latter criterion. Few ever achieve it.

The six poets walk and talk together for a little while but Dante coyly refuses to tell his audience what they discuss. The subject was, he says, 'things about which it is good manners to be silent'.[5] Scholars may argue but most writers will tell you it was probably about money. Virgil and Dante eventually take their leave, 'the company of six loses two', and the lightest moment of the *Inferno* has passed. From now on every step downwards will take them to a progressively more evil place.

They descend to the second level which is the circle of the lustful. Those who are here have 'let reason be slave to appetite' and given in to that most ubiquitous of temptations. They are guilty of sin but they are still only on the outer edge of Hell; there are much worse things than a bit of lustful behaviour. Unsurprisingly, there are once again many souls in this circle. Dante sees them swirling together like flocks of starlings at dusk.

The never-ending hellish storm whirls and strikes the spirits as it torments them. When they meet their judgement they shriek, weep and moan, cursing

the power of God. I understood that carnal sinners are condemned to these torments, they who subjected their reason to their lust.

(*Inferno*, 5:31)

Virgil identifies some of the lovers as they are swept by. There are those of whom we have heard: Cleopatra, Helen of Troy, Dido Queen of Carthage (it is Virgil again who wrote about her fling with Aeneas which is the reason she is there). Others are not so well known: Semiramis, for example, who became ruler of Assyria when her husband died and was so prey to lust that she made licentiousness a legal obligation in her country. Men are represented as well – Paris, Tristan and Achilles – but, of those we hear about, the lustful women easily outnumber them. James Joyce memorably called the *Inferno*

'Through Hell with the Papes (mostly boys)'.[e] That is fair comment; in fact, it is only in the circle of the lustful that gender equality is properly respected. This may be possibly an insight into Dante's psychology but it is more likely a sad but predictable manifestation of the inherent misogyny of the Middle Ages.

Dante's attention is caught by one particular couple. They are pressed tight together, floating 'weightless in the wind'. He asks Virgil if he can speak to them. If you call them in the name of their love they will speak, he is told. When he calls out they peel away from the main body of souls and glide towards him, not storm-tossed now but like a dove approaching its dovecote with its wings locked for the final glide. It transpires that they are a celebrity couple from the late thirteenth century, Paolo Malatesta and Francesca da Rimini. They died when Dante was about 15 years old and it is just possible that he had met them – we know that at least one of them visited Florence at that time. Francesca was married to Paolo's brother, the Lord of Rimini. When the brother discovered their affair he killed them both. We are told that a place much deeper down in Hell is being kept open for him. The couple themselves will fly in the wind for eternity, locked together naked as they were when they died. The audience is left to judge for itself whether this is the consolation of perpetual togetherness or the endless punishment of sharing a single bed when one is no longer a teenager.

Francesca does the talking while Paolo remains mute and tearful. She is charming and eloquent. When Dante asks her the key question, 'How was it that you came to start the affair?' her answer is prefaced with another famous line from the *Comedy*: 'There is no greater pain than to remember past happiness in present sorrow.'[6] She follows the remark with an observation which includes Virgil in the conversation: 'and this your teacher also knows.' Perhaps she does this out of good manners or perhaps it is out of a desire to make herself feel better by reminding Virgil that he is only one level better than she is.

She recounts the simple tale of how the couple's close proximity turned effortlessly into sexual liaison. One day she and her brother-in-law decided to pass the time by reading a book together. They chose the medieval classic *Lancelot du Lac*, the story of which revolves around Lancelot's adulterous affair

e 'Skim over Through Hell with the Papes (mostly boys) by the divine comic Denti Alligator' (*Finnegans Wake*, Book III.2, p. 440). If a reader ever gets bogged down by the technicalities of the *Inferno* a good cure is to read this quotation aloud in a cod Irish accent.

with the married Guinevere. 'We were alone without any qualms … our eyes often met and the colour drained from our faces … it was in one moment that we were overcome.' When they read how Lancelot finally kissed Guinevere it was all too much for them. Paolo kissed Francesca and, as she puts it, 'we did no more reading that day'.

Her description is good drama, expressed in language which echoes slightly the poetic style of Dante's friends, the *Fedeli d'Amore*. It is noteworthy, however, that she is completely unwilling to take any kind of responsibility for the incident. She seems almost to be blaming the book for having caused their affair. It is also significant that she has apparently 'misremembered' the plot of *Lancelot du Lac*. In the story it is in fact Guinevere who first makes a move on Lancelot, not the other way around.[f] Francesca stops far short of expressing any kind of regret for what happened. It is hard not to admire her fortitude: even Hell cannot make her turn her back on her love. Dante the theologian must presumably unequivocally endorse her condemnation – a sin is a sin. Dante the novelist, on the other hand, has given us in a few brush strokes an insight into a real personality operating in the real world of desire and self-deception.

When Dante wrote this scene the pictures must have played in his head, as did all the pictures in the *Comedy* – that is how he wrote. It is hard not to imagine that, as the naked couple floated before his inner eye, he did not also think about that other famous couple, Dante and Beatrice. We can never know what Dante thought as the ideas of love, nakedness and Beatrice were all buffeted together inside his mind. Dante chooses not to tell us and to a modern mind it leaves an almost painful gap in our understanding. The closest we will get to any indication that the question was also important for Dante comes in the very next event in the story. The traveller is so overcome with emotion at the story told by the lovely, naked Francesca that he faints clean away and falls down on the ground like a corpse. The erotic episode of Paolo and Francesca has come to a close.

Dante regains consciousness in the next canto to find himself in the third circle. He switches briefly to the immediacy of the present tense to describe

f   In many details the description of shared study turning into physical contact is similar to the twelfth-century philosopher Peter Abelard's autobiographical account of the beginning of his celebrated affair with Heloise. Once again the incident is represented (this time by the Abelard himself) as having happened at the man's initiative and being a complete surprise to Heloise. Once again one has one's doubts.

the scene: 'I am in the third circle, of eternal, accursed, cold and heavy rain: a never changing downpour. Large hail, foul water mixed with snow pour down through the shadowy air: and the earth on which it falls is putrid.'[7]

This is the circle of the gluttonous who, like the lustful, have been unable to get a grip on their natural appetites. It is guarded by another mythical creature who Dante has imported into his *Inferno*: Cerberus, the three-headed dog who guards Virgil's Hell, is also on duty here. His eyes are crimson, his beard is foul and black, his belly vast. His party piece is to catch souls with his claws, strip off their skin and rip them into pieces. We will learn later on in the *Inferno* that souls may be mutilated, dismembered or even shredded but afterwards their fate is quietly to reconstitute themselves in readiness for the next torment. Cerberus barks enough to make a ghost wish it was deaf and the tormented souls of the over-indulgent bark back in their turn. Just like Charon before him, Cerberus is not pleased to see Dante. But Virgil has a trick ready for him. In the *Aeneid* the hero buys Cerberus off with some honeyed cakes. Dante selects an option which is more in keeping with the mood of the scene and has Virgil throw mud into its mouths. This is enough to distract all three of Cerberus' heads and, while this dog is still thinking about it, the travellers slip past him.

They pick their way onwards, walking over the shades of storm-lashed gluttons, 'setting our feet upon their emptiness that looked like people'. Quite suddenly one of the dead sits up and calls to Dante: 'Hey you, the one being led through this Inferno, see if you can recognise me. You were made before I was unmade.' Dante does not recognise him but he replies with diplomatic charm: 'Perhaps your awful punishment is pushing you out of my memory but I don't think I've ever seen you. But tell me who you are and why you are suffering like this.'

He gets an almost civil answer. 'Your own city – so full of envy that it is overflowing – was my home during my sweet life. The citizens called me "Ciacco" and now I lie here in this rain because of the wicked sin of Gluttony.'

Ciacco, which appropriately means hog, is usually thought to have been a nickname. Although we don't know this person's real name we do have a little background on him thanks to Boccaccio, who includes him as a character in one of the stories of the *Decameron*.[8] Ciacco comes over as a rather likeable, Falstaffian rogue who spends his time getting into scrapes and outwitting fellow members of the minor aristocracy. He has made an appearance in the *Comedy* for a specific reason: he is there to predict the future of Florence.

The convention is that the souls whom Dante meets in Hell have no direct knowledge of the world of the living at the moment of speaking. They do, however, have knowledge of the future.[g] The effect of this on the narrative is to give them plenty to talk about. The souls ask Dante about what is going on back on earth and in return they can tell him what is going to happen. Their predictions tend to be quite accurate in the short term, of course, because Dante was writing a few years after April 1300, when events in the near future of the characters had already happened. Nonetheless, the act of describing recent events in the guise of predictions opens all sorts of possibilities for incorporating opinions and comment. Ciacco pulls no punches in giving his views on the city he describes as 'like a sack overflowing with envy'.

He is the first of many who will pronounce on the state of Dante's city. Here Ciacco gives a brief picture of the immediate future. A long period of feuding will end in bloodshed. 'The rustic party' (la parte selvaggia) will drive out their rivals but they will themselves soon fall and be held down by their enemies for a long time. He is telling a familiar tale of Florentine factionalism and tit-for-tat vengeance driven, as he colourfully puts it, by the sparks of pride, envy and greed. What is special about this schism is that it is the one that will cause Dante's own downfall.

The traveller asks for details. He mentions several notable Florentines who have been involved in Florentine politics in recent decades – Farinata degli Uberti, Tegghiaio Aldobrandi, Jacopo Rusticucci, Arrigo de' Fifanti, Mosca de' Lamberti. Since they have all passed on by now, Ciacco will know how they have fared in the afterlife. What was the final judgement on their lives? Were they deemed to have been good or bad? 'They are all among the blackest souls. Their various sins drag them deep into Hell. If you go down that far you will meet them.' Ciacco refuses to say more.

After his Jubilee visit to Rome, Dante returned to Florence in March 1300. By then nobody in Florence would have needed a prophecy to tell them what the latest dispute was about or who the warring factions were. The sides had already taken names for themselves: the Blacks and the Whites. Previous factions had chosen the names Guelfs and Ghibellines which at least reflected something of the historical origins of the dispute. This time the combatants

---

g   Even this knowledge is temporary. After the apocalypse, when the world will be remade and Christ will reign supreme, the damned will remain as they are but their foreknowledge will disappear and their memories fade, leaving only the pain.

had adopted names that expressed only pure belligerence: wherever there are the Whites we can expect to find opposing Blacks and vice versa.

The Black party comprised those who, by and large, supported the actions of Pope Boniface VIII. Its core constituency were the old-school aristocrats who once would have sided with the emperor and now supported the Pope (who demonstrably had imperialist tendencies). The opposing Whites tended to be the merchants and minor aristocrats who had more to gain from a truly independent Florence and who, anyway, hated the old-style ruling classes.

At one level this latest schism was a reflection of the politics of the Italian peninsula. But in Florence the origins of a fight were as likely to be found in the spaces between front doors as in the political landscape of a continent. It could be equally well argued, for instance, that this particular feud had started two years earlier, when the Cerchi family had applied for planning permission to build a new road to link their home directly to the palace of the podestà.

The Cerchi, who by the time Dante returned to Florence were the de facto leaders of the White faction, were considered by everyone to be embarrassingly nouveau riche. The chronicler Dino Compagni slightly spitefully calls them 'men of low status but good merchants'. They had been landowners from the small hill-town of Acone outside Florence who had done well and bought a palace in the city twenty years earlier. These are the people whom Ciacco calls 'the rustic party' – one could even translate the phrase more freely as 'the country cousins'. Apart from being arriviste upstarts, another reason for the unpopularity of the Cerchi was that their new riches were much bigger than other families' old ones. They were just good at striking deals and making money. It was, for example, their leader Vieri dei Cerchi himself who had made the deal with Guglielmo, the treacherous and belligerent bishop of Arezzo, when he decided to lease his land to the Florentines as their army approached his city on its way to the battle of Campaldino.

The planning application for their new road survives in the city records. It was to be the centrepiece of a major upgrade of the Cerchi houses which involved knocking three dwellings together to make one huge palace. Dino Compagni agrees that it was the house that triggered the trouble. Archaeologists are still able to see evidence in the existing (much modified) buildings of the new hall that was created with ostentatiously large windows and pointed arches. Local residents were doubtless of a mind that it was totally out of keeping with the style of the neighbourhood. The whole project was a shameless piece of social climbing but the road was the last straw. It was more than just a road, it was a statement that the Cerchi had arrived and were now entitled to be in direct contact with the leader of the nobility. In order to realise this symbolic link, not only would a number of houses have to be demolished but the ancient abbey of the Badia Fiorentina would lose most of its cloisters.[h]

It was unfortunate for the Cerchi and also for the city of Florence that local residents included the Donati, whose family head was the leader of the Black party. He was none other than Corso Donati, who liked to be called *Il Barone* and whose loyalty Pope Boniface VIII had recently taken the trouble to purchase with lucrative political appointments. Corso was one of nature's gangsters who, despite his ancient noble origins, cultivated an aggressively foul-mouthed style of speech and action. He hated Vieri and took a delight in insulting him and mocking his pretensions. He called him the Ass of Porta San Pietro and used to amuse passers-by when he walked out of his house in the morning by demanding, 'Has the Ass brayed yet?' It seems that, at this level of informed debate, he was always able to get the better of Vieri who Dino says was good looking but not very bright. Corso's antics were apparently so successful that itinerant street jesters began to take up the theme of Vieri the donkey. He had managed to turn Vieri into a running gag. That must have hurt more than any amount of disagreement about the legitimacy of papal claims in Tuscany.

The chronicler Villani has a story that, as tension rose in the city, the Pope himself invited Vieri to Rome to discuss what measures they could take to reduce the tension. Boniface was no doubt sincere in his desire for peace. Most rulers who wish to gain control of foreign territory are – it makes their job so much easier. Vieri, however, refused to discuss a negotiated peace. He simply stonewalled the Pope saying that he had no idea what he was talking about since he, Vieri, had no quarrel with anyone. Villani rates him as a wise man in most respects but on this occasion has to admit that he was foolish. Vieri had plainly heard one donkey joke too many.

On 1 May 1300 – just three weeks after Ciacco makes his prediction of it – the first blood was spilt. Traditionally on that day there was a dance in the Piazza Santa Trinità. A group of aristocratic young Black party members, including one of Corso's nephews and some boys from the Spini family (the Pope's favourite bankers), enjoyed a good dinner together before going on to

---

h   Records of the outcome of the planning application are lost but we do know that the Cerchi road was constructed at some time because it exists to this day as the Via dei Cimatori (Cloth Shearers' Street). The only bit that failed to get through the system was the final section which would have linked them to the palace of the podestà, the part that was intended to go through the cloisters of the Badia monastery. That was never going to happen.

the party. At the end of the meal the young blades all vowed to take action to sort out the upstart Cerchi once and for all. Dino Compagni (who is telling us this story) remarks that the Devil chooses to act through youth because they are easier to deceive. When the Black revellers arrived at the dance they found the young Cerchi and their team already in place. There was some name-calling, some pushing, swords were drawn and in the fracas somebody sliced off the nose of Ricoverino Cerchi. The Donati followers retreated to the nearby Spini palace but as news of the incident spread through the city, whatever partisanship had remained latent up until then was brought into the open. Suddenly Florence was in the grip of a full-blown feud.

Dante must have observed all this while still shaken by his vision of Beatrice. He could scarcely have missed any of it since his house was close to both the Cerchi and Donati palaces.[i] Inside his mind he was at the greatest turning point in his life – the moment that the entire *Comedy* commemorates. He certainly

---

i We know from several sources the district of Florence in which Dante lived but there is scant evidence that it was on the site of the house on the Via Santa Margherita, which is today called 'la Casa di Dante'.

already had doubts about the wisdom of a political career. In his imagination he may even have been beginning to play with the fictional elements that would go to make up the *Comedy*. To the outside world, however, he was still a rising politician, probably with great things ahead of him. He was even a successful businessman: records show that at this time he and his brother were borrowing large amounts of money to finance property deals.

His public career had its own momentum. His articulate speeches and good judgement in the councils had been noted and seven days after the incident of Ricoverino's nose we find the records showing that he was sent on a diplomatic mission to the nearby town of San Gimignano to try to persuade the citizens to sign up to the Florentine way of looking at things. The document refers to him as 'that noble man' and he must have been deemed a successful diplomat because in June he was elected to serve on the six-man Council of Priors. This was the ultimate authority among the merchant popolo class. Since the Ordinances of Justice had radically reduced the power of the nobility it was effectively the governing body of Florence.[j] Priors were elected from the council for a three-month term only. Dante, therefore, had until August to use his diplomatic skill and intelligence to save Florence from yet more violence and chaos.

j The priors together with the standard bearer and one other officer were collectively also known as the signoria, after which the Piazza della Signoria, site of the demolished Uberti houses, is named.

14

THE FIGHT FOR PEACE

he *Comedy* can, at first sight, seem to have an episodic structure which borders on the chaotic. The reader is presented with a rapidly changing series of encounters with the souls of the dead, each one unique, startling and different from its predecessor. Episode follows episode and character follows character. The experience is rather like a good party where one is hurried on from one fascinating guest to another or perhaps like a walk down the main street of a city where you are on speaking terms with a high proportion of the inhabitants.

It is all very intriguing but, rather like life itself, it gives little impression that any of it is obeying some pattern or guiding principle. But Dante was, by temperament as well as by the age he lived in, committed to the view that the world is subject to a fundamental order. As we have seen, he read numerical significance into every incident of his experience and he believed that the twin principles of mystical religion and rational philosophy provided an overall explanation for the entire universe. Unsurprisingly, therefore, the world of the *Comedy* which he created is, on analysis, almost overburdened with order. Taken overall the three parts show patterns of character, time, place and events that reflect Dante's understanding of the universal pattern of Creation. In the same way the apparent jumble of assorted sinners that we meet in Hell turn out to be organised according to a medieval moral schema.

What makes the *Comedy* work for the reader (or, rather for the listener, as the first airing of the work was almost certainly a series of readings) is the tension between that well-defined order imposed by Dante the theorist and the ambiguity and uncertainty of the realistic dramatic encounters written by Dante the novelist. Without the theory the story would be rambling and pointless; without the story the theory would be just another late medieval treatise. There is no point in having structure in a work if your audience does not notice it and, although some of it will be evident to a reader as they accompany the travellers on their journey, it falls to Virgil to explain the general principles on which Hell is organised. When they are a little further down the pit Dante manufactures a break in the narrative for him to do so. The pair are waiting on the edge of a precipice from which they are about to descend into the circle of the violent. This is bounded by a river of boiling blood. They cannot descend straight away because they need to take time to accustom themselves to the awful stench that rises up from it.

Virgil fills in the time by giving a breakdown of the broad types of sin and the infernal locations for which their practitioners are destined. Sin, according to Dante's analysis, is what occurs when human beings deviate from the will of the all-loving Creator. The different types of sin are categorised according to the reason for that deviation. We have already seen that those who were prey to lust or gluttony find themselves in the upper reaches of Hell, where they suffer light punishments (it is all relative). This is because they have only committed sins of weakness: they deviated from the plan of universal rightness because they gave in to temptation instantaneously and possibly even with simultaneous feelings of guilt. Anyone who has ever tried to lose weight by eating less will understand this situation, although it is worth noting that it is the sin of material greed that is condemned. There is no suggestion in Dante that either being overweight or eating unsuitable foods are in themselves sinful.

Next down from the gluttons we find souls who were guilty of weaknesses related to material wealth: misers who gave in to the temptation to hang on to their wealth and gloat, and their opposites, the spendthrifts who ruined the lives of their families and themselves by profligate spending. These two are opposite polarities of the same weakness (which Virgil calls 'mental blindness') so we find both of them in the same circle, rolling heavy boulders round but each travelling in opposite directions. As they go they bang into each other and shout. Their degradation and the undistinguished life they led on earth has made them unrecognisable but Virgil does confirm Dante's suspicion that the many tonsured heads he can see (he is looking down from above) belong to anonymous popes and cardinals 'in whom greed is most likely to prevail'.

Last in the category of the sins of weakness we find those who had given way to anger. We hardly need to be told the bad consequences of this sin and it does seem reasonable that this should be the furthest down and therefore the most serious lapse of control. For example, it might be appropriate to put in this circle the unnamed member of the Black party who, after a good dinner and fired up with partisan self-righteousness, sliced off the nose of poor Ricoverino Cerchi on the eve of St John's day. That is one possibility but, although Virgil's analysis helps us through the story, it is not without ambiguities. We might, for instance, equally well argue that our young hothead deserves to be in the circle of the violent which is to be found a further two levels down.

We have made the assumption that Ricoverino's assailant acted while his rational mind was clouded by anger. From the description of the event this does seem credible. We can imagine that he was, in a way, himself a victim of the web of pride, greed and envy spun by the major figures of the two parties. His sin was merely to have been too weak to resist the frenzy of anger which such situations engender. He was only a pawn in their game.

There is, however, another possibility. Suppose that the mutilation of Ricoverino's nose was premeditated; that the assailant had planned the assault over a period of weeks; that on the evening in question he had even put young Ricoverino off his guard by feigning friendship. Most people would agree that this would make it a worse sin and legal systems tend to recognise such a distinction in their classification of crimes. To stretch the hypothetical a little further, if the incident had happened in the United States and had Ricoverino died of his wounds then this distinction would be precisely the difference between a charge of first or second degree murder. This distinction is also the major division of sins in Dante's Hell. The lower regions and the even more dire punishments that go with them are reserved for those whose actions were made consciously by a misdirected rational mind – the sins of malice.

As the travellers leave the circles of the sins of weakness they pass by the souls of the angry. Virgil chivvies Dante once again. He tells him to hurry up because the stars that were rising when they set out are sinking now. This helpfully tells the audience that the time is past midnight on Good Friday, but the question on all readers' minds is how does he know. Virgil is well below ground and we know that spirits like him have no direct knowledge of the world above. Does he have some sort of accurate internal clock and telling Dante about the stars is just a way to be picturesque? Dante likes to give technical explanations but he never gives one for this. In terms of the mechanics of the story it remains a mystery but its effect is to keep the travellers in touch with the great clock of the universe against which the entire *Comedy* is played out.

The souls of the angry are to be found in a bog. Covered in filth, they brawl together, flailing, punching and biting their companions. Dante can also see bubbles rising out of the mire. Virgil explains that these come from the souls of the angry who kept their emotion bottled up in the form of smouldering resentment and 'were sullen in the sweet air'. Like their own feelings they never come to the surface and will remain buried in black ooze for all time.

The bog feeds into the River Styx, the most famous of the rivers in Hell. It runs in a circle around the pit, surrounding the walls of a city like a moat. The city is called Dis and within its walls are the souls of all those whose sins were more serious than moments of weakness. The approach to Dis marks a change of mood in the *Inferno* and the first substantial barrier that the travellers are obliged to overcome. In ancient mythology Dis was the name of the king of the underworld but Dante has turned him into a place name. There is no Christian precedent for the idea of a city within Hell but there is such a thing in the Islamic tradition. It would be mere speculation to suggest that this is an idea that Dante picked up from conversations with Muslim acquaintances. Curiously, however, we can be certain that Islam was on Dante's mind when he wrote about the walls of Dis, because he remarks that beyond them he can make out the forms of mosques glowing red with fire. There is no further reference or explanation for the mosques of Hell which makes their inclusion rather puzzling. It is just possible that they are there by way of an acknowledgement of the Islamic origin of the idea of an infernal city, but if that is the case it is a gesture which is, by modern standards, ill-judged to say the least.

The travellers cross the River Styx in a boat piloted by an irascible boatman called Phlegias, who once again makes it plain that he is not happy about carrying mortal passengers. The boat is approached by one of the swimming souls who asks, 'Who is this here before his time?' The exchange that follows comes as a shock.

> 'I am here but not to stay, who are you, wallowing in filth?'
>
> 'Just a weeping soul.'
>
> 'Well you can carry on weeping ... I know who you are, despite all that muck.'
>
> (*Inferno*, 8:34–9)

Dante is making no pretence of civility. When the soul tries to get into the boat Virgil pushes him back into the water and then turns and embraces Dante, congratulating him extravagantly on his sound judgement of character, 'blessed is she in whose womb you were conceived'.[1] Virgil adds that the man in life was full of arrogance and there are no good memories of him.

Dante carries on the theme and says that he would really like to see this soul being tormented. Virgil remarks that 'such a wish is worthy of fulfilment' and sure enough Dante does indeed see Filippo Argenti, as the attendant demons identify him, being torn to pieces until he gnaws at himself with his own teeth.

It is almost as if the traveller has absorbed some of the pathological anger from the damned spirits around him. We know nothing of the historical Filippo Argenti and we can only guess that some personal score is being settled or some in-joke is being played out. To modern readers this is a repellent episode and it is very sad to see Dante, whom we have begun to respect for his sensitivity, get caught up in this orgy of spite.

Now the travellers must enter the city of Dis, descend to the centre of the earth and observe the worst tortures of Hell on the way. To mark the importance of this transition Dante the writer presents them with a serious obstacle. They finally meet some objectors to Dante's presence who do not back down at a word from Virgil. Hundreds of devils line the parapet above the gates. They speak in an eerie unison as they make it clear that under no circumstances will Dante be allowed to enter: 'He will have to go back by himself if he can. And you who led him through this dark land, you are going to stay right here.'[2]

Dante is understandably terrified and his brief response to Virgil can be paraphrased as 'Don't leave me!' Virgil reassures him, 'Don't worry, nothing can prevent our journey', before leaving him in order to talk to the devils.

We sympathise with Dante's fear as well as his panicky suggestion that they give up now and turn back. But the dramatic problem that the author faces is that we know that this episode will turn out all right in the end. The pair will continue their journey – otherwise there would be no book. It is not a moment of genuine tension. Almost all scripts which involve action face a similar problem at some time. The audience knows that heroes always survive, at least until the final reel (especially if they are played by expensive stars). The solution is to distract the audience with intriguing details and surprising action to keep their mind on the story and off their knowledge of the rules of drama. In the succeeding 100 lines of the *Comedy* we are able to observe an object lesson of how it is done.

Virgil returns from his chat with the demons to the sound of a gate slamming behind him. He assures Dante that this setback is only temporary and that, even as they speak, help is on its way. But the next canto opens with Virgil expressing nervous concern about how long it is taking: 'He stopped speaking like a man listening intently, for his eye could not see through the murky air and fog. "But we must win this fight," he said, "or else ... But help was promised us." How long it takes for someone to arrive!'[3]

Anxiously, Dante asks Virgil if anyone has ever actually done this before; that is, have they ever descended from the outer circles into the depths? Virgil gives a surprising response. In a moment which seems to be pure invention on the part of the author, he replies that yes, he has himself done it before. He briefly tells the story of how once, a long time ago, he was summoned by a witch called Erichtho who required him to descend to 'the lowest place, the darkest and the farthest from Heaven which encircles all'[4] in order to retrieve a soul. Virgil does indeed know the way.

Scholars can find parallels for this surprise episode. Erichtho is mentioned by the Roman poet Lucan (whom Dante met in Limbo). We are told that she had once fetched the shade of a freshly killed soldier back from the underworld so that he could reveal the outcome of the war between Pompey Magnus and Caesar. But Virgil cannot have been the soul-fetcher on that occasion because he wasn't dead yet. Virgil is referring to a separate, previously undocumented adventure of his own. The audience is no doubt intrigued but they are also left with unanswered questions – 'Really? Tell me more. Who was this spirit?' – which threaten to take their minds off the plot. This is never a good thing in a story but Dante has an answer. He provides a diversion. It is so effective that it works both for the audience and the narrator:

> And he said more, but I do not remember, for my eyes were drawn to the high tower's blazing peak where all at once, erect, had risen three demonic Furies stained with blood. They had the limbs and the shape of women; their waists were bound by green hydras. Thin serpents and horned snakes entwined, in place of hair, their savage brows.

> (*Inferno*, 9:34–7)

The snake-covered furies are yet more creatures from classical mythology. Their function is to act as agents of the gods and deliver vengeance to those who have offended them, so they are in the right place. Virgil, of course, knows about them and, while the girls claw at there own breasts in paroxysms of rage, he tells Dante their names. 'That's Megaera on the left. The one wailing on the right is Alecto and Tisiphone is in the middle.'

The furies tell the travellers that they are going to summon up a secret weapon in the shape of the Gorgon Medusa, the famous monster of Greek mythology (also with snakes for hair) who had the ability to turn humans to stone. Presumably this power does not extend to insubstantial spirits so it is only Dante who is in danger, but if he catches a glimpse of the Medusa it is the end of the story. Virgil acts quickly. He tells Dante to turn around and cover his eyes and, just for safety, he covers them with his own hands as well.

They remain huddled together, cringing in expectation of the onslaught of the Medusa. Then, out of nowhere, there comes the sound of a howling wind, 'like a mighty storm, made violent by waves of heat, that strikes the forest and with unchecked force, shatters the branches, hurls them away, and, magnificent in its roiling cloud of dust, drives on, putting beast and shepherd to flight'. Virgil sees him first. He takes his hand away from Dante's eyes and tells him to look into the distance where the mist over the bog is thickest.

A tall figure is emerging, walking on the water. He approaches along a straight path. The condemned souls in the water scatter before him like frogs in a pond that have been startled by a snake. His gaze remains unflinchingly on the portal of the infernal city but intermittently he brushes his hand in front of his face in a fastidious gesture, fanning away the foetid air. He goes straight up to the gates and, without a word, touches them with a wand whereupon they open spontaneously. He directs some scathing remarks at the dumbstruck demons on the walls to the effect that he cannot understand why they bother with resistance when they know it is pointless. He turns, ignoring the travellers, and goes back across the lake – mean, moody, magnificent.

Dante is sure that he has seen an angel but regrets that he doesn't even know his name. Dante the writer (who has a complex relationship with proper names) has discovered something that would later be used to great effect by the makers of the Lone Ranger, as well as the great film director Sergio Leone. In the right circumstances, the dramatic impact of a character can be enhanced if they have no name. Before the angel appears, Dante takes one line to tell his audience to pay attention to the poetic meaning of the episode. But he must have known that was something for the pub afterwards. As soon as the 'Angel with No Name' makes his appearance we are not thinking about theology, nor are we concerned by the inherent lack of tension in the narrative. Our eyes are glued to the screen. Dante the writer has taken an unpromising moment of non-tension and thrown intriguing anecdotes, monsters from Greek mythology and a cinematic angel at it so that it has turned into a memorable scene.

When, in June 1300, in the first few weeks of Dante's priorate, Cardinal Matteo d'Acquasparta arrived at the gates of Florence they were not bolted against him. In fact, he was welcomed fulsomely by those from both ends of the political spectrum, some of them doubtless through teeth more gritted than others. Whether, in his own heart, he thought of himself as a visiting angel who would overcome intransigence and aggression by dint of magical power is not known. He might possibly have had some such idea of his role because he was a papal legate, a representative of the Pope, sent from Rome on a mission to restore peace in the city.

Acquasparta was about 60 years old. He had been, in his time, the head of the Franciscan Order of Friars Minor. He was also a philosopher, capable of profound theological and spiritual thought as well as decisive action; he had written about eternity and the nature of time. In other circumstances he would probably have got on well with Dante. There is unfortunately no record of their meeting but they must have spoken because Dante, as a prior, was at the time a member of Florence's eight-man[a] governing body, the signoria, with which Acquasparta had come to negotiate. Dante is unlikely to have hit it off at a political level with the cardinal who was self-evidently the creature of Pope Boniface. Acquasparta had been the papal adviser during the fight with the Colonna and his elevation to the position of legate, the first rank of the Pope's representatives, was a reward for his support. As an agent of the Pope he was predisposed to support the Black party, but the chronicler Villani does insist that at the beginning all sides were trying for a peaceful settlement and that the White-dominated signoria did its best to help him in his work.

The cardinal investigated the situation and came up with a proposal which must have seemed logical at the time. It is always easier to be logical when you are outside a dispute. He proposed altering the voting system in such a way that it would automatically institute power-sharing into the city's governance. He had grasped that, in a wholly polarised electorate such as the one Florence had become, voting is based on party loyalties rather than the worth of the candidates. This is how the Whites perpetuated their dominance of the signoria and in these circumstances the effect of any election would only be to exacerbate the problem of sectarianism. The chronicler Villani confirms that tension was coming to a point where any election caused a riot. The cardinal therefore proposed that each side should draw up a list of its supporters who were deemed worthy of becoming priors. The names on the list from each party should all be put in a bag from which the names of those who were to become priors should be drawn at random.

The scheme would indeed have produced a balance between the White and Black factions and an end to the flash-point elections every three months. It

---

a   The signoria comprised six priors, the standard bearer and one other officer.

also meant, however, that the Whites would have to relinquish power. Very few groups in history have ever done that voluntarily and the Whites were not to be one of them. They ceased to co-operate with the cardinal and the peace process stalled.

Matteo d'Acquasparta had no further moves to make. He became very unpopular. The Whites didn't like him for the obvious reason that everything about him marked him out as a Black partisan. The Blacks were becoming hostile also because many of them thought that by tinkering with procedural reforms he was failing in his mission of consigning the White government to the pages of history. His unpopularity was brought home to him in a way more deadly than any opinion poll when, one evening, somebody with a crossbow took a shot at him in the bishop's palace, where he was staying. The bolt thudded harmlessly into the window shutter but it is not hard to imagine the effect the incident had on the legate and his retinue. They moved out the next day to a house on the other side of the Arno which was not surrounded by towers.

The White government was not slow to realise the potentially bad political fall-out of this event. They decided to try to make amends by paying Cardinal d'Acquasparta compensation. It was the chronicler Dino Compagni himself who was delegated to deliver the money. He tells us that he arrived, as instructed, bearing the sum of 2,000 florins in a silver cup. He apologised to the legate and explained that this amount was the maximum that legally could be voted by the priors without the ratification of the full Council of One Hundred. The legate gazed at the money for a long time but in the end did not take it.

On 23 June 1300, the eve of the feast of St John, the patron saint of Florence, the guilds traditionally held a procession. This was a worthy civic event but in the strained circumstances of the Black/White dispute it had acquired the highly charged political significance that one might associate with an Ulster Loyalist march. The guilds were the heartland of White party support. Doubtless there was much defiant waving of banners, drumming and chanting. Members of the Black party, aristocrats who had seen their own power and status ebbing away since the institution of the Ordinances of Justice, felt anger and frustration welling up as they watched the guildsmen strutting by. To them they were just grubby little tradesmen who had got above themselves. The Blacks were outraged by the sheer ingratitude of the Whites. Florence would be nothing without the fighting prowess of the nobility. 'We gave you the victory of Campaldino and you repay us by taking away our honour and our jobs' is the slogan that Dino Compagni heard repeated as tension mounted. The age-old conflict between nobility and guilds burst on to the streets once more as the parade degenerated into violence.

Once they are through the gates of Dis the travellers, rather surprisingly, find themselves in a graveyard. Dante tells us that it resembles the Roman graveyard at Arles in the south of France. The area, known as the Alyscamps, exists to this day. It is a pleasant spot where Roman sarcophagi lie sprinkled among the pine trees and it remains a tourist attraction and a picnicking spot. Dante is here demonstrating a personality trait that is of great use to historians and biographers. He is very fond of throwing references to places he has visited (especially outside Italy) into the *Comedy*. This is of great use when trying to piece together an account of his movements during the ill-documented period after his departure from Florence. Thanks to this passage we can, therefore, be confident that Dante had at least once visited Arles.

The graves which the travellers see are, unlike the pleasant ones in Arles, glowing with heat. They contain the souls of heretics. Virgil is careful to explain that each grave is occupied by many souls. In fact, all those who hold (or rather held, since some of them will have revised their opinions since arriving in Hell) to the same heresy are stuffed into the same grave. Virgil's explanation is rudely interrupted when a soul rises out of a nearby tomb: 'A living Tuscan passing alive through the city of fire and with such courtesy of speech! Stay here for a while, if you please. Your way of talking shows you were born in the noble city to which I was perhaps too cruel.'[5]

Dante moves instinctively away but his guide suggests that he ought to speak to Farinata degli Uberti. 'But choose your words carefully,' he warns. Farinata had been the head of the Uberti family in the previous century and had witnessed two cycles of the back-and-forth tide of fortunes between the Guelfs and Ghibellines around the time of Dante's birth. He had presided over a Ghibelline takeover in 1248 only to see it reversed in 1250. Again in 1260 a military victory had allowed the Ghibellines to affect a coup only to find themselves deposed six years later. This latter incident had been characterised by particularly fierce fighting and bitter vengeance and its memory was etched in the minds of every Florentine. It was especially prominent in the minds of the Uberti family themselves because as a result of it their houses had been demolished and left as the open space that is now known as the Piazza della Signoria. The piazza bears this name because of the newly built palace of the signoria (now known as the Palazzo Vecchio) which abuts the square. Its strange non-rectangular shape is the result of it having been scrupulously built not to encroach on Uberti land in order to avoid any later dispute.

Farinata is arrogant and defiant even in his present predicament. He gives every impression of thinking that the whole of Hell is a tiresome inconvenience which would be beneath his dignity to acknowledge. His heretical refusal to follow the orthodox beliefs of ordinary little people also seems to be entirely in character. We do not know very much about the details of his alleged beliefs beyond Dante's claim that he had denied the immortality of the soul. Boccaccio backs Dante up on this point in the *Decameron* and records also show that he was condemned posthumously for heresy along with his wife, and that his children and nephews were 'deprived of their heredity' in 1283, nineteen years after his death.

Farinata begins the conversation with the traditional opening gambit of the aristocracy: he asks Dante 'who his people were'. When he is told, Farinata realises that he is dealing with somebody who is, by descent, a Guelf. Farinata remarks that he had been obliged to throw them, meaning his family or possibly the Guelfs in general, out of Florence not once but twice. Dante is ready with a good answer. They may have been expelled twice, he says, but at least they came back afterwards and 'that is a trick your side never quite got the hang of'.[6]

Farinata acknowledges the truth of the remark and agrees that it causes him greater pain than the grave he is in. He offers a word in his own defence in answer to the many Florentines who still hate him. After the second Ghibelline victory he tells us that such was the ill-feeling among the victorious side that there was a move to raze the whole of Florence to the ground as a warning to other Guelfs. Farinata says that it was he who argued against this move and wants that to be taken into consideration by his critics. He has a point: had Farinata's argument not carried the day and Florence been knocked down, the history of Western culture would have been significantly different. Farinata ends the conversation with his own comeback. Using the power of prediction of the spirits in Hell, he looks into the future a little further than the old hog Ciacco had done. The moon will not be full fifty times he says, before Dante will himself learn just how hard it really is to make a return from exile.

With its formal statements and lightning ripostes, the conversation between Dante and Farinata is a little bit like a televised debate between representatives of the two major parties. It has even had an unscheduled interruption. During the conversation another soul had popped up in the same grave (Virgil has given us the information to deduce from this that he is also an immortality denier). Farinata does his best to ignore the entire incident but Dante recognises instantly that the intruder is Cavalcante dei Cavalcanti, the father of Dante's best friend Guido Cavalcanti. The father is also quick to grasp the situation.

With the logic of a proud father (or perhaps that should be the misguided self-obsession of a heretic) he reasons that they must now be giving tours of Hell to talented young poets. If Dante is there it stands to reason that Guido is likely to be with him. Perhaps this is a different version of the poets' boating trip that Dante had written about to Guido. The father asks the only question that is on his mind: 'Is my son Guido with you?'

We do not have details of the emergency meeting that the priors called within twenty-four hours of the violence at the St John's Eve parade. Dino Compagni, who was there, says that the decision they came to was a joint one. On the other hand, Leonardo Bruni, the sober humanist historian, says that Dante (also at the meeting) was later blamed for it. It is entirely credible that such a decision might have been Dante's idea or that, even if he was not the instigator, he might have argued for it more vigorously than most. He was, we know, a good speaker and in the wake of his successful diplomatic mission to San Gimignano he would have been listened to. The decision does indeed seem to bear the hallmarks of someone who, deep inside, is disillusioned with the political process; someone exasperated with stupid human sheep who wilfully throw themselves into the well of misery.

It probably seemed, to Dante and to the other priors, a decisive move which in extreme circumstances might just bring peace to the city. They effectively said 'a plague on both your houses' and summarily arrested all those whom they considered troublemakers from both sides. Dino Compagni names those who were arrested from the Black party: Sinobaldo Donati, Rosso and Rosselino della Tosa, Giachinotto and Pazzino de' Pazzi, Geri Spini, Porco Manieri and, of course, the ringleader of the Blacks, Corso Donati. They were all required to withdraw from the city and stay in Castello della Pieve, about 100km to the east of Florence. Dino says that the Blacks were ready to stage a coup rather than do this. They had secretly sent to Lucca to ask for military support. When the priors got wind of this they wrote a stiff letter (which Dino says he drafted) to the rulers of Lucca warning them of the consequences of any breach of Florentine territorial integrity. The army from Lucca turned back and Corso and his companions were obliged to go into exile after all.

In order to show their even-handedness, the Whites who were arrested had to be of equal significance to their party. They were: Gentile, Torrigiano and Carbone de' Cerchi, Baschiera della Tosa, Baldinaccio Adinari, Naldo Gherandi and, Dante's best friend and fellow poet, Guido Cavalcanti. It should be no surprise that Guido was on the list. He had had no choice but to be on the front line of this dispute since Corso Donati had tried to kill him while he was in France and he had retaliated by attempting to stab him on his return. The White detainees were sent to the town of Sarzana, about 100km to the north-west.

The short, sharp shock of instant exile proved ineffective. It was not possible to bang the heads of the factions together and make them stop fighting. The White exiles were recalled to Florence ahead of the Blacks. The biographer Bruni says that Dante was again blamed for showing his innate pro-White prejudice by arranging their early return. That may be true, but there is another possible reason: Sarzana was a health hazard. Malaria was endemic and, in the month of June, the risk must have been great. Dante may have argued for the recall of the Whites because he knew his friend Guido had already become gravely ill. As it happens we have a copy of Guido's last poem, written in exile. As Dante once did when writing for Beatrice, he addresses the poem itself (the 'ballata'). He says he realises that the poem must already be able to sense his failing faculties but he needs it to go on one final mission. It must find the lady he loves in the city he will never see again:

> Because I never hope to go again, Ballata,
> into Tuscany
> You must go, soft and gentle,
> Straight to find my lady
> And she will, from her high courtesy,
> Do you great honour.

> For her sweet intellect;
> And out of charmed respect
> You'll always stand with her;
> For, Spirit, you adore her too
> Forever for her excellence

(Cavalcanti, Rime, xxxv)

Guido, in fact, did live to see Tuscany again, but only just. He returned to the city but died of fever a few weeks later, at the end of August 1300, just at the end of Dante's priorate. The chroniclers Villani and Dino Compagni are united in mourning the loss to Florence of such a brilliant young man. History remembers him mostly as Dante's best friend.

When, back in Hell, Guido's father asks Dante where his son is the correct answer is, of course, Florence. The exile of Guido was several months after

April 1300 when the conversation is taking place. But Dante the author has already shown by including Guido's father at all that the incident is on his mind. Dante the character reflects the author's concern by making a slip of the tongue: 'I am not on my own: he who stands there waiting leads me, perhaps to one your Guido held in scorn.'[7]

Guido's father shows no interest in whom his son did or did not hold in scorn. He focuses on one word that Dante has uttered: 'held'. Past tense. Is Guido dead? 'What? Did you say "he held"? Is he not living? Do his eyes no longer see the sweet light?'[8]

The thing that often confirms the truth of an unpleasant fact spoken aloud is the pause that precedes any attempt at denial. Dante tells us that he paused and, before he could come up with an answer, Guido's father had slipped back into his eternal grave. Farinata, whose speech has been interrupted, just carries on talking. At the end of the conversation, however, Dante does try to get him to explain, the next time he sees him, that his son is still living and that Dante's hesitation was due to the fact that he had not quite yet grasped the logic of the souls' ability to see the future.

It is a lame excuse which brings to a close a confused but intriguing episode. Dante the writer did not have to include any of this. The fact that he did so perhaps is a sign of his distress at having indirectly caused the death of his best friend when all he wanted was to bring peace to his city.

After the exile the Blacks became increasingly concerned that they not only might not prevail, but were in danger of suffering the same obliteration as Farinata degli Uberti and his family. They called an emergency meeting in the church of Santa Trinità, in the square where the incident of Ricoverino's nose had occurred. There was open talk, for the first time, of the Blacks asking for outside help in the form of a military 'peacekeeping' intervention. There was only one candidate who could broker such a move and that was Pope Boniface. Even to plan the act of inviting foreign soldiers into Florence was plainly treason, but the discussion was kept at a hypothetical level and no arrests were made. Dino Compagni, who seems to have been present as an observer, was horrified by what he had heard. He tells us that before the meeting broke up he felt the need to ask a question: 'My Lords, why do you want to disturb and ruin so good a city? Against whom do you wish to fight – against your brothers? What victory would you have? Nothing but mourning.'[9]

Dino says that they replied with the words that are used by belligerents and pacifists alike, 'We only want peace'.

After the meeting a rumour spread that there was a baker in town who had already started increasing production in order to provide provisions for an army of occupation (Florentines have never been slow to spot a business opportunity). The effect of this rumour, true or not, was to induce the rank and file of the White party to arm themselves in the interests of peace. When the Blacks saw this they rushed to the priors complaining of White aggression. Then they armed themselves in order to preserve the peace. The peace of Florence was now guaranteed by not one but two armed groups roaming the city.

Outside Florence things were also happening. Corso Donati had broken the terms of the exile and gone to Rome to talk to Boniface. The Pope had then scheduled a meeting with the king of France's brother, Charles de Valois. Charles was already on a military expedition in Italy. He and his army were occupying the town of Parma. Everyone in Italy was aware of his presence and he had already received delegations from both the White and the Black parties of Florence. The Blacks had even been generous enough to make a donation of 70,000 florins to 'help with the campaign'. Charles also has a meeting with Corso Donati in Siena. When he later met Pope Boniface in his home town of Anagni in September 1301 the campaign fund was topped up with a further 200,000 florins. At the meeting the Pope conferred two new honours on Charles. First he made him the Count of Romagna and then, in the name of the imperial throne (which was vacant at the time), he gave him the title of *Paciaro*, 'Peacemaker'.

15

NATURAL JUSTICE

'Like a green log on a fire burning at one end only while, at the other, hot sap and air hiss out of it.'[1] Anybody who has ever gazed into a wood fire can bring this picture to mind. Dante has just torn a small branch from a living bush in the seventh circle of Hell. It is the wound left when the branch was ripped that he describes in this way, except that it is not sap but blood that is oozing, while at the same time the bush is crying out in pain. This incident takes place in the circle which is reserved for souls whose sin was violence.

The soul of Piero della Vigna has been transformed into a bush because he committed suicide. In life he was a philosopher, a wise man attached to the court of the Holy Roman Emperor Frederick II. He fell out of favour and Frederick had him blinded and imprisoned. In despair, Piero killed himself by smashing his own head against the stone walls of his cell. All suicides are to be found here, all changed into trees. They destroyed their own bodies in life, now in Hell they are without even their shadowy forms. They form a wood, encircling this level of the pit, which is inhabited by harpies: more creatures from Greek mythology with human faces, wings and taloned feet. To increase the torment of the souls the harpies eat the leaves of the trees. On the day of judgement, when tradition says that the souls of those who are not damned will regain their bodies, the suicides of the seventh circle will also collect their bodies, except that they will never wear them; instead they will hang them like discarded clothes on the branches of the trees. The souls will then return to their trees to continue to serve their time in vegetal eternity.

In the circle of the violent the travellers also meet assorted murderers, tyrannical rulers who have oppressed their people and profligates who (as opposed to the spendthrifts whom they met in the upper circles) are there because their wild spending amounted to violence. With this last group Dante is singling out the uncaring super-rich who seem to be an inevitable by-product of wealthy nations. One of their number, Giacomo da San Andrea, cared so little for his possessions that he set his own houses on fire for a laugh. When he was restless, he had himself lulled to sleep by the sound of his servants ripping the finest silk fabric. To Florentines, whose wealth was based on the textile industry, that must have been particularly distressing. Another, a Sienese called Lano, reputedly died in a moment worthy of *Absolutely Fabulous*, when he refused to run away from the danger of an advancing army on the grounds that people like him did not travel on foot.

Emerging from the wood, the travellers find themselves on the edge of an area of red hot sand on to which fiery rain is falling like snow. Dante cannot walk on the sand but fortunately they are able to cross it by way of a raised pathway.

They see a group of souls approaching on the sand. As the oncoming spirits look them over with interest, one of them recognises Dante and cries out, *Qual maraviglia!* 'How marvellous!' This is the only soul in the whole of Hell who expresses any pleasure at seeing Dante. It is Brunetto Latini, a scholar and writer from Florence who was born in 1220, so was forty-five years older than Dante. It is obvious from his greeting that Dante knew Brunetto and that, despite their age difference, they had many ideas in common. Like Dante, Brunetto was concerned about the just governance of Italian city states. He believed, also like Dante, that a just, independent republic was possible if citizens were properly educated. Brunetto was also a writer. He had written, among other things, a book called the *Tesoretto* which, like the *Comedy*, recounts an allegorical journey of discovery and begins with its protagonist lost in a wood of error. The *Tesoretto* pre-dates the *Comedy* by about fifty years and, although it lacks the dramatic richness of Dante's first-person narrative, it would be a brave historian who denied that it was a prototype. Dante seems to be acknowledging this as he tells Brunetto how much he misses his fatherly presence on earth and remembers how it was he who taught him 'how a man makes himself eternal'[2] – by which he presumably means achieving immortality as a writer – and finally 'how much gratitude I owe'.

Brunetto wants to talk to Dante but he explains that he has to keep walking because if he were to stop he would be obliged as punishment to lie motionless on the sand for a hundred years, unable to fend off the constant fiery rain.

Dante tells us that, although he did not dare get down on the sand beside him, he walked along bowing his head, both in order to hear what was being said and as a mark of respect.

Although he is in the circle of the violent, the sin for which Brunetto is there is more of a theoretical kind of violence. It is sodomy, categorised as the violent distortion of the natural order of things. In late medieval Italy sodomy seems to have meant homosexuality in general. Sexual acts between men were a crime for which prosecutions are recorded, although they tended to concentrate on cases where the activity could be construed (rightly or wrongly) as the rape of young boys. The death penalty could even be imposed, but although we know that it was carried out in some instances, it seems also to have gone hand in hand with tolerance of the 'don't ask don't tell' variety.

Brunetto begins with encouragement for Dante: 'If you follow your star you cannot fail to reach a glorious gateway, if I observed correctly when in sweet life.'[3] He continues with a warning about the fate of Florence, rather as Ciacco did, but this time it concerns Dante directly. He warns that as the 'malignant thankless rabble' of the Blacks pollute Florence, it is not fitting that 'a sweet fig' like him should grow among such bitter berries. Brunetto warns that eventually not just the Blacks but both parties will wish to devour him. But fortunately by then, as he puts it, 'the grass will be far from the goat'.

Brunetto lists some of his fellow sinners in this area. All of them in his particular sub-section, he explains, were clerics or scholars. Among them are mentioned Priscian, a celebrated Roman grammarian, Francesco d'Accorso, a noted thirteenth-century jurist who taught at Bologna and later moved to Oxford, and Andrea dei Mozzi, who was bishop of Florence from 1287 to 1295. The bishop was relieved of his post at short notice by Boniface VIII and moved to Vicenza where he died, or, in Brunetto's phrase, where he 'left his sin-stiffened sinews'.

Neither Dante the writer nor Dante the traveller displays any shock or disgust at the sexual choices of Brunetto and his companions. Not only is Brunetto greeted with affection by Dante but Virgil does not, on this occasion, show any disapproval of his evident sympathy for the sinner.

In recent years several writers[4] have pointed out that Dante's treatment of homosexuals in the *Comedy* is invariably sympathetic. The traveller always treats them with courtesy, whereas gluttons and flatterers are frequently the objects of contempt. In the next canto, for example, Dante meets three more gay men. This time they are soldiers whose naked souls circle around Dante eager for news of Florence. Virgil actually advises him that they 'deserve courtesy' and when he hears who they are Dante is so impressed that he tells us that he wished he had been able to climb down on to the sand to be with them. Later, in Purgatory, Dante will meet the souls of those who, although guilty of sexual peccadilloes, have been forgiven and are undergoing cleansing before admission to Heaven. They are divided into two groups: straight and gay. It is obvious from the passage that each group is about equal in number. The groups walk in opposite directions and as they meet each other they exchange extravagant showbiz kisses (*Qual maraviglia!*, Darling, how marvellous!). Dante says that they resemble columns of ants on meeting who rub their antennae together in greeting.

In the light of this one might be tempted to wonder whether Dante himself might have been gay. It should be noted immediately that there is a formal sense in which such a question is quite meaningless: firstly, the truth about the physical sexual behaviour of Dante Alighieri is something which has long ago slipped below the horizon of history and, secondly, it is difficult to designate as gay somebody who lived in a culture which did not itself recognise the idea. That having been said, what remains of the issue can best be summarised hypothetically: if someone were to write a fictionalised account of Dante's life and were the author to make the central character gay, then there is very little in the way of evidence which would make that view untenable (that probably includes Beatrice) and there are even some scraps of evidence that might support it.

Brunetto has to go. He can see another group of souls gaining on him in the distance and he has to move off. Dante watches him depart, running to catch up with his group. He says that he looked like a competitor in a race, padding along behind, struggling to keep up with the field, and then he says '*e parve di costoro quelli che vince, non colui che perde*': 'He seemed to me more like a winner than a loser.'[5]

In this one extraordinary and unexpected remark we can see the effect that the writing of fiction has on moral certainty. Dante believes in the whole edifice of the theory of just punishment but if you are crafting a fictional account of taking leave of an old friend it is not credible to do so without some sympathy. It was fiction that made him write the line. If he had ended the story with 'and serve him right' it would have been a bad story: we would have believed a little less in Brunetto, Dante or, for that matter, the entire *Comedy*. For a modern reader there is a feeling that, just for an instant, hundreds of years of prejudice, misunderstanding and hatred have melted away.

The sins which we meet in the seventh circle are grouped under the heading violent but in fact they are a rather mixed bag. They amount to a slightly

ill-assorted run of tragic, poignant and mildly amusing episodes, almost as if they are leftover, hard-to-categorise sins which have ended up squeezed in between the victims of moral weakness outside the walls of Dis and the spitefully fraudulent in the pit below. From now on, however, as the travellers descend, they will meet sinners whose deeds are sorted in ascending order of evil. This sorting is not just a story-telling device, intended to shape the *Inferno* into a slow build-up to a climax. It does that as well, but its origins go back to Aristotle.

The idea of good and evil is woven into the fabric of Dante's universe. Aristotle believed that all matter was composed of a mixture of four elements: earth, water, air and fire. Different substances appear different because of the varying proportions of those basic ingredients. He ranked the elements according to a quality which is normally translated as 'nobility' and added a law of motion: noble things rise, less noble things sink. These simple laws provide a surprisingly good explanation of the world we see around us. Earth, for example, is the least noble element so it sinks towards the centre to form a round muddy ball which is 'the Earth'. Next is water, more noble than earth; it sits on top of the land. Sometimes it rises into the sky but eventually it will obey the fundamental laws and come back down as rain. Nobler still is air which rises and stays there. But fire is the noblest element of them all. It flies upwards through the air where it can be seen as light: the brightness of the sun in daytime, the stars at night.

A bubble rising through a glass of champagne, a flame pointing upwards from a candle, a stone sinking into a pond or a hot-air balloon ascending into the sky are all instances of Aristotle's laws. From his explanation we can understand why the earth is spherical and we also know why people do not fall off it: their bodies are held there by less noble elements within them.[a]

The *Comedy* relies on this picture. As Dante descends to the centre of the earth he experiences increasing evil (lack of nobility) until at the centre he will meet the most evil thing in the universe. When (as he will) he returns to the surface and takes off into space he will ascend through spheres of increasing nobility, characterised by increasingly high-ranking angels and ever holier spirits of the dead, until he arrives at his ultimate destination: the light-filled outer sphere which contains everything, the highest Heaven to which his sighs ascend.

This picture of the universe is, of course, wrong. It turned out to be an untenable model which eventually collapsed under the repeated application of scientific rigour. It was fiction, and like the best fiction it retains the virtue of credibility. I defy anyone to stand on a hill on a starry night, look up at the sky and not understand what it would be like to believe in the earth at the centre of a system of ever-moving, light-filled spheres. The picture, and the feeling that goes with it, can without difficulty be expanded to include the elements, ascending and descending according to their nobility. Beyond it all it is even possible to imagine the great mystical sphere of the Primum Mobile, sweeping round with a constant motion which turns all the other spheres in its wake. It is a story of a balanced universe: a machine in which all things – good, evil, hope and despair – play their part.

The appeal of the imagined world of Dante is that, because it incorporates good and evil, it has a place for humanity. In our own time the Large Hadron Collider may labour and physicists may trace the elegant equations of string theory, but they will never produce a line which has anything to say about damnation or bliss. When it comes to those questions we are now, thanks to modern science, profoundly on our own.

The travellers prepare to leave the circle of the violent and enter the deeper (and therefore more evil) eighth circle, devoted to deceivers and fraudsters. Dramatically this is another significant step and, just as with the entry into Dis

---

a If the reader is wondering why, if all this is correct, earth and water have not sorted themselves out properly so that all the land has sunk leaving the planet earth as one vast ocean, let them be reassured that they are not alone. After he finished the *Comedy* Dante himself devoted a short book to this very question. It was his final work.

and the arrival of the Angel with No Name, the transition is marked with its own spectacular moment.

On the inner edge of the sand they approach a cliff. Dante cannot see the bottom and conversation is almost impossible because of the sound of the waterfall as the infernal River Phlegethon plunges into the abyss. There is apparently no way down but Virgil has a plan. He asks Dante to hand him the cord which is tied round his waist. Virgil dangles it over the edge of the cliff, shaking it, rather as if he were playing with a kitten. What flies up from out of the darkness, however, is not a kitten but Geryon, 'the monster that stinks out the world'.[6]

The name is borrowed from Greek mythology but the monster has been completely refurbished by Dante's imagination. Now equipped with wings, he is designed to be the embodiment of fraud. He has the plausible face of an honest man but as we move further down his body we see that the rest of him starts as a hairy animal with vicious claws and then, as one moves backwards, turns into the poisonous sting of a scorpion.

For a creature that symbolises fraud, though, he does seem to have been very easily fooled when he was attracted by the simple scam of a dangling piece of string. As the monster (who for some reason does exactly what Virgil tells him) crouches on the edge of the precipice, Dante climbs with Virgil on to its back. Virgil sits behind in order to protect Dante from the slashing tail. Dante can see what is coming and gives a good evocation of what it is like to go on a white-knuckle (or as he would have it, a white-nail) ride:

> Like a man in a shivering-fit of malarial fever, so ill his nails have lost all colour
> who shivers all over at the sight of shade, I was stricken at his words ... I tried
> to say – though my voice did not come out as I intended – 'Make sure you hold
> me fast!'
>
> (*Inferno*, 17:85)

For the sake of the passenger, Virgil instructs Geryon not to dive vertically, but to descend in gentle spiralling circles. Dante is then able to look down on to the broad expanse of the eighth circle and the torments below.

The episode of Geryon does more than provide a dramatic moment for another transition in the story. It also solves a problem for Dante the writer. His story requires that the travellers descend from the surface to its centre in two days. Anybody at the time of writing who was educated would know that this was impossible because the distance in question was about 4,000 miles. The Geryon episode at least allows the story to maintain a fig leaf of credibility: we are not told how far down the monster flies so we can imagine that it might have been enough to leave only two days of walking for the travellers.[b]

As Dante spirals down on Geryon's back he eventually relaxes enough to observe the structure of the circle below him. He sees that the eighth circle is a broad one, subdivided into ten concentric ditches to which Dante gives a special name, the *Malebolge*, which means something like 'evil pockets'. Each *bolgia* (the usual shortening) contains a different and (following Aristotle's theory of the universe) successively worse type of fraud.

In the first ditch are seducers, driven on by devils with whips. They are the ones that are so numerous that the devils have to employ the same methods of crowd control that were used at Boniface's Jubilee in Rome. In the crowd Dante recognises one Venedico Caccianemico from Bologna, who pimped for his own sister. He also sees Jason, the ancient Greek hero who captained the *Argonaut* in its quest for the Golden Fleece. Jason finds himself there for talking his way into the affections of a girl called Hypsipyle and then leaving her when she was pregnant.

Next, Dante grabs his readers' attention with a ditch full of excrement. This is the eternal home of flatterers. They sit in a ditch coated with slime, 'disgusting to the eyes as to the nose'. Now, instead of the honeyed, insincere words that brought them to this condition they emit snorts and grunts. Among them he sees a woman, 'foul and dishevelled … scratching herself with her shitty fingernails while standing and squatting'. The description of her is vivid and horrible. In the next lines we discover the nature of her flattery. Her name is Thaïs and she is a fictional character in a play by the Roman writer Terence. In the play, when asked by her lover, 'Have I found favour with you?', she gives the answer, 'Oh most wonderfully'. This hardly counts as one of the great acts of flattery of history and, even for a fictional character, her punishment seems very unfair. One has the feeling that Dante might have included her only for the fascinating horror of her disgusting plight. When we discover that, in fact, in the play the so-called flattering line is actually spoken by a quite different (male) character we might wish that on this occasion Dante had kept his talent to shock to himself.

b   By the time the travellers make their way back up, however, it seems that Dante the writer is confident that the audience is enough on his side for him not to bother. He baldly states that, having escaped from the devil, the pair make their way up, without incident, through a convenient tunnel.

Natural Justice

We are much closer to moral certainty when we come to the ditch which is exclusively reserved for clerics who have sold spiritual benefits for money, the sin of simony. Here Dante sees the hole in the ground which awaits Boniface VIII. He, of course, committed simony when he handed out indulgences in order to obtain support in his war against the Colonna. One day he will end up head down in a furnace while flames lick around his feet, but Dante does not have the satisfaction of seeing him in place because in April 1300 he is not dead yet. The poet has to content himself with praising God for creating such appropriate punishments: 'Oh highest Wisdom, how great is the art you show in Heaven and in the wicked world and what justice you dispense!'[7]

He does take the time to exchange a brief word with the present occupant of the hole, Pope Nicholas III, who mistakes Dante for Boniface, arrived ahead of schedule. Nicholas is not pleased to see him because this means he will be pushed further down by the new soul. The traveller does little to comfort him. Presumably he is too preoccupied with imagining the time when it will be Boniface's little red shoes kicking in the flames.

For most of the time Dante seems to have been able to keep the wild fantasies of degradation and revenge from impinging on his daily life. Part of him remained always the secretive adolescent of the *Vita Nuova*, preoccupied with keeping the workings of his innermost room from the prurient gaze of those around him. This must account for his success as a diplomat. He remained outwardly calm and reassuring, able to broker treaties, and even on one occasion was chosen to be part of a special mission to the court of Boniface himself. There are only two recorded occasions when the rage that flickered so brightly on the screen of his inner cinema broke through and affected the behaviour of the diplomat. Each of these incidents was to cause a disastrous downturn in Dante's fortunes.

The first one happened in June 1301. The sole topic of conversation in Florence at that time must have been the inevitability of the arrival of Boniface's official peacemaker, Charles de Valois, and what effect it would have on the conflict-riven city. By chance, a record survives for that month of Dante's contribution to a debate in the Council of One Hundred. This was the body which had ultimate control over the city's finances on which Dante, as a prior, was obliged to sit. The motion under consideration was whether a small force of 100 soldiers should be sent in support of another one of Boniface VIII's military campaigns. This time he was fighting the Santafiora family, who came from the Sienese Maremma. It was normal for the city to give token support to the papacy, doubtless out of a combination of loyalty, religious deference and enlightened self-interest. At a time when Florentines were expecting any minute to receive a visit from an army under the command of a man who was, in all but name, the Pope's official representative, it would have been insulting and dangerous to say no.

Knowing all this, it must have been obvious that the motion was going to be carried. And indeed it was, by eighty votes in favour and one against. The one was Dante. In the debate he had spoken passionately against giving any support whatsoever to Boniface, ever. Then he voted as a lone voice in a sea of compromise. To place oneself in a minority of one over an issue which is a foregone conclusion is simply to mark oneself out pointlessly and make enemies in a time of crisis. This was the act of a diplomat who has temporarily been taken over by the enraged poet who had been hiding inside him. His one-man protest was a brave, eloquent but totally futile gesture. Sensible politicians do not make futile gestures; poets, on the other hand, have been known to live by them.

Dino Compagni, in his increasingly despairing secret history, takes up the story of the events surrounding the arrival of Charles de Valois. He shares Dante's anger and also his conviction that it is moral failure that led to his city's misfortune: 'Words falsely spoken did more damage to Florence than the points of swords.'

Dino relates the jockeying for position of the Black and the White parties in the run-up to Charles' arrival. Ambassadors from the Black party visited Rome and warned Boniface that, left to their own devices, the Whites would turn Florence into a base for resistance for his old enemies, the Colonna. In case that did not clinch it, 'they reinforced these lies with a great deal of money'. The White ambassadors, to Dino's fury, arrived late because one of their number had insisted on stopping off on the way to argue about his rights to a certain castle. By the time they got to Boniface the arguments of the Blacks had already sunk in, along with the money, with the result that His Holiness was utterly charming to the White ambassadors. He told them not to worry, that he would ensure that Charles acted even-handedly. He then sent two of the ambassadors back to Florence to pass on his message while the others remained with him.

Back in Florence the White party was cautious, unwilling to risk losing the advantage they already had by taking on the Blacks in a fight. The Blacks, on the other hand, were worried that if they were seen to step back from confrontation they would make themselves vulnerable to the kind of retribution which had been a part of Florentine life since the destruction of the Uberti houses in 1266. Charles sent ambassadors to Florence ahead of his arrival. The ruling Whites received them with courtesy. Dino's recollection of Charles' chief emissary was that he was a French knight who was stupid, untrustworthy and spouted irritating platitudes. With hindsight he is bitterly regretful that the Whites followed papal instructions and kept talking 'when we should have been arming ourselves'.

Dino himself made a final attempt at peacemaking by organising a meeting of all interested parties. He begged the assembled Black and White political heavyweights to take the path to peace, 'let everything be set aside and forgiven for love of your city'.[8] In the sacred atmosphere of the ancient Florentine baptistery they all agreed and, at Dino's insistence, made an oath and kissed the Bible. Dino in retrospect feels guilty that by insisting on a solemn oath he had transformed their casual falsehoods into perjury: 'I have shed many tears over this oath, thinking how because of it so many souls were damned for their malice.'[9]

> No barrel with a missing stave gapes open quite as wide as the soul I saw split
> from chin down to the place where we fart. His guts hung down between his
> legs and I could see his innards and that foul sack that turns what we have eaten
> to shit.
>
> (*Inferno*, 28:22)

There is an anatomical accuracy about Dante's description which makes us wonder if he has not finally made use of his experience of the battle of Campaldino. The soul which Dante is looking at is one of the sowers of discord. In life they ripped communities apart with deceitful words; down in Hell it is they who are split apart. In the time it takes them to walk around the circle (we are told that it is now only 22 miles in circumference since they are close to the bottom of the cone) their wounds heal. As they pass the starting point a devil with a sword mutilates them again.

In this ditch Dante sees a selection of people – some with their heads severed, others with open throats or missing jaws – who have been responsible for discord and dispute in cities of Italy, including his own. Less predictably, the Prophet Muhammad is there along with his son-in-law, Ali. It is not surprising that a medieval Christian would put the Prophet in Hell, but we might expect him to be there for heresy or some offence against the Christian world. Dante seems to have picked up on a slightly obscure tradition that Muhammad was in fact a Christian cardinal who went to the bad and formed his own breakaway religion. It would be a little surprising if Dante really had given much credence to such an unlikely story – elsewhere he displays a relatively good understanding of Islam. Even in this episode he shows enough familiarity with the life of the Prophet to know that if he is to give him a companion, Ali, who was among the first to follow him, would be the right choice. One could almost argue that by putting the Prophet here Dante is being sympathetic to Islam. The decision to put him in this circle may be bad for the Prophet but it avoids condemning the religion as a heresy. Where there is schism now, there was once union.

The Prophet speaks to Dante, but he does not talk about his own history or his present plight. Instead he has a message for Dante to pass on to an Italian who is still alive: Fra Dolcino, the leader of a slightly obscure radical sect of Christians who believed in sharing property and, according to their detractors, their women also. Every now and again Christianity throws up a sect which believes in freedom and equality for all. During the thirteenth and fourteenth centuries there were many such groups (the followers of Francis of Assisi are probably the most famous) and the Church took on the task of eliminating or neutralising all of them. Dolcino's 'Apostolic Brothers' managed to hold out against papal forces for over a year. Muhammad's message to Fra Dolcino was that unless he fancied a trip to Hell he had better stock up on food. The message does not seem to have got through: the brothers were starved out and Dolcino and his female accomplice Margaret of Trent were burnt at the stake in 1307. It is not clear whether the Prophet is merely offering friendly advice to Fra Dolcino or whether he does not in some way sympathise with the heretics because of their obstinate opposition to Western values.

The souls of those who have told lies and deceived others have a ditch of their own. When Dante looks into it he sees them trapped in parcels of flame moving along the bottom of the gulley, 'each one wrapped in the fire which burns him'. The one in whom Dante takes the most interest is Ulysses. He was known for his ability to con his enemies with convincing lies. He appears in Homer's *Iliad*, the story of the Trojan War, where it is he who thinks up the idea of using a giant wooden horse to trick the Trojans into letting Greek soldiers into their city. He is also, of course, the principal character of the *Odyssey*, the story of his own epic sea voyage to exotic lands.

As an intrepid traveller through dangerous lands who can weave a convincing tale, we should not be surprised that the author himself has a lot of sympathy for Ulysses. He is a kind of doppelgänger for Dante; the scholar Patrick Boyde memorably calls him 'Dante's evil twin'.

A quirk of fate helps Dante to write a new story for Ulysses. The text of the *Odyssey* was not available to him translated into any language that he spoke. He knew about the story because it is mentioned in some detail in books that he did know. As a consequence he did not realise the importance that Homer's epic places on Ulysses' return to his home in Ithaca and his wife Penelope. Without that knowledge Dante feels bold enough to invent a new end to the voyage.

In Hell, Ulysses explains to Dante that once he had escaped the clutches of the enchantress Circe, where he had been imprisoned for a year, he could not resist the urge to set out on one more voyage. Even his desire to see his wife Penelope again could not overcome his need to see the rest of the world and 'know all man's vices and all human worth'. He is a perfect confirmation of Aristotle's line that all men by nature desire to understand.

The great tourist and his crew set out for the final time, leaving the Mediterranean by way of the Straits of Gibraltar. In classical times these were known as the Pillars of Hercules,[c] set in place to warn mortals never to go beyond that point. They pass them anyway and steer to the left, heading for the southern hemisphere which was believed at the time to be composed entirely of water. The crew is old and exhausted. Ulysses knows that as they leave the known world he will have to encourage them:

> 'O brothers,' I said, 'through a hundred thousand perils you have at last reached the west. During the brief period of wakefulness of our senses that remains to us, do not deny yourselves this chance to know the world where no one lives.'
>
> Remember where you came from. You were not made to live like brutes or beasts. You must follow virtue and knowledge!

> (*Inferno*, 26:112)

The old persuader had not lost his touch. He tells us that when he had finished speaking he could scarcely hold the crew back and, 'setting our stern towards the sunrise, we turned our oars to wings in our mad flight'.

It would be hard not to find this speech a little inspiring. It is indeed intended as a keynote speech for the great travel book of the mind that Dante is writing. Even beyond that, it would function equally well as the inspirational theme for any of the succession of individualistic 'mad flights' that have characterised

---

c The two pillars, together with the slogan in Latin 'No further' (*Ne plus ultra*), became a common motif. When the Spanish started to explore the New World in earnest, 200 years after Dante, they changed the slogan to 'Further' (*Plus ultra*). The stylised picture of the two pillars with a banner bearing the slogan curling between them like a letter S became a part of the Spanish coat of arms. It is thought by many people to be the origin of the S with two vertical lines through it that is the dollar sign.

the development of the modern mind. From the journey of Marco Polo (which was happening in reality as Dante was writing) to the later formation of empires as Europeans went in their shiploads beyond Hercules' forbidden pillars. It could even be applied to the early twentieth-century wanderings of Ulysses' own patient, understanding alter ego through the streets of Dublin. From the time of Dante onwards, 'mad flight' is what Europeans have been all about.

Ulysses and his crew sail south until they see stars that cannot be seen in the northern hemisphere. After a five-month voyage they catch sight of land. Something which, had they listened to the theoreticians, they could have expected. Ulysses does not know it, but he has seen the island mountain of Purgatory. This is where the souls of the dead make their slow climb towards Paradise as they atone for their sins. It is the location for part two of the *Comedy* in which Dante will climb the mountain, meet the soul of Beatrice and finally take off from the summit on his journey to the stars.

But Dante's tale of brave Ulysses ends in disaster before land is reached. A freak wind spins the ship round and it is dragged under. In this version of the story he is never to be reunited with his Penelope. The waters close over him in the last line of the canto:

> We rejoiced, but soon our celebration turned to grief for, from that unknown land, a whirlwind came that struck the ship head-on. It spun her round three times and on the fourth it lifted up her stern. Down went the prow, obedient to Another's will, until the sea closed over us.

> (*Inferno*, 26:136–42)

Determination and intelligence had got Ulysses a long way but without knowledge of the divine grace that Beatrice brings to her chosen traveller, Dante's evil twin can go no further.

16

THE PLACE WHERE FORCES MEET

Arise, wicked citizens full of discord: grab sword and torch with your own hands and spread your wicked deeds. Why delay any longer? Go and reduce to ruins the beauties of your city. Spill the blood of your brothers, strip yourselves of faith and love, deny one and another aid and support.

(Dino Compagni, Chronicle, II)

The words are not one of the outbursts from the *Comedy* but Dino Compagni's impassioned opening of the final book of his Chronicle. The other chronicler of the time, Giovanni Villani, says that a comet appeared in the skies above Florence in 1301 as a portent of the events that would follow the arrival of Charles, Count of Valois. In the *Comedy*, when Dante is ascending the mountain of Purgatory, it is Hugh Capet, the founder of the entire dynasty of French kings ('I was the root of that malignant tree which now overshadows all of Christendom'[1]) who summarises what is to follow: Charles will arrive armed with his own treachery, 'carrying the lance of Judas with which he will burst open the guts of Florence'. But it is the on-the-spot chronicler, Dino Compagni, who is left to give a detailed account of Florence's descent from a prosperous republic to a city run by violence, treachery and corruption.

Charles arrived with very few troops of his own but he was soon backed up by forces from Lucca, Siena, Perugia, San Miniato, Volterra and San Gimignano, all of which had good reason to hate Florence and relish the spectacle of its humiliation. The governing White priors were terrified. They welcomed Charles with full honours and then held an emergency meeting. Dino, who was there, catches the atmosphere: 'the party of unity lost its vigour and malice began to spread'. One of the party advised giving up, taking the city gates off their hinges and inviting the exiled Blacks to return. Then there was a lengthy filibuster from a man called Bandino Falconieri about how safe he felt under the protection of Charles de Valois. Dino complains that he took up half a day of the committee's time, 'and we were in the shortest days of the year'. A move to elect new priors was rejected as illegal under the Ordinances of Justice. The meeting broke up with no decisions made.

Meanwhile, Charles set up his headquarters not in the vicinity of the Dominican church of Santa Maria Novella, as would have been normal, but on the south side of the river in the Oltrarno. It was not lost on anyone that this was strategically a superior plan since it provided a highly defensible fall-back position in the event of a military reversal.

The Blacks, who had the aristocrats on their side and everything to fight for, prepared for battle. They called in supporters from the surrounding countryside while those wealthy members who had palazzi near the river could be seen preparing to defend the Oltrarno stronghold by assembling rock-throwing devices on top of their homes (they must presumably have had these machines ready in their cellars all along). When the White Scali family, whose palazzo was on the north side of the bridge, tried to make the same preparations, their neighbours, the Spini, the Pope's bankers, talked them out of it on the grounds that this would make them traitors to their class.

A new 'coalition signoria' was belatedly appointed, representing both Blacks and Whites. Dino insists that this new cross-party committee did its best to prevent violence. On the advice of a member of the clergy, they staged a religious procession in the hope that it would calm things down. It did not work. As the priors realised that they were indeed on the verge of civil war, they finally called up the rural militia, a part-time force from the surrounding countryside. Few of them turned up and those who did quickly deserted to the Blacks. The priors then passed strict emergency laws forbidding any kind of public mayhem or brawling. To show that they meant business they set up an execution block in the middle of the vacant lot which was already becoming known as the Piazza della Signoria. While the signoria debated further action,

White supporters fortified their homes as best they could. Dino comments that decency is of no avail against great malice.[2]

The city was like a pile of dry straw that needed only a single spark to ignite it. On 1 November Corso Donati, exile, hero of the battle of Campaldino, champion of the Black party, protégé of Pope Boniface VIII, a man described by Dino as 'having his mind always set on evil doing', entered the city of Florence. He had come directly from a meeting with the Pope. He made for a gate in the northern section of the nearly completed walls that was near his own house and he and his men broke it down. His arrival was the signal which released all the pent-up violence stored within the city. There commenced a cycle of vengeance and destruction: the prisons were opened, houses were burned. Dino says that 'the city seemed to belong to Corso' as he not only orchestrated the violence but, at the same time, set up a system for the collection of money by extortion. Even children were robbed. Over the following days Dino also says that rape and 'forced marriage' were commonplace.

The priors appealed to Charles de Valois. 'A noble city is dying under you', they said. Charles replied that he knew nothing about it; he only wanted peace. In a final desperate act the priors attempted to summon a spontaneous meeting of all the people of Florence. They rang the great bell on top of their new palace in the Piazza della Signoria. Nobody came.

In Dante's version of Hell the sin which is worst, and therefore placed lowest, isn't lust or heresy – it is betrayal. The bond of trust between two human beings is lodged in the innermost part of the soul. To break that bond is an offence against the part of the soul that perceives love. The treacherous are lodged in the ninth circle, close to the point of the cone and the centre of the earth. To get there the travellers must cross a final barrier: a cliff which surrounds the central well of Hell. It is ringed with giants, half-forgotten creatures from the dawn of time whose existence is hinted at in both Greek mythology and the Bible. Virgil addresses one of their number. He promises that if he carries them past the final obstacle the mortal who is with him will make him famous in the world above. The ruse works and the pair are carried gently down on to the floor of Hell. To mark the final section of this part Dante introduces a contrast: the lowest circle of the Inferno is freezing cold. They find themselves standing on ice, the frozen water of the river that the travellers have crossed more than once as they descended. Here the atmosphere sickens the soul – the absolute zero of the moral spectrum. Dante feels it: 'I did not die but I was not living either.'[3]

They set out across the ice towards the centre of the earth, the 'central point of the universe where all weights converge'. Dante sees 'a thousand dog-like faces, broken by the cold'. These are the souls of the betrayers – 'better for them if they had lived as sheep or goats' – they are frozen into the lake with their heads or torsos poking up like frogs in a pond. Some have their faces pointed downward but the worst sinners look upwards so that their tears collect around their eyes and freeze into a solid, icy visor: 'here weeping puts an end to weeping'.

In the gloom Dante inadvertently stumbles against one of the heads. The soul objects, 'Why are you kicking me? Have you come to take revenge on me for Montaperti?' The name Montaperti would be known to all Florentines. It was the battle in 1260 where the Guelf republic lost to Ghibelline forces with the result that Florence suffered a short but brutal period of Ghibelline repression. It could be argued that it was this battle that started the oscillating cycle of coup and counter-coup of which the havoc wrought by Corso Donati and the Blacks was only the latest episode.

Intrigued, Dante asks the soul his name but he refuses to tell him. No offer of a mention in Dante's book will persuade this one, 'you don't know what works as flattery in these depths'. Dante flies into a blind rage (the only time in the *Comedy*) and starts tearing the soul's hair out. It will not be moved: 'strip me bald if you like, you'll never know my name'. Dante persists, 'I had already pulled out more than one fistful when he squealed like a dog with eyes shut tight'. One of the neighbouring spirits objects to the noise and calls out, 'What's the matter, Bocca?'

Bocca. That is the other name that all Florentines would know. Florence had been winning the battle of Montaperti until, just at the last minute, one of the Florentine soldiers near the standard bearer rushed forward and cut his hand off at the wrist with his sword. The effect of seeing Florence's standard fall was to spread despair through the army and allowed the enemy to make a final push and win the day. It was a premeditated act of treachery which brought Florence to ruin, and the name of the traitor was Bocca. Dante leaves him.

The travellers continue out on to the frozen lake, Dante catches sight of something unusual: two souls, frozen together in the same hole. They are so close that 'one head used the other for a cap'. To his horror he becomes aware that one of the souls is eating the brain of his companion. Dante promises once again to include the story in the book: 'I'll repay your confidence in the world above, unless my tongue dry up before I die.' This soul has no inhibitions about telling his story. First, though, Dante the writer, in a moment of finely crafted cinema, lets the well-mannered soul prepare to speak by wiping his messy lips in the hair remaining on the chewed-up skull of the other.

His name, he tells the travellers, is Count Ugolino della Gherardesca. He conspired with one Archbishop Ruggieri (with whom he is sharing the ice hole) to gain control of Pisa in the run-up to the battle of Campaldino. When the partnership went wrong, Ugolino and his four children were arrested by Ruggieri and locked up together in a cell. Ugolino recounts how he listened to his children sobbing for food, and then: 'It was at the time they brought our food. Each one of us was full of dreams of dread when from below I heard them driving nails into the door. I stared in silence at my flesh and blood. I did not weep, inside I turned to stone.'[4]

The archbishop had boarded up the cell and left the entire family to starve to death. Dante lets Ugolino supply heart-rending details of their last days. Seeing their father's anguish, the children suggest that he should eat them; that would be preferable to watching his pain. 'The fourth day came, and my child Gaddo fell down before me, crying: "Why don't you help me? Why father?" There he died.' All the children eventually die, leaving the distraught Ugolino alone and helpless: 'By then gone blind, I began to grope over their dead bodies. For two days I called to them although they were dead. Then hunger proved to have more power than grief.'[5]

Dante does not make clear what Ugolino means when he says hunger had more power than grief. He could, of course, simply intend us to understand that starvation killed him, as of course it did, and thus put an end to his grieving. But there was another rumour current at the time. It was one of those tales which was so fascinating in its horror that people eagerly passed it on to each other even though no evidence was ever offered to support it. Ugolino was said to have kept himself alive by eating the corpses of his own children.[a] Dante shamelessly plays on this idea both by making the remark about hunger overcoming grief at the end of the story and, earlier, by having the children actually suggest it to their father.

The scene finishes with Dante the traveller expressing a reaction with which most modern readers would agree: the really innocent victims were Ugolino's children. He curses the city of Pisa for its cruelty. Ugolino meanwhile resumes his attack on the unspeaking archbishop.

---

a To this day the Gherardesca family is trying to clear themselves of the allegation of cannibalism. In 2001 they commissioned a chemical analysis of what are believed to be the bones of Ugolino with the intention of proving that he had never consumed human flesh.

The gruesome story of Ugolino is the climactic encounter of the descent into Hell. Critics have pointed out that his consumption of his children is itself a parody of the central mystery of Christianity. In the ceremony of the Eucharist adherents eat the flesh and drink the blood of Christ. This act is seen by believers as a joyous moment in which they make themselves one with the body of Christ and approach divine bliss. In the depths of Hell, Dante offers his audience an act of cannibalism that was caused by betrayal and contains no element of the divine: a kind of negative inversion of the sacred meal – the opposite of bliss.

The story surely also has a political interpretation: there is probably no better metaphor for the irreconcilable conflict which was tearing Florence apart than two people who hate each other stuck together in a hole for eternity.

After the arrival of Corso Donati, Florence underwent six days of lawless destruction and then a new set of priors was appointed, all staunch Black party men. A new podestà was also sworn in, Cante dei Gabrielli da Gubbio. He had arrived in the city with Charles de Valois. The new rulers made some show of even-handedness by arresting malefactors from both Black and White parties but Dino bitterly reports that the Whites were kept without bedding for long periods, while the Blacks were generally released the same day.

Under the new government extortion became institutionalised. Trumped-up charges and false claims were made against the vulnerable and the newly disempowered. Men were accused, tortured into confessing and then fined. A family called the Bostichi, who quickly rose to prominence, made a point of torturing late payers publicly in the New Market in order to encourage future victims. Charles de Valois himself took part in this. Dino tells the story that when he later asked Pope Boniface for payment to cover his expenses, the Pope said no on the grounds that he had already 'put him at the golden fountain'.

Not surprisingly, under these circumstances it became the norm to lie and cheat one's way out of trouble, 'many fortunes were hidden, many people changed their tune from day to day'. Any action resembling a stand on principle would have resulted in death. Florentine society was in a state of vindictive chaos, 'many who had formerly been unknown became great through wicked deeds … no pity could be found … the greatest man was the one who shouted loudest: "death, death to the traitors!"'[6]

Dante's own house was destroyed and his possessions looted, probably during the six days of licensed mayhem that followed Corso's arrival. We cannot be certain about where he himself was at this time. He certainly doesn't mention having been in Florence to witness the chaos. Boccaccio says that he was on a diplomatic mission to the papal court and Dino lends credence to this idea by confirming that Boniface had sent some of the White ambassadors home whilst retaining others (he doesn't mention Dante in this connection, though). Quite why he might have done this is not clear. Perhaps he had taken a shine to Dante and admired his intellectual powers. Perhaps he feared Dante as a troublemaker and was cunningly keeping him out of the city at a crucial time, although there is very little evidence that at this stage Dante was capable of making trouble for anyone apart from himself. If Dante was indeed detained in Rome and having meetings with the Pope, any account of their conversations would surely be one of the great treasures of fourteenth-century Italian history. Sadly, no such account exists.

The loss of his house, whether he was in the city at the time or not, was an illegal act for which he was entitled to redress. Or rather would have been, had not the new podestà, Cante da Gubbio, effectively legalised the theft retrospectively. Among the many acts of condemnation issued at that time there exists a copy of one issued against four ex-priors: Palmieri degli Altoviti, Lippo Becchi, Orlanduccio Orlandi and Dante Alighieri. The charges were, broadly, that they had used their position to gain money. Remarkably, the new podestà was apparently able to accuse them of 'illicit gain and unjust extortion' and keep a straight face. The charges are listed without detail, sometimes not even bothering to specify who is being accused: 'they or some of them are accused of ...'

The document moves on to specify the punishment – there is not even a cursory mention of a trial. There will be a 5,000-florin fine. In addition they are obliged to repay the money they extorted to anyone who can furnish proof of entitlement. If they fail to pay the fine within three days all their property will be confiscated and destroyed. Even if they do pay the fine within that time they will still be obliged to stay out of Tuscany for two years.

Dante's position in respect of all this was clear. As he was outside Florence the chances are that by the time he saw the charges the three-day period would have been up. But that probably did not matter since his house and possessions had been destroyed anyway. The bottom line was that he was exiled. The condemnation document specified two years of exile if he did pay the fine; if he didn't pay we can assume that it was for an indefinite period.

As Virgil and Dante continue across the frozen lake of Cocytus, Dante the writer has one more new idea about damnation with which to surprise his audience. He meets the soul of a man who is not dead. In exceptional cases, we are told, damnation precedes death. Friar Alberigo had invited his enemies in a family feud to dinner with the expressed aim of fostering a reconciliation. During the fruit course, however, Alberigo gave the order to have them murdered. In response to this act of gross betrayal a devil arrived, took Alberigo's soul and cast it directly down to the lake of ice. Meanwhile, the devil took control of the friar's empty body until the allotted time for its death. Now Alberigo languishes in the depths, a victim of instant damnation, not knowing what is happening to his zombie body.

Then Dante sees the Devil. From a distance he looks like a windmill (the largest machine in existence in Dante's time); closer, he is an even more vast figure, stuck in the ice up to his waist. His bat-like wings beat back and forth, creating the wind that cools the lake of Cocytus to freezing point. He has one head but three faces, parodying the Holy Trinity. In each of the three mouths the soul of a sinner is constantly being chewed. They are all three iconic traitors from history. Two of them, Brutus and Cassius, betrayed the empire when they conspired together to kill Julius Caesar. The third is Judas, who betrayed the Son of God Himself.

The Devil is at the very centre of the earth, which is where he has been since the first minute of Creation. When the universe was made he was Lucifer, God's most beautiful and most favoured angel. But he and a number of other angels became arrogant and thought they were above God's power. They rebelled against Him and the Almighty hurled them out of Heaven. Lucifer, in particular, was thrown straight down towards the earth which he hit with the full force of the divine lob. He plunged into the exact centre of the earth and stuck there, leaving a conical impact crater which is the cone of Hell (quite how the crater was roofed over with the surface of the earth is not explained).

The origins of the rebellion story seem to go back as far as Babylonian myth. There are only the scantest references in the Bible, yet by Dante's time it had built into a fully fledged story by successive additions – one of the greatest examples of team writing in history. Dante does not dwell much on the rebellion. He notes that the Devil, who was once the beautiful Lucifer, is now 'as foul as once he was fair'. He also mentions *en passant* that the rebellion of the angels and their expulsion happened at the very moment of Creation 'in as much time as it takes to count to twenty'. Rather like the formative events, all of which are said to have happened in the first five minutes after the big bang, the angelic rebellion happened fast because it is in the nature of things. The angels can see God's mind; He can see their minds: the whole scene was played out with lightning inevitability.

Dante is awestruck and terrified at the massive figure of the ruler of Hell 'from whom all grief derives' but the Devil takes no notice either of Dante or Virgil. Although he is the figurehead for all evil he is not an active participant in the drama. He does no more than flap his wings and chew. In Dante's version of Hell the Devil does not roam the earth tempting humans to sin because he does not need to. Throughout *Inferno* we have seen that acts of evil are the result of people's own decision to ignore the will of God. To blame their sins on temptation by another agency would be to let them off the hook.

The travellers have reached the end of the infernal leg of their journey. Virgil announces, 'Now it is time to leave; we have seen it all'.[7] Fortunately he has a plan. He tells Dante to hang on to him as, waiting for the right moment in the cycle of Satan's wing strokes, he slips down between the ice and the Devil's thigh, clambering down the coarse hair with Dante on his back. He is alarmed when, halfway down, Virgil apparently turns round and climbs back up again. When they emerge out of the confined space on to a flat surface Dante thinks he is back where they started. But when he looks at the Devil he sees not his head but his legs with their cloven hoofs pointing upwards. The travellers have passed the centre point of the earth,[b] where all forces meet. Now they are no longer descending: down is now the direction from which they came. From now on it is up all the way.

It is the end of the *Inferno*, neither author nor audience is in the mood for too much fuss about the 4,000-mile journey back to the surface. We are told there was a hidden passage leading upwards and that the pair climbed it without talking. They emerge into the light of the early morning of Sunday 10 April 1300. They left Hell on Saturday night and Dante is fully aware of the time difference between Mediterranean time and Purgatory time which they are now using. The relief is palpable in the last line of the *Inferno*: 'We climbed up with him in front and I behind, far enough to see through a round opening some of those beautiful things that are in the sky. Then we emerged, once more to see the stars.'[8]

---

b From Dante's description it seems that the centre point of the earth is situated precisely between the Devil's thighs. It is a slight source of irritation to the more studious amongst us that Dante did not take his phenomenal powers of visualisation one step further and realise that, at the centre of the earth, the forces that meet are coming from all directions and would therefore cancel out, leaving him and Virgil apparently weightless. That would have been a brilliant and prescient piece of reasoning from which the poet was only one step away.

***

Unable to return to Florence, Dante went to join his fellow White exiles. Less than a month after his condemnation, the White leaders assembled in the small, isolated hilltop town of Gargonza, perched in rugged wooded hills about 70km to the south of Florence. The purpose of the meeting was to plan a daring military exploit that would restore White rule and justice to their city.

The plan was to capture the small town of Puliciano and thereby establish a bridgehead in the area known as Mugello to the north-east of Florence for a surge into the city. Dante's signature appears on an agreement that the Whites will compensate for any damage their campaign might do to the property of the local castle-owners, a family called the Ubaldini. This sort of agreement was not uncommon in conflicts at the time, but nevertheless it does seem to be an action more typical of the merchant class than the hard-nosed warlike aristocrats. The Whites were actually supported by at least one group of aristocrats: the Uberti, whose houses had been destroyed to make room for the Piazza della Signoria and whose arrogant ancestor Farinata had discussed Dante's future in Hell. In Florentine style they were presumably just happy to side with anyone, even people who might be considered their natural enemies, who was going to make trouble for the Pope-supporting Guelfs.

With exile comes a desperate kind of comradeship and a fervent faith which can too easily generate wild fantasies of victory. It creates an atmosphere where even to make a realistic assessment of the situation invites an accusation of treachery. The White escapade was hasty and ill thought-out. Security was leaky and the Black government in Florence had been aware of the plan from the start. Barely had the Whites reached Puliciano than the Blacks turned up in overwhelming strength. Promised support from Pisa did not materialise and the Uberti preferred not to fight.

The Whites were routed easily. The Blacks made a point of ravaging the property of the Ubaldini (it is not recorded whether the defeated Whites were able to make good their promise of compensation). They also tortured and executed those Whites whom they captured. Exiled Whites now counted automatically as enemies of Florence. Even while the attack was being planned Black attitudes were hardening: it was during the preparations that Dante received the news that the podestà had issued a further condemnation against him and thirteen others for non-appearance at their 'trial'. His sentence had been increased. From now on if he, or any of them, should come within the limits of the commune of Florence they were to be burned to death.

17

I AM BEATRICE

A lady appeared to me with a white veil and a green mantle, dressed in the colour of living flame …

For a long time the inside spirit had not been overcome with the awe that used to make me tremble in her presence … now, through the hidden force that came from her, I felt again the power of that ancient love.

(*Purgatorio*, 30:28)

Dante hears, '*Guardaci ben! Ben son, ben son Beatrice!*' – 'Yes, look at me! I really am Beatrice!' This is the first line of dialogue we have ever heard Beatrice speak, unless you count the 'hello' that prompted the vision of the Lord of Love in the *Vita Nuova*.

This reunion happens at the top of Purgatory, the world's highest mountain on the other side of the world and the island which was the last thing Ulysses saw before his ship was dragged beneath the waves. The summit, which is the part of the earth closest to Heaven, is also the Garden of Eden, where man and woman were first created. Adam and Eve lived there in bliss until they, like their descendants after them, misused the gift of free will and went against the divine will. As punishment, they were exiled from the perfection of the garden and obliged to populate the imperfect rest of the world.

Dante's first glimpse of the soul of Beatrice was through a swirling storm of white petals – he says that she looked like the sun as it appears through

mist. The petals, which provide an image worthy of Busby Berkeley, have
been thrown into the air as part of a mystical pageant. The show, which has
been put on for Dante's benefit, has an impressive cast: the twenty-four elders
of the Church, the four beasts of the apocalypse, various maidens and three
girls dressed in green, white and red representing the theological virtues
of faith, hope and love respectively. The colours of the latter trio (it is probably
not a coincidence that they are also the colours of the Italian flag) are, of
course, echoed in Beatrice's outfit. She rides in a chariot drawn by a gryphon,
a mythological beast with four legs, a beak and wings so tall they reach out
of sight.

The *Comedy* is officially divided into the three parts of *Inferno*, *Purgatorio*
and *Paradiso*, but it could also be split into pre-Beatrice and post-Beatrice parts.
This scene marks the transition into part two. The pre-Beatrice section is the
story of Dante's struggle which leads eventually to his purification from sin.

Only when he has achieved this is he allowed to see Beatrice and move on to his journey to the stars.

To get to this point in the story not only has Dante descended into Hell but he has also climbed the purifying mountain of Purgatory.[a] In doing so he has gone through a sort of fast-tracked version of the process of purgation which awaits all souls of the dead who are fortunate enough to have escaped damnation but have not been quite good enough (or have not been prudent enough to obtain a plenary indulgence) to go directly to Heaven. At the foot of the mountain an angel with a sword inscribes the letter P in Dante's forehead seven times. The P is for *peccato*, sin. The letters will be removed one by one as Dante purges his various sins in turn. The travellers embark on a journey through an enchanted land, aided by angels and other poets. As he progresses Dante loses the Ps that represent pride, envy, sloth, miserliness, prodigality, greed and gluttony successively.

Finally we come to lust. It is here that the two columns of souls, divided according to whether their interests were heterosexual or homosexual, circle the mountain greeting each other with a kiss. Dante witnesses this scene through a wall of flame. It becomes apparent that for him to progress he will have to pass through the fire. He knows about the fear of fire. He tells us that he has seen what human bodies look like burned to death[1] and he can hardly have forgotten that this was now the penalty that awaited him should he return to his native city. Virgil tries to encourage him, pointing out that he looked after him all the way through Hell. Then he reminds him who he is on his way to meet, 'only this wall keeps you from Beatrice'. That does it. Dante walks into the flames and, although he tells us that he would gladly have jumped into molten glass to find relief from the heat, he emerges unscathed.

In the Garden of Eden, Virgil confirms that, purged of sin, Dante is now truly master of himself, 'I crown and mitre you over yourself'. He may now relax and enjoy the delights of the garden 'until those lovely eyes rejoicing come'.

When Beatrice does arrive and he hears her voice again, Dante's reaction is to do what he has always done since he was in the dark wood: tell Virgil about

---

a Purgatory is the poor relation of the three parts of the *Comedy*. It frequently gets no more than a brief mention in books about Dante (see below) but it does contain great poetry and some very fine examples of Dante's jaw-dropping imaginative powers. It also has a point of interest over the other two parts in that, according to medieval Christianity, because few of us are either irredeemably evil or unfeasibly saintly, most of us are going to end up there.

it. He already knows what he is going to say. He is going to tell him that he has 'recognised all the signs of that ancient flame', which is actually a quote from the *Aeneid*. Virgil would have enjoyed the compliment but he never hears it because when Dante turns 'with all the trust that makes a child run to its mothers arms', Virgil is not there. He has slipped away quietly while his friend was distracted by the procession. Dante's reaction is immediate: 'But Virgil had departed leaving me bereft, Virgil sweetest of fathers, Virgil to whom I entrusted myself for salvation ... not all that our ancient mother lost could save my cheeks from being stained with tears.'[2]

By 'our ancient mother' Dante, of course, means Eve and what she lost is all the special joy of the Garden of Eden. Dante's analyst, had he had one, might well have been interested that he has used the word mother twice in the space of eight lines (the first time being when he turns to Virgil on which occasion the Italian word he uses is actually 'mamma'). This incident is poignant because it seems to be mostly about emotion. Virgil's symbolic role as representative of the Roman Empire, or even as the literary figure Dante has to beat, is not referenced in the exchange. He is simply 'the sweet father', the friend.

There is only one word Beatrice can use here to bring Dante's attention back to her and, for the first and only time in the *Comedy*, she uses it: 'Dante', she says, 'do not weep because Virgil has departed ... do not weep yet ... there is another sword to make you weep.' The other sword that Beatrice refers to is a combination of regret and shame. These emotions dominate his encounter with Beatrice in the garden. He looks at her and is so overcome that he lowers his head 'like a guilty child facing his mother' (third mention). Unfortunately he then sees his own reflection in the river which increases the agony of his guilt, so he lowers his head even more to avoid the feeling. As so often with Dante, if we visualise this picture in detail we are left with an almost comic image. Beatrice stands high on a chariot looking down on Dante whose chin is now forced into his chest in a contorted pose of abject self-effacement.

The elements which make up Dante's shame are clear to us: he deserted Beatrice intellectually by placing too much emphasis on philosophy at the expense of spiritual revelation, and he deserted her emotionally by devoting himself to the love of the *Donna Gentile*/Lady Philosophy. We can add to these any amount of what Beatrice calls 'being led astray by present things' and what Dante the protagonist calls 'false joys offered by the world', which can presumably include any non-spiritual diversion from sex to idle gossip. It is clear that out of these ingredients was fashioned a weapon that caused Dante deep pain. But how they were combined – *exactly* what it was that made Dante feel guilty – is very hard to fathom.

Dante the writer has Beatrice upbraid his own fictional persona on and off for three cantos. She offers no sympathy. The theme is the same throughout: after my death you should have got the message and devoted yourself to higher things but instead you allowed yourself to be distracted. She states unequivocally that 'your estrangement was a sin'. The words seem almost to issue from a deep pool of her own resentment: 'There was a time when my countenance sufficed ... but that man you see strayed after others. No pretty girl or other brief attraction should have weighed down your wings.' Dante is in no doubt as to the strength of her feelings – he 'felt the venom of her words'. This is plainly the Beatrice that Dante the writer wants. There can be no doubt about the genuineness of his pain. It would be ridiculous for a modern audience to expect anything resembling the chattiness of a real relationship – 'I've missed you so much! ... So have I! ... You look great! ... Do you like my chariot?' – but it is a little surprising that, in this the lengthiest account in any of his writings of an exchange between the two of them, love is hardly mentioned at all.

Only at the very end of Purgatory is Dante let off the hook. He is allowed to drink from the River Eunoë, one of the two rivers of Eden, the other one being the more famous Lethe, river of forgetfulness. The name Eunoë was invented by Dante from Greek words which mean 'well mind'. The effect of its waters is the opposite to Lethe: it brings back memories but only the ones about good deeds in the past. When he drinks Dante feels much better. *Purgatorio* closes with Dante feeling good and ready for Paradise. The final word is the one which closes all three parts of the *Comedy*: 'I returned from the most sacred waters like a new plant with new-grown leaves: eager to rise, now ready for the stars.'[3]

Paradiso begins in self-confident mood. Dante the author addresses his public with a bold, fiction-writer's lie: he says he has been there.

> The glory of Him who moves all things pervades the universe and shines in one part more and in another less ... I was there in that Heaven which receives His light the most. I saw things I can neither know nor say. But what treasure as I could store from the holy kingdom shall now become the subject of my song.
>
> (*Paradiso*, 1:1–12)

Dante may be confident but as a writer he is facing huge challenges of description and of drama. He has already begun with what will become a familiar rhetorical ploy as he enlists our sympathy by confessing how difficult it is going to be to describe. The result is that we want him to describe it even more. The dramatic challenge is simply to keep Heaven interesting. This is a problem for all those who depict Heaven: with everybody happy and no bad deeds being done the obvious elements of a story are ruled out. But, by measuring Heaven against his own experience and keeping the narrative in touch with events on earth, Dante succeeds in overcoming this problem as well as any writer ever has.

We are still in the Garden of Eden. Beatrice stares up at the sun. Dante tries to look at it too which he finds easier than usual. He sees sparks of fire in the light then the day becomes brighter, 'as if one day shone on the next', and he experiences a strange sensation, so strange that he has to invent a word for it, 'transhumanisation'.

Beatrice explains. They have just left the earth's surface – 'lightning never shot downwards as fast as you are now ascending'. Without the ritual of a countdown, Dante is already on his way into space. He did not notice because he was concentrating on Beatrice but the sparks he saw and the increasing brightness were due to his passing through the sphere of fire which separates the mundane world from the heavens. This is possible, within the terms of Aristotle's physics, Beatrice explains, because of the transhumanisation he experienced. That was the process of draining the ignoble elements from his body.[b] Because of that he is now rising naturally, just as fire rises through the air. Beatrice feels this is so natural and so obvious that she finishes her explanation with the remark that, knowing all this, it would be surprising if he had *not* risen towards the stars.

Suddenly the couple are enveloped in a cloud of pearly light – 'a solid object but without solidity' is how he describes it. They are passing through the moon. To Dante it is not a world on which one can stand but a semi-gaseous mass. In fact, the moon is the only one of the seven[c] planets that he describes at all. In the rest of *Paradiso*, which is deliberately shorter on detail than the other parts of the *Comedy*, he will concentrate on the sphere of the planet rather than the heavenly body itself.

While they are there Dante has a question. Why are there areas of light and dark on the surface of the moon? Since it is a heavenly body one might expect

b There is some debate about whether it is Dante's body or just his soul which rises.

c The seven planets are, in ascending order of distance from the earth: Moon, Mercury, Venus, Sun, Mars, Jupiter, Saturn. To geocentric Dante, of course, the earth is not a planet but the sun is.

it to be featureless, an evenly lit pearl. It seems a slightly trivial question for the first astronaut in history to ask, but it is there because the answer involves the whole universe. Beatrice explains that the light of God's wisdom, which pours into the spherical universe from the outside, is refracted and modified by the rotating spheres as it makes its way downwards. The effect of this is to produce diversity; not just the patches on the moon but all the diversity that we see around us. What she tells him is actually the answer to a much wider question to which Dante will return at the end of his life: how come the universe isn't the same all over? In theological terms the question is, 'why are there all these objects and living creatures everywhere when God could have just created a glowing pool of His love?' In modern cosmology the same question occurs in different form: 'Why, after the big bang, did the universe not just settle down as a pool of pure energy? Why are all these planets and stars here?' Dante was right to be concerned about this question because the stakes are high – in the homogeneous universes which grand theories suggest we would simply not exist.

It is time for a human story. While still in the moon Dante sees some shadowy figures which look like reflections in an imperfect mirror. They are so like reflections that Dante tells us he turned around to see what they were reflections of. But they are not reflections, they are just ethereal. Dante has met his first souls who have a place in Heaven. Beatrice confirms that they are 'real substances', souls who are assigned to the lowest sphere because they broke vows.

Dante speaks to one of them – 'oh well created spirit who in eternal life tastes the sweetness which untasted cannot be understood' – and asks her name. She is Piccarda Donati, sister of the famous Corso Donati. All of Florence must have known her story. She was plainly the quiet, spiritual member of the family because, early in her life, she joined the convent of St Clare in Florence. The Poor Clares, as they were known, were the women's arm of the Franciscan movement and as one of their number Piccarda would have renounced all material wealth and devoted herself to charity. Her brother, however, remained in the material world and when he needed to strengthen an alliance with the powerful Tosa family, he dragged her out of the convent and forced her to marry one of them. Piccarda's goodness guaranteed her a place in Heaven, but by marrying she had technically broken her vow of chastity so her place is the lowest possible.

Dante asks her if she minds this. Does she not yearn to be higher up? No, she says, 'the virtue of love calms our desire'. She answers with 'such joy that she seems to be on fire'. To want more would not be in accordance with God's will and that would be a negation of the divine love which brings them bliss. 'In His will is our peace.'

The gift of being content with whatever God or fate has happened to give you is probably a good quality to have when in exile. Dante certainly had the capacity to derive pleasure from the simple contemplation of nature – the frogs, birds and other wildlife that he mentions in the *Comedy* are always evidence that the universe is fundamentally well-ordered – but he never lost his capacity to complain:

> I have travelled like a stranger, almost like a beggar, through virtually all the regions to which this language of ours extends, displaying against my will the wound of fortune for which the wounded one is often unjustly accustomed to be held accountable. Truly I have been a ship without sail or rudder, brought to different ports, inlets, and shores by the dry wind that painful poverty blows.
>
> (*Convivio*, 1.3.4–5)

He had spent all his life in the relatively small, close-knit community of Florence. Now he was obliged to stay where people spoke differently and dressed differently. For survival he had to 'eat another man's bread and walk another man's stairs'. Florence was integrated into Dante's entire being. All his memories of Beatrice were there, linked with streets, buildings and corners. The *Comedy* is as much about Florence as it is about Heaven or Hell. The city is frequently addressed as if it were a person, even if it is normally being admonished for its wickedness. There is no doubt about his constant desire to return: 'Florence cast me out of her sweet bosom, where I was born and bred up to the pinnacle of my life, and where, with her good will, I desire with all my heart to rest my weary mind and to complete the span of time that is given to me.'[4]

He gives us no details of his circumstances at the time beyond saying that he lived in poverty. Boccaccio tells us[5] what Dante, of course, does not: that his wife Gemma stayed in Florence. She was, after all, a member of the victorious Donati family and was therefore probably not in physical danger. Boccaccio says that she was able to 'defend from the infuriated people a small portion of his property by claiming that it was her dowry'. The implication is that the rest of Dante's money was gone. 'The dry wind of poverty' was indeed blowing severely.

He must have survived, to put it bluntly, on charity. This was probably not too difficult in the months after his condemnation. To anyone who had some sympathy for the Whites (and that included all of Florence's many enemies) he was a celebrity refugee and looking after him was a worthwhile political gesture. Soon, however, he would have to face the agonising indignity of asking for help. A year or so later we find him having to lace natural good manners with unsubtle hints as he writes to the Counts Oberto and Guido da Romena apologising for not having come to their uncle's funeral.[d] The final third of the letter is a rather pathetic account of his circumstances, obviously included in the hope of eliciting sympathy because 'poverty has thrown me into her prison'.

It was time of unaccustomed petty humiliations. He was evidently not always treated with sympathy. He talks about the 'wounded one being held accountable for his own wounds', which today we term 'blaming the victim'. His expulsion had led to him being perceived in a new way. He was no longer the bright young Florentine poet; it was too easy to see him now as a sad political refugee who also wrote a bit. He had suffered a sharp loss of status:

> And I have appeared before the eyes of many who perhaps because of some report had imagined me in another form. In their sight not only was my person held cheap, but each of my works was less valued, those already completed as much as those yet to come.
>
> (*Convivio*, 1.3.4–5)

Over the next decade he was to travel from city to city. It is impossible to reconstruct his movements accurately. His own phrase that he travelled 'over virtually all the regions where this language [Italian] extends' gives as accurate an impression as anything. Boccaccio gives a list of the families he stayed with: Count Salvatico in the Casetino, Moruallo Malaspina in Lunigiana, the della Faggila family near Urbino and also the towns of Bologna and Padua.[6] Other people have slightly different ideas. Verona was also to be a very important city in his exile and we can add the small town of Forlì to the list as public records place him there in the autumn of 1302. It was the home town of the commander-in-chief of the White forces during the disastrous adventure in the Mugello so there is a strong likelihood that he was there on party business.

Meanwhile, back in Florence, the Black government was not finding it any easier to maintain peace than its White predecessor. Corso Donati once again

---

d   There is reason to doubt Dante's sincerity because he seems to have also placed the uncle, Alessandro da Romena, in the circle of traitors for forging florins.

was at the centre of the trouble. Flushed with his success in overthrowing the Whites, he now became concerned that he was not being accorded the status he deserved as the 'saviour of Florence'. He took action in the best Florentine tradition and, as the chronicler Villani puts it, formed another faction. Also following tradition, he was not too fussy who his allies were so long as they were against his enemies. Among others he teamed up with were the Cavalcanti family, even though he had in the past tried to have Guido Cavalcanti murdered, and the Tosinghi, who had been on the White side in the previous conflict. On the opposing side Villani lists the Spini, Pazzi, Gherandini and some of the Frescobaldi. Tension escalated. Rock-throwing machines were again seen on the roofs of palaces (once a family had assembled it, it was much easier to do it a second time). Having expelled one faction, it had taken the city of Florence just two years to recreate an almost identical sectarian schism within the remaining one.

18

A PARTY OF ONE

I n 1303, in the town of Anagni to the south of Rome, something happened which gave new hope to many people in Italy. The soul of Pope Boniface VIII, famous to historians for being arguably the most powerful pontiff in the history of the papacy (so far) and famous in Dante's Heaven as the man who had turned the throne of St Peter into a sewer, departed this life.

The story of his death is as extreme as the story of his life. Fittingly, it is also the culmination of his long-running dispute with the French king, Philip IV. The fight had started as a dispute about whether Philip had the right to tax the clergy but it soon became a trial of strength. In a succession of moves, declarations and counter-moves, pope and king had each raised the stakes. While both of them waged other wars and pursued other interests all over Europe, neither of them ever neglected to maintain their duel. Boniface's employment of the king's brother as his agent in his attempt to gain influence over Florence provided a respite. The result, while not a disaster for Boniface, had not been sufficiently clear cut to warrant gratitude either. Very soon the fight was as fierce as ever.

Late in 1302 Boniface produced a summary of his wildest assertions of papal power in the form of the papal bull called *Unam Sanctam*. It was the ultimate official proclamation of papal power: 'for every human creature it is necessary for salvation to be subject to the authority of the Roman pontiff.'

Philip responded to this familiar absolutist claim by summoning a council. It met in the fortified stronghold in the centre of Paris, known as the Louvre.

The agenda was ostensibly nothing to do with *Unam Sanctam*; its job was to produce a list of Boniface's crimes. Philip's chief lawyer, a man named William of Nogaret, set about the task of writing the charge sheet with vigour. The story is that he had reason to hate the Pope because his own parents had been killed in Boniface's continuing persecution of the heretical sect known as the Cathars.

The charges included things for which a case could undoubtedly be made, such as corruption and simony. It then moved on to crimes that may just have been true but were going to be difficult to prove: failure to believe in the immortality of the soul, the condoning of sexual sins and practising most of them, including, but not restricted to, buggery. Beyond that, William of Nogaret and his team seem to have discovered, like Dante, the pleasures of writing pure fantasy fiction and included such charges as keeping a private demon (an idea with great fictional potential) and consulting sorcerers. They naturally included heresy because it was the only crime for which all a pope's previous edicts could be annulled. Philip would have found that useful. It was the will of the council that Boniface attend a later meeting to answer all the charges. They wanted to put the Pope on trial.

Boniface responded with a council of his own which, under his instruction, drafted the bull *'Super Petri Solio'*, which declared in ringing tones that Philip IV, King of France, was to be excommunicated. It called on all those loyal to the Pope to swear allegiance and obey the edict. The bull was to be officially published, and thereby brought into effect, by being hung on the door of the cathedral of Anagni,[a] the Pope's home town, on 8 September 1303.

Rulers in the Middle Ages seemed often to manage to survive excommunication unscathed but Philip was in a weakened state. He found himself in a beleaguered Paris ringed by hostile elements from nobility and commons alike. Excommunication would have undermined his already tenuous authority so he took the deadline seriously.

William of Nogaret was dispatched from France to Italy. Early in the morning of 6 September he arrived in Anagni, where he knew the Pope to be staying. He was accompanied by 300 mounted soldiers and 1,000 infantrymen. The force had been supplied by various local lords who had a grudge against Boniface. Most prominent among these were the two members of the Colonna

---

a   The small town of Anagni, which was even smaller in the Middle Ages, is distinguished by having supplied the Church with no less than four popes. Only Boniface, however, has the honour of having a speciality regional dish, Timballo alla Bonifacio VIII, named after him.

family who had been cardinals until Boniface had dismissed them in his fight with their family. The ruins of the Colonna town of Palestrina, which Boniface had destroyed, were almost close enough to be visible from Anagni. It must have been a special day for the ex-cardinals.

History is fortunate to have an eye-witness account of what followed. William of Hundleby, a visiting English cleric from Lincolnshire, sent a letter home describing the events very soon after they happened. William tells us that as the soldiers arrived men and women were leaping from their beds demanding to know what was going on. Although it was not the case, the popular answer on the street was that the soldiers had come to kill the Pope. Boniface was evidently not popular in the town because, on hearing this, a large section of the community turned out in support. Some of them started enthusiastically to assist the soldiers by looting the many houses in the town which belonged to Boniface's cardinals.

The raiding party surrounded the palace. When the Pope asked what they wanted they responded with short-term demands, obviously drafted by the people who were there at the time. They demanded that Boniface hand over all the treasure of the Church and reinstate the Colonna cardinals. When Boniface refused the soldiers attacked the palace. After a spirited defence by the occupants the raiders gained entrance by burning down the door of the cathedral (presumably the very one on which the proclamation of Philip's excommunication had been due to be posted in two days' time) and forcing their way into the palace by a stairway.

Boniface, who was in his eighties, was found in his room in full papal regalia clutching a cross. William of Nogaret managed to prevent other members of the party from killing him, which would have been a disastrous own goal for the French monarchy. Instead the Pope was locked in a room while his palace was stripped of its rich treasures – 'No one could believe that all the kings of the earth could have had such a treasure'. William leaves us with one of those details which, if it were in the *Comedy*, would make the reader suddenly sympathetic with a previously unlovable character. William records that Boniface sat in his cell resigned to his fate and to his impotence muttering quietly to himself the words of the Book of Job: 'the Lord giveth and the Lord taketh away.' William of Hundleby sums up with the kind of understatement for which his people are still renowned: '*Papa habuit malem noctem*', 'The Pope had a bad night'.

The following day a remarkable thing happened. The fickle people of Anagni decided that they did not want foreigners interfering with their pope. It was, after all, an unprecedented and so far unmatched outrage against the throne of St Peter. Historians still refer to it as the 'Outrage of Anagni' and even Dante refers to it as a 'second mocking of Christ'. Perhaps, having reflected on this, the citizens of Anagni staged a counter-attack in the early morning and drove back the raiding party – some historians believe that they were helped by those of the raiders who had seen the error of their ways. William of Nogaret himself was wounded and he and the others fled. The Pope was released by the people, brought into the town square and given wine and food. 'Everyone could speak to the Pope as with any other poor man', remarks William, amazed as people often are by the discovery that famous people are human. A little later Boniface made a speech of gratitude to the citizens of his home town. He absolved them of any sin over the incidents with the cardinals' houses. He also asked that his treasure be returned. Some of it was.

Boniface went back to Rome protected by an armed guard and took up residence in the Lateran palace. But the shock had been too great and he went into a decline. Some say that he went mad, gnawed at his own hands and dashed his head against the wall. All are agreed that he eventually passed away peacefully in the evening of 12 October 1303. What happened to him next is fiction.

A new pope was elected only ten days later. Benedict XI provided an encouraging contrast. He was a much more moderate man, indeed he is the only pope who lived during Dante's lifetime who is not mentioned either as being in Hell already or as being certain of going to Hell. Then again, Dante does not mention him in connection with Heaven either. He just did not make as big an impression as Boniface, but being a nice-but-dull pope does have advantages: there have, as we know, been five subsequent popes who have taken the name Benedict; there have been no more Bonifaces.

With Boniface out of the way there was a feeling that a shadow had been lifted from Florence and that peace was possible. One of the new Pope's first acts was to send a special emissary to the city. Cardinal Niccolò da Prato seems to have sincerely wanted to make things better; Villani, who probably had met him, heaps praise on him: 'sensible, clever, wise, prudent and highly capable'. When he arrived in Florence on 10 March 1304 the citizens, who still had to endure barricades and armed groups wandering the streets, greeted him with joyous relief.

The cardinal set about his work in a businesslike manner. He wrote to the White exiles calling on them to renounce violence and return to the conference table. For their reply the exiles turned to their 'tame writer', Dante. He drafted a letter in which he displays all his skills as a fourteenth-century diplomat. It assures the cardinal that the Whites have always only wanted peace and liberty. All they want is justice for those who seek violence. It thanks the cardinal for his compassion in trying to bring peace to the city and assures him that the White party will put away its swords and submit to his will. Although to modern eyes it is flowery and rambling, it is probably in exactly the style that was required and, for all its floweriness, its message is clear.

In the new atmosphere of hope Dante moved from the north to Arezzo. The advantage of this was that it was much closer to Florence. There he was able to monitor developments more easily and, who knows, perhaps even be ready to return if the time came.

Over and above the conflict between Blacks and Whites, the cardinal also needed to work on the split that had just opened up among the Blacks themselves. He made great progress on this front. He managed to persuade Corso Donati and Rosso della Tosa, the leader of the opposing faction, to meet in a public ceremony in the piazza in front of the Dominican church of Santa Maria Novella. Dino Compagni was there: 'in the presence of the signori, having made many peace agreements, they kissed one another on the mouth in the sign of peace.' Such was the euphoria at the dawn of this new era that even when heavy rain fell during the day no one left. They did not even seem to feel the downpour. In the evening great bonfires were lit and all the church bells sounded.[1] But Dino does add that by the evening Rosso della Tosa was beginning to become indignant because the reconciliation had gone further than he would have wished.

A few weeks later, as part of the traditional May Day guild celebrations, the company of Borgo San Friano, who had a reputation for innovative spectaculars, put on a show. It was staged on pontoons on the River Arno and the audience was placed on the wooden Carraia Bridge to the west of the Ponte Santa Trinità. Perhaps they had already heard rumours of the amazing epic on which the exiled traitor Dante Alighieri was working; perhaps it was a genuine case of parallel invention, but the show was about Hell. The publicity promised that 'anyone desiring news of the other world could obtain it by visiting the banks of the Arno that evening'. It was a sell-out. The audience loved it. Villani describes men disguised as demons horrible to behold, cries and shrieks and actors who 'had the appearance of naked souls'. The company of Borgo San Friano knew how to put on a show. Then the wooden bridge began to collapse in several places. There was panic; some people were crushed to death, others were drowned. Villani cannot resist making the dark joke that many in the audience did indeed get news of the other world that day.

With this unpleasant omen, the honeymoon with Cardinal Niccolò da Prato seemed to be over. The ruling Black party were no more willing to give up power than their White predecessors. They made the right noises but agreement was never quite reached. Dino, as ever, sums it up: 'Cardinal da Prato made many peace pacts between the citizens of Florence but then their ardour cooled and many quibbles were found.' He was tricked into getting involved in disputes with neighbouring cities. They asked him for his advice about selecting a podestà but then rejected all four of his suggestions. He did manage to arrange face-to-face talks between the Whites and the Blacks. They started well but then broke down, Dino says because of continued Black intransigence.

The cardinal left Florence in despair. His final act was to place an interdict on the city, which is roughly the equivalent of excommunication for cities. In his final letter, dated 9 June 1304, you can hear the exasperation of a man who has been biting his tongue for four long months: 'You want to be at war and under a curse. You have no wish to hear, let alone obey, the messenger of the vicar of God.'[2]

Just to show that it was business as usual, on the following evening Florence erupted in street fighting. Dino describes how the Corso Donati faction wanted to take action against the Cavalcanti so they started fires in the area of their houses. It spread much more rapidly than anyone expected, destroying 1,900 dwellings. Dino notes the usual looting and failure of the podestà to do anything to help. The Cavalcanti were ruined and fled the city.

The death of Benedict XI on 7 July put any further hopes of peace on hold. It was now the turn of the Whites to revert to type. They put into action another of their daring plans. It was launched just two weeks after Benedict's death and displayed all the hallmarks of having been planned entirely in the aftermath of the pontiff's demise. Dino, who is entirely pro-White, manages to describe the plan as bold and intelligent but ultimately has to admit that it was also foolish and premature. This time they did actually manage to get inside the new walls of Florence but they were soon repulsed. The Blacks pursued them and they were resoundingly defeated at the town of Lastra, 12km away. The Whites had gone from being the government of Florence to bungling exiles for whom victory would remain forever no more than a self-deluding dream.

In the sixth circle of Hell, just inside the walls of Dis, Dante had taunted Farinata degli Uberti[3] that he and his fellow Ghibellines had never learned the trick of making a comeback.[b] Farinata's reply was that Dante himself would soon be learning how hard a trick that was to master. This is what he meant.

***

'Whoever on earth laments that we must die to find our life above knows not the fresh relief found there in this eternal downpour.'[4] We should not fear death because Heaven is so wonderful. Dante is prompted to this thought because where he is, in the sphere of the sun, he is able to sense God's grace as it comes down as an eternal downpour from the outer edge of Heaven. It is not an original sentiment and it has convinced very few people in life that death is not to be feared.

In the sphere of the sun he has been surrounded by the triumphant souls of a kind of A-list of medieval thinkers and writers: Thomas Aquinas, the ultimate theological authority; Isidore of Seville, scholar and theologian; the Venerable Bede, historian and the only Englishman Dante meets in Heaven; Siger of Brabant, theologian with a reputation for unorthodox beliefs; Bonaventura, third head of the Franciscan movement; Hugh of St Victor, philosopher and early champion of technology; and Joachim of Fiore, a mystic whose dire predictions of the imminent end of the world were very influential. It has been suggested that these are the authors who have influenced him. Like all the souls in Heaven they glow – 'our brilliance is in ratio to our love'. He talks to Thomas Aquinas for a while until, as the conversation finishes, the group begins to glow even more brightly until Dante's vision is disturbed. He tells us he seems to see another circle of souls around him but he cannot quite make them out.[5] Nobody knows who these souls are meant to be: a vision of some future age; the ghosts of great writers to come?

Dante turns back to Beatrice and she smiles. All at once he becomes aware that they are alone and that the light around him has turned red. They have been transported to the sphere of Mars. Dante does not tell us his idea of the distances between the spheres but his key source,[6] who does give numbers, estimates the average distance between spheres as about 9 million miles. Dante has travelled this distance in six lines of poetry.[7] Dante the writer has faced the problem of travelling over large real distances in a fictional story before. In Hell he solved it with a flight on the back of the monster Geryon; in outer space

b So complete was the expulsion of Farinata's family that, following their expulsion of
  1258, not one of them entered the city for fifty-six years. The first of the Uberti who was
  allowed in after that time was Azzolino, who was part of the negotiating team brought
  in by Cardinal Niccolò da Prato for the ill-fated face-to-face talks. Dino recalls that the
  disaffected people actually cheered the Uberti arms as they were borne through the streets.
  To them anything was better than the present lot.

he invokes the possibility of instantaneous travel. He moves when Beatrice smiles. Later science-fiction writers would coin a phrase for this: beaming up.

The souls in the sphere of Mars swarm in their millions like the stars in the Milky Way or specks of dust in the beams of the sun. They form up in a vast cross from which Dante has a vision of the power of Christ. Dante describes almost nothing about it except the music: 'Until that moment nothing had existed that ever bound my soul in such sweet chains.' When the vision has passed, one of the souls descends to Dante from the starry cloud like a shooting star.

It is his great-great-grandfather, Cacciaguida, a nobleman and a hero of the crusades. As a noble ancestor Dante addresses him with enormous reverence. He expresses surprise that he cares about such things in Heaven because, as he rightly says, 'Our pride in noble blood is a trivial thing'.[8] But nevertheless he is proud and even finds himself speaking in a more refined manner than usual in Cacciaguida's presence.

At Dante's request, Cacciaguida gives his assessment of the state of Florence. His reply starts with a diatribe against the shameful way in which the women of Florence now behave (no details) and then broadens into what is in essence a collection of observations about how things were better in the past. The fact that it is a little predictable does not, of course, mean that it is not true.

Cacciaguida is aware of Dante's exile from the city. On the subject of his fellow White exiles and their ill-fated antics he does not equivocate: 'What will weigh you down most will be the despicable, senseless company whom you shall have to bear in that sad vale.' He mentions a serious quarrel between Dante and his fellow exiles, of which this is the only record: 'all ungrateful, all completely mad and vicious they shall turn on you but soon their cheeks not yours shall blush from shame.'[9] The row will cause an irretrievable breakdown in their relations. Dante will reject the Whites and at the same time reject the politics of partisanship. From then on he will go it alone and become, in a famous phrase, a *parte per te stesso*, a party for you yourself – a party of one. All artists are parties of one.

19

THINGS CAN ONLY GET BETTER

I n the period which followed the disastrous defeat of the Whites at Lastra in 1304, Dante's role seems to have developed from that of a recipient of handouts to a sort of freelance diplomat, writing letters (as he had done for the White exiles) and even taking part in negotiations. There is one record, for example, of his helping a family called the Malaspini to negotiate their way round a dispute with the local bishop in a town called Castelnuovo di Magra.

As a party of one, newly decoupled from the polemics of exile, he must have had time to collect ideas for the *Comedy*. Everything he saw was potential material. The sparks in a fire, frogs in a pond, birds at dawn, columns of ants: all these things became the metaphors and visual texture of the *Comedy*. Places too were absorbed into his long-running movie: a tower in Bologna gives the scale of mass of a leaning giant in Hell and the workers in the busy shipyard of the Arsenal in Venice become the band of demons that plunge sinners into boiling pitch.

These references also provide evidence of the cities he had visited. Beyond the Italian peninsula we can check off Bruges, where the dykes become the walkway over the fiery sand; and Arles, where Roman tombs become the eternal resting place of atheists. There are strong indications that he visited Paris. Boccaccio insists that he did so, as does the chronicler Villani. The

Comedy mentions a Parisian street, the 'Street of Straw',[a] where one Siger of Brabant was alleged to have cooked up heretical ideas. Dante is not always complimentary about the French. In an outburst against the Sienese he lapses into wild hyperbole and accuses them of being 'even more vain than the French'. He certainly knew the French language because he shows off by providing a few lines in French when he meets the soul of a troubadour in Purgatory.

If 1307 were the year in which he had visited Paris he would have been witness to one of the most famous events of the century. In the evening of Friday 13 October of that year, King Philip IV's troops rounded up the independent order of warrior monks known as the Knights Templar. The story of the trials, torture and eventual elimination of the order is well known even today. The reasons for the move are not crystal clear although it does seem that Philip's motive was probably financial gain. The king was in severe difficulties. He had already resorted to desperate money-making schemes, such as the devaluation of his currency and the persecution of Jews to extract money from them. The Templars were next on the list. Philip's persecution of the Templars set a standard for European oppression. The prosecution tactic in the hearings that followed of inventing lurid and ludicrous rituals – the Templars were alleged to have passed the time by worshipping a made-up deity called Baphomet and kissing each others' bottoms – created the pattern that has lasted into our own time. It was also tried on Boniface and was used in almost all subsequent witch trials.

Writers, including the Dante namesake and enthusiast D.G. Rossetti, have tried in the past to connect Dante more directly with the Templars in some way. It is slightly surprising that he only mentions them once and then only in passing[1] (if conjectural gnomic references are discounted), but that could be explained by the fact that by 1307 he had the plan of the *Comedy* already well worked out. In addition, the situation was developing until there came a time when saying the wrong thing about the Templars could lead to a charge of heresy and, although Dante does not display many inhibitions about upsetting the powerful, as a diplomat he might have seen fit to impose limits on his outspokenness.

If he had been in Paris in 1309, on the other hand, he would have had a close view of an event with which he does concern himself: the removal of the

a La Rue de Fouarre still exists in the 5th *arrondissement* of Paris. Its literary fame has been acknowledged by letting it lead into the Rue Dante.

papacy to the French town of Avignon. The successor of Benedict XI, Clement V, never set foot in Rome, probably because he feared an attack. After Anagni popes must have been aware that they were not invulnerable. Clement set up shop in Avignon on the River Rhône and that is where all popes had their seat for the next seventy-eight years. This was effectively the annexation of the papacy by the French crown. Dante is quite clear that this was a bad thing and that Clement was, in his opinion, no more than the creature of the king of France.

We do know that, by the year 1310 or soon after, Dante settled for a longer period in the town of Verona in Lombardy in the north of Italy. This move was the beginning of a new phase in his life. A more permanent home would give him the opportunity to take stock of his situation and prepare to write *Paradiso*, the final and most important part of the *Comedy*.

Dante was the guest of the new dynamic Lord of Verona, Cangrande della Scala. He had been christened Can Francesco della Scala but everybody seems to have been agreed that *Can' Grande*, 'Big Dog', suited him rather well, one way or another. Cangrande was to be a major player on the Italian political stage. Opinions of him as a person vary but Cacciaguida, in his lengthy speech in the sphere of Mars, not distinguished by praise of many living people, prophesies a great future for him: 'His generosity will be so widely known that even his enemies will not be able to stop their tongues from praising it ... Look to him and trust his gracious deeds. Through him many people will be altered; rich men will change places with beggars.'[2] We can probably deduce from these lines that they were written while Dante was staying in Verona.

Verona was a city comparable to Florence in size and even approaching it in wealth but in other ways it was radically different. As it had grown over the previous century it had gone through an opposite history. In Florence the opposing interest groups of merchants and noblemen had been given a more or less equal share of power, which left them permanently in conflict. In Verona this had not been allowed to happen. Back in the 1220s one Ezzelino III da Romano had, by decree, converted the office of podestà, which he held at the time, into a permanent lifetime lordship. His successor, Mastino I della Scala, went one step further and made it an inherited post. From that moment on, the running of Verona was the family business of the della Scala. The Scaligeri, as the family are also known, had no need to fear the constant opposition of a signoria elected by the merchant class or indeed any other body. They were in charge and they ensured that they would remain so by specifying severe punishments for anyone who questioned their authority. They had abolished what little democracy there had been but the result was that Verona escaped the incessant cycle of schism and conflict that so marred Florentine life.

There were other aspects of Verona that Dante would have found a congenial contrast to what he had left. Unlike Florence it had a collection of fine Roman buildings to remind him of the golden age when the bright sun of empire shone on the road down which humanity travelled. The city's cathedral had a library which was one of the major resources in Italy and in Western Europe at the time. The Scaligeri also, being secure in their position, actually ran a court where artists and writers were encouraged to meet and talk. In Florence anyone in authority had been too busy wondering how to survive the next riot to pay any attention to the arts.

It is very easy to imagine (although there is no evidence) that periodic public readings of the emerging cantos of the *Comedy* might have become part of court life. Courtiers would have eagerly awaited the next reading to find out which celebrity the poet had slandered this time, rather in the way that certain sections of British society rush to the magazine *Private Eye* to feast on the latest outrageous revelations.

In undemocratic but stable Verona, Dante must have felt a little like a child from a disrupted home who finds himself taken up by a traditional family and feels relief at the certainty and predictability of a firmly run world. He did not come from a 'broken home' but both his parents died early and it would be quite understandable if the breakdown of his Florentine 'mother' left him with a desire for good order and calm.

He came increasingly to believe that the only hope for the human race was imperial government. There is no suggestion that he is merely excited by the idea of firm government and, before we accuse Dante of being a proto-fascist, it should be said that in all his political writings he emphasises that he is talking about just rule exercised out of love. But from now on, in the political arena, the desire for a strong and effective empire is something that increasingly preoccupied him. In the political jargon of his age, Dante was turning from a Guelf into a Ghibelline.

It was while he was in Verona that he devoted some of his time to writing the short book called *Monarchia*, an analysis in Latin of the history and function of empire which argues that the Roman Empire and its legitimate successors were ordained by the will of God. The book is directly opposed to the opinions of Boniface expressed in *Unam Sanctam*. It was attacked very soon after Dante's death and put on the Church's index of proscribed books. The ban was lifted in 1881 and *Monarchia* is now considered to contain within its pages a concise statement of official Catholic policy.

The Scaligeri family were, even by the standards of the Italian nobility, unswerving supporters of the Ghibelline imperial cause. Their coat of arms even incorporates the great symbol of empire, the eagle. In the sphere of Jupiter Dante lets the souls of just rulers express his ideas about empire through the medium of a talking eagle.

When the conversation with Cacciaguida is over Dante turns to Beatrice. She is now glowing with even more intensity and, without even a smile, they are transported to the next sphere. The red glow of Mars turns pale 'like a girl recovering from a blush' and they are in the silver sphere of the planet Jupiter. It is here that the luminous souls of past good rulers fly like flocks of birds in the evening, forming up in lines and curves words that eventually spell out the Latin sentence that is the political message of the *Paradiso*: *DILIGETE JUSTITIAM QUI JUDICATIS TERRAM* – 'Love justice you who rule the world'.

The slogan flashes up letter by letter but, when it is finished, the final M remains in the sky, golden against the silver background like some richly chased medieval chalice. Further glowing souls fly up to add to it, like sparks from a log in a fire when it is hit. The extra souls cluster on the central angle of the M and build it up. At first the central spike which they create makes it look like a Florentine fleur-de-lys but that is only a fleeting impression. The central point curves over, the sides of the M become wings and Dante finds himself looking up at a golden imperial eagle.

'And what I have to tell you here and now no tongue has told or ink has written down nor any fantasy imagined it.'[3] The amazing thing is that the eagle speaks as one entity. The souls speak in unison; they use the words 'I' and 'mine' where one might expect 'we' and 'our'. There is no need for them to broker deals or negotiate a joint position. They are of one mind and they speak with one voice – just as one unified glow of heat comes from many coals.

The eagle understands God's justice more than anyone from the spheres below, let alone from the earth. Dante has a question: 'you know the question whose answer I have hungered to hear for so long.' The eagle knows. It stretches its neck and starts to speak. It begins with a discourse on the unknowability of the will of 'He who drew the boundaries of the world with a compass and within them drew distinction both hidden and clear'. The gist of its preamble is that God's will is so vast that no one, not even the eagle, can understand all of it. Dante in particular cannot expect to see the true nature of divine justice any more than he can see the floor of the ocean.

But Dante still has a question. The eagle knows what it is and summarises it for him in a general form:

Consider a person born far away on the banks of the Indus where there is no knowledge of Christ. He is sinless in word and deed but will die unbaptised with no understanding of God's grace and will therefore not be allowed to enter Heaven and feel the bliss of God. Is that fair?

It is a good question and one which, as the eagle points out, Dante has asked before. In his mind, of course, it has a more personal formulation: 'Why can't my friend Virgil come with me into Heaven?' The eagle gives its answer with all the gravitas of a considered legal opinion straight from the sphere of divine justice. It can be paraphrased simply: 'this ruling comes from the will of God and the will of God is good therefore this ruling is good. Who are you to question the judgement of God?'

It may be possible, especially if you are a devout late medieval Christian, to stare at that answer long enough until, not unlike those magic pictures that were in vogue a few years ago, it unexpectedly acquires the appearance of solidity. Perhaps Dante did stare long enough and it did turn into an answer which satisfied him. But if it did the solidity was not permanent because Dante the writer revisits the issue in the following canto. There the eagle lists the souls of rulers who make up its eye (remember it is a composite bird). It turns out that two of them were pagans: the Roman emperor, Trajan, and Ripheus, a minor character from Virgil's *Aeneid*.

As Dante says, 'how can this be?' How come they managed to get into Heaven? The eagle has its answer ready. In the case of Trajan, he was brought back to life and then baptised. Ripheus, who led a blameless life and loved righteousness, had his eyes opened to the truth and 'faith hope and love were there in place of baptism'. In this way he became a Christian even though he lived before Christ. The mind resounds with questions which, for once, Dante does not ask, such as: 'if you allow these special cases then anyone could be converted to Christianity irrespective of where and when they lived, so why didn't God in His infinite love do that for all the poor pagans who are stuck in Limbo?' There is no future in asking such questions of the past and we must be content to note that if Dante had been entirely satisfied with the answer he would not have mentioned these bizarre cases. 'The tongue goes where the tooth hurts,' as Leonardo Bruni put it.

Having spoken to its own satisfaction, the eagle flies up and circles around 'like a stork that has just fed its young'. The bird's next task is to give a comprehensive list of the major political injustices of the age. But, for an instant, Dante is left looking up at it as he stands on the fault line between overarching theory of moral principle and an immediate intuition of what seems right. It is a place which has always been a fruitful location for both poet and dramatist.

In October 1310 a man called Henry of Luxembourg crossed the Alps into Italy via the Mont Cenis pass. Accompanied by only a light force of troops, he and his retinue were travelling at speed, with his queen, Margherita of Brabant, riding by his side, sitting astride her horse like a man – less ladylike but faster. Henry was the new Holy Roman Emperor and his visit to Italy was of the utmost importance because only by means of a coronation by the Pope in Rome could he confirm himself truly as the emperor.

Most people seem to have agreed that Henry had the potential to be a great emperor. He was not German or Italian but from Valenciennes, a small town in what is now the north-eastern corner of France and therefore free from the more obvious loyalties that might prevent an emperor from acting justly. The Pope supported him. It was one of the few things that Clement

V ever did that went against the will of Philip IV of France, but the only other candidate had been none other than Philip's brother Charles de Valois, and the Pope drew the line at letting one family have power over the whole of Europe. So in September, Pope Clement V had issued an encyclical from his palace in Avignon, urging all Italians to recognise and welcome the new emperor.

By all accounts Henry was not as corrupt and greedy as the usual contenders for the post. He was already behaving like an emperor. He had sent ambassadors ahead of him, calling on the cities of northern Italy to welcome back their exiles and cease the sectarian conflict that was the day-to-day business of Italian politics. With the full ceremony of a Roman coronation and a commitment to proper imperial rule, he was set fair to be the first real Holy Roman Emperor in sixty years. His existence was proof to Dante that the machinery of the Roman Empire was still capable of functioning. In fact, there seemed to be a chance that the world would once again see the balanced rule of the two suns overseeing the human family.

Dante needed to believe in an imperial miracle, 'we have long wept by the waters of confusion and unceasingly prayed for the protection of a just king'. Fired up with faith in the new age, he wrote a magnificent letter to the 'Princes of Italy' urging them to support the emperor. Henry VII was ready to take his place in the cosmos:

> And we too, who waited through the long night in the wilderness, shall see the long-awaited joy. For a giant of peace shall appear, and justice which like a heliotrope deprived of his light had grown faint, shall receive his rays and rise up again. All they that hunger and thirst shall be satisfied in the light of his radiance, and they that delight in iniquity shall be put to confusion before the face of his splendour.

> (Dante, Letter 5)

Henry's first objective was to consolidate his support in northern Italy. Dante had also written to the Lombard rulers urging them to embrace the ideals of the Roman Empire and give the new candidate their support. Lombardy was traditionally an area of Ghibelline cities and, as soon as the lords of Lombardy realised that Henry was a serious contender, there was no question but that they would be on his side.

The triumphant Henry spent Christmas in Milan and on 6 January was crowned king of Italy with the famous iron crown which was believed to have been made by Constantine the Great (the first Christian Roman emperor) out of the nails from the Crucifixion. Dante attended the ceremony, as he excitedly tells Henry in a letter to him personally. This time, in his enthusiasm, he compares him to Christ: 'When my hands touched thy feet, and my lips paid their tribute. Then my spirit rejoiced within me and I said secretly within myself: Behold the Lamb of God, which taketh away the sins of the world.'[4]

He addresses Henry as 'the most glorious and most fortunate conqueror, by divine providence king of the Romans' and 'the successor of Caesar and Augustus' and signs himself, as he does in several of his letters, 'Dante Alighieri, a Florentine undeservedly in exile'. He is writing to Henry to urge him to turn his attention to the city of Florence. He describes the situation in language that would not be out of place in the *Comedy*. Florence is 'the viper that turns on her own mother', she 'pollutes the running stream of the Arno' and she 'defies the ordinance of God and worships the idol of her own will'.

In the city of Florence Dino Compagni, the one-time White prior, now banned by law from standing for office or even from taking part in an assembly with his fellow ex-priors, also saw a glimmer of hope from across the Alps. He did not write to Henry; instead he started work on his invaluable and instructive chronicle of the events which had brought such sorrow to his city. He was to describe Henry as moving from city to city, 'making peace as if he were an angel of God'.

But the Black government of Florence did not wish the new emperor to come upsetting the balance of power in Tuscany. For Henry to arrive and start reviving the strength of the Ghibelline empire supporters would mean that Florence would once again find herself surrounded by a ring of Ghibelline cities – Pisa, Arezzo and Siena being the main players. Florence would lose control of the lines of communication which were vital for trade. They had not fought the battle of Campaldino for that to happen.

They were fortunate that Pope Clement V was, at the time, in the process of turning against Henry, perhaps to please his French paymasters, or perhaps out of nervousness about the scale of the Henry phenomenon. The Pope instructed Robert, King of Naples and Duke of Calabria (who was technically Henry's vassal), to organise resistance to Henry's 'invasion'. The signoria was delighted. From that moment on official Florentine documents are all headed, 'In honour of the holy church and his majesty King Robert and to the defeat of the German king'.[5] There had been so much feeling whipped up against the 'German king' that when Henry's ambassadors arrived in the city they were set upon by a mob, nearly killed and had to be rescued and helped back to the city gate by the podestà's troops.

In the growing excitement Dante wrote to the signoria in Florence. The letter is addressed to 'the most wicked citizens within the city'. After a brief statement of his standpoint on the nature of empire, the letter moves on to accuse the Florentines of 'transgressing every law of God ... insatiable greed has urged you all too willingly to every crime', calling them 'senseless and perverse'. Insults, however, are not enough for him, as he goes on to describe with Biblical relish the just retribution which the emperor will inflict on their city. The following is just a sample:

> ... the eagle shall swoop down upon you ... What good shall it do you, wretched men, when you are standing in his presence ...
>
> ... to your grief you shall see the buildings which you have raised crumble beneath the battering-ram, and devoured by fire ...
>
> ... you shall see the destruction of your temples and your children suffering in shock and ignorance for the sins of their fathers ...
>
> ... your city, worn out with endless lamentation, shall be delivered at the last into the hands of the stranger, after the greater part of you has been taken in death or captivity; the few that shall be left to endure exile ...
>
> ... O most foolish of the Tuscans, deluded both by nature and by corruption, who neither consider nor understand in your ignorance how your diseased minds go astray in the darkness of night! ...

(Dante, Letter 6)

Long before the letter comes to its end it is obvious that Dante has passed the point of no return. The Black government would never allow somebody who held these opinions to come back. Only the total overthrow of the Black government would ever get him through the gates of the city of his baptism now.

In the *Comedy* it is Thursday 14 April 1300. Dante has been travelling for a week. Now he is in the sphere of Saturn among the souls of those who have led a contemplative, monastic life. This sphere is silent: there is none of the music and singing which has, up to now, been the background of his cosmic journey. Dante asks the reason for this of St Benedict, the founder of European monasticism, whom he has just met. He is told that it is because of him; he is not yet spiritually strong enough to cope with the music of this high Heaven. He must undergo a further process of purification before he is able to withstand such power. Dante then asks St Benedict why it was he, St Benedict, who was chosen to come down and explain things to him. This could be construed as light conversation but the saint chooses to interpret it, probably correctly, as a question about the fundamental nature of God's plan. Dante is given a severe reply. The bright glow which is all that the traveller can see of the saint begins to spin like a millstone at full speed. Benedict explains that he is in direct touch with the power of God, that is the source of his bliss, 'I see the highest essence from which the power flows'.[6] But, continues St Benedict, not he and not even the highest angel who is closest to God can answer that question, 'for what you have asked is buried deep in the valley of God's eternal law'.

Just then their conversation is interrupted by a shout from the assembly of souls, 'the sound of which has never been heard on earth'. Dante is terrified and runs to Beatrice 'like a child who returns to the one he trusts most'. She comforts him 'like a mother quick to help her breathless son'. 'Don't worry, you are in Heaven and everything is for the good up here', she says. 'If you are so shaken by a single shout just imagine what would have happened if they had sung.' It turns out that the words he could not hear for the noise – 'the prayer within the shout' – was a statement of the vengeance yet to come against evil on earth which, Beatrice clearly states, Dante will himself witness before he dies.

Then it is time to move up to the sphere of the fixed stars. Together Beatrice and Dante ascend the celestial ladder which leads to this, the most distant part of the universe that is visible from earth, the sphere which contains all the others so far. On earth the fixed stars are seen to rotate full circle once every twenty-four hours, taking the sun (and the other planets) with them, thus giving rise to night and day. The stars are fixed in the sense that they do not move in relation to each other. In Dante's universe they form an unchanging pattern on the outer wall of the cosmos.[b]

They arrive in the constellation of Gemini, the location of the sun when Dante was born: his birth sign. Dante calls on the constellation itself to give him strength for the last and most difficult part of the journey. The next stage for the traveller will be a series of viva voce examinations to make sure he is prepared for the final phase.

b   In reality, of course, the stars do move in relation to each other and they are not points of light on the inner surface of an enormous ball. Nonetheless, modern astronomers still talk of the celestial sphere and sometimes of the fixed stars. The reason being that stellar distances and time scales are so large compared to those of the solar system that the idea of a celestial sphere is a serviceable approximation for many tasks such as, for example, navigating a spacecraft to Saturn.

Beatrice tells Dante to look back down towards the earth. It makes him smile because it looks so insignificant. From the harmonious calm of God's great Heaven he recalls the pounding of misfortune and misery that has filled him with rage and calls the earth 'the threshing floor that makes us wild'.

The Black government of Florence was evidently concerned about the imminent arrival of Emperor Henry VII. By way of insurance, they took measures to restore normal relations with the exiled Whites. On 2 September 1311 they introduced a bill revoking the exile sentence on a large number of Whites in the hope that, in the event of Henry's victory and yet another swing of the pendulum, the vengeful wrath of the Whites might be slightly assuaged. Unsurprisingly, Dante was not on the list. His letter, with its overt references to the destruction of the city, marked him out as an extremist whom the Blacks could legitimately exclude from any future negotiations. Dante's only hope of return was in Henry's total victory.

But the emperor was slow to leave the north. He had difficulty persuading his allies to mobilise. Meanwhile, his opponent, King Roger of Naples, was building up substantial funds, thanks to papal support and the encouragement of Florence and the 'Guelf League' it had hurriedly formed. Dante wrote again to Henry to urge him on, 'in our uncertainty we are driven to doubt ... are you the one who will come or should we look for another?'

But it was to be nearly a year before Henry felt confident enough to make the journey south to Rome and the coronation which would place him in the long line of emperors, stretching back to Augustus. When he did make it (by ship, thereby avoiding Florence) the absence of papal support made his life difficult. When he attempted to go to St Peter's he was repulsed by soldiers loyal to the Pope. The people of Rome, however, turned out to be on his side, perhaps because imperial coronations had traditionally been occasions for largesse and celebrations. Henry could not go to St Peter's but he managed to get himself crowned in the ancient (though not traditional) church of St John Lateran which was, at the time, virtually in ruins. Clement V issued a statement from his palace in Avignon telling Henry to leave Rome immediately and ordering him to observe a twelve-month truce. He did neither.

Henry waited for some months in Rome and then quite suddenly, almost as if he had decided to heed Dante's pleas, he marched to Florence and laid siege to the city. The Florentines were taken unawares but managed to bar the gates. Soon afterwards, a force of Guelf League reinforcements managed to sneak past Henry's army and enter the city. The Florentines started to feel more confident but they did not launch a counter-attack. Instead they continued with business as usual, allowing traffic in and out of the city and checking that incomers did not include any imperial Trojan horses.

It was a strange kind of siege. The truth was that without reinforcements Henry did not have the troops to mount a full attack. The support he had hoped for failed to materialise and in March he withdrew to the Ghibelline city of Pisa. Henry had realised that victory would never be possible without the defeat of Roger of Naples and, to this end, he set out for Naples by sea in August, backed up by the Pisan navy. He left behind him Dante's dreams of a just empire for Europe, peace for Italy and a return to Florence for himself. The situation only worsened when, on his way there, Henry of Valenciennes, Holy Roman Emperor, died.

In Florence, Dino Compagni stopped writing his chronicle. He did not bother to describe the abortive siege or the death of Henry. He knew, just as Dante did, that all hope of a return to justice was gone. He packed his manuscript away. It remained unread for almost three centuries. Two copies were made somewhere along the line but his story and the wealth of insight and detail it includes were not recognised until the eighteenth century. The manuscript ends boldly, echoing Dante's dire warning that imperial justice would soon come to the city:

> Oh wicked citizens who have corrupted and spoiled the whole world with bad practices and illicit profits! You are the ones who have brought every bad habit into the world. Now the world is beginning to turn against you: the emperor and his forces will seize and plunder you by sea and by land.
>
> (Dino Compagni, Chronicle)

By the time he hid his book away Dino knew that this would not happen.

***

> If ever it happens that this sacred poem to which both Heaven and Earth have set their hand (so that it has made me lean for many years) should conquer the cruelty that expels me from the fair sheepfold where I slept as a lamb.
>
> (Paradiso, 25:1–3)

In the sphere of the fixed stars Dante is speaking about his hopes. With another reference to childhood, he tells us that he still longs to return to Florence. He is actually talking about more than a simple return. It would be a vindication. If this were to happen he will return a changed man: 'I shall return a poet with another voice and, at the font where I was baptised, take up the laurel crown.'[7]

Return would be the crowning validation of his life. The child who gazed up at the baptistery ceiling, who turned into the introspective love poet of the *Vita Nuova*, will have become the voice of his age, reminding humanity of its transgressions and celebrating the glory of God's great creation. It sounds reasonable to us, viewing it 700 years later. It probably sounded so to Dante but by then he knew it was only a dream. The first word of the passage is 'if' not 'when'.

This speech comes in the middle of the three tests that Dante has to undergo before he can go on to the next stage of Heaven. He is required to show his understanding of the three theological virtues: Faith, Hope and Love. Dante's examiners are three saints: St Peter examines on Faith – Dante explains that it is God's gift of understanding the mystery of the universe (not, as many people think, the ability to believe things that are not true); St James on Hope – it is hope of Heaven, not fear of Hell that should make people good; St John on Love – it is love that has brought him here; love is what the *Comedy* is about. To heighten the drama at this point, before he can give his answer, Dante loses his sight. Then the canto ends.

In the next canto St John reassures him that the loss is only temporary. Dante tells him that everything about his life and about the universe have combined to bring him from 'twisted love' back to 'just love', back to the straight pathway that he had lost in the dark wood: 'The world's existence and my own, the death He bore that I might live, all these have drawn me from the sea of twisted love and brought me to the shore where love is just.'[8]

And Dante in his turn loves the universe: 'I love the leaves of good which the Eternal Gardener bestows on his garden.'[9] He is fond of the image of a tree for the universe: it implies that all experience and all knowledge are connected – all just facets of one beautiful system.

The souls of the fixed stars begin to sing. There is a flash of light and Dante's blindness is gone. He can see clearly now.

20

THE STARRY DYNAMO
IN THE MACHINERY OF
NIGHT

It seemed to me that I saw the universe smile.

(Paradiso, 27:3)

With his newly restored and newly modified vision, Dante sees the smiling universe and is transported with joy: 'O happiness! O indescribable joy! O fulfilled life of love and peace! O riches held in store!' Even in the middle of a difficult and painful life he had the ability to remember what joy felt like.

This is the beginning of Canto 27 and it comes, after three cantos of theological instruction, as a blast of joy for reader and protagonist alike. It is not an accident that this gem (Dante manages to include the phrase '*il dolce canto*' in the second line) is number 'three times three times three' in the third part of the *Comedy*.

Dante is looking into an infinitely receding field of glowing souls and they are all moving upwards. One of the great sights to be seen on a winter's night, now as then, is a sky filled with gently falling snow, lit from below. The effect is disorienting, as if space itself were moving before your eyes. Dante says that this is what the multitude of souls looked like, except that they were glowing red and rising instead of falling.

He continues to gaze at them until Beatrice tells him to look down once more towards the earth. Because of the diurnal motion of the heavens they have travelled on since his last look. Then they were over Jerusalem, now they have moved ninety degrees onward to the west and are over Cádiz (we can deduce from this that Dante's examination in the three theological virtues took six hours). He remarks that he can now see the course of Ulysses' mad voyage beyond the Mediterranean. Mentioning him now is a reminder of Dante's own daring, and arguably even madder, voyage to the edge of space.

Then Dante looks at Beatrice and all the art in the world seems as nothing in comparison with her smile. With this they move up to the next sphere, the one that sweeps round every twenty-four hours giving the world day and night. It is the first mover, the Primum Mobile.

The Primum Mobile is not visible from earth. Its existence had to be inferred indirectly by scientists – just like the particles of modern physics. It is an innovation which was added after the time of Aristotle to account for the mysterious slow drift of the fixed stars which had been observed since Roman times. Dante scholar, Patrick Boyde, points out that the mysterious and scientifically novel Primum Mobile exercised a fascination for Dante and his contemporaries in just the way that black holes do over journalists and television producers today.

The closeness of this final sphere to divine perfection means that it is homogeneous: it has no features. Dante regrets, therefore, that he cannot indicate to his readers which part of it Beatrice put him in because all parts are exactly the same.

In twelve lines Beatrice, 'with her smile showing the joy of God on her face', explains the mystery of the Primum Mobile. Firstly, it is the source of all motion: 'The nature of the universe, which holds the centre still and moves all else around it, starts here as from its origin.'[1] Outside this outermost sphere there is no space and no time. This is the end of the universe; beyond it there is only one thing: 'This Heaven has no other "where" but in the mind of God, in which burns the love that turns it and the power that filters down.'[2] In other words, the entire sphere of the universe is embedded in the mind of God which is itself outside the space-time continuum. It will remain forever a mystery to all but God: 'Light and love enclose it in a circle, as it contains the rest. And only He that bound it comprehends how they were bound.'[3]

She returns to the image of the tree: the roots of time disseminate the power of God into the universe like a plant with multiple branches and leaves. Each leaf contains a fragment of divine love.

But even here there is politics. Human beings start their lives in a state of moral goodness but greed makes people turn against it. Beatrice uses the shocking image of an innocent, loving child who grows up to hate his mother and wish her dead. This should not surprise you, she says, when you remember that currently there is no one to govern the human family. In other words, there can be no good without an emperor.

When he was writing the *Vita Nuova* (it must have seemed so long ago) Dante managed to free himself from the introspective dead end of the troubadours' idea of love. The poem he wrote at the time that best expresses the broadening of his vision begins with the line: 'Even beyond the widest circling sphere. There's where the sigh goes when it leaves my heart.'[4] The widest circling sphere is where he is now. Beyond it is where he is headed.

In Canto 27 Dante gives us the picture of the universe that informs the entire *Comedy*. It turns out that we all exist in a bubble in the mind of God. Within the vast sphere of Creation, the machinery that turns the stars is driven ultimately by the power of that which flows into it. The horror and misery that blight our existence only happen when humans unnaturally turn against the loving force that nurtured them. Yet in the myriad leaves of experience we can see the connection with the force of cosmic love that feeds the roots of the tree. The Eternal Gardener has ordered things so that we can all potentially see the universe smile.

Some Italian historians count the death of Henry VII, in 1313, as the end of the Middle Ages. Without engaging in a debate about that claim, it can be agreed that it marked the end of an era for Italian history. The Guelfs and the Ghibellines, the political schism that gave the world Romeo and Juliet, was from that moment on of declining relevance. The Holy Roman Empire itself would survive in some form, as we have seen, until 1806 but it was to be, even in its own estimation, more of a loose political alliance than a true successor to the empire of Augustus.

Within two years of Henry's death, all the major characters in the story of Dante and the *Comedy* had gone. In Florence, although strife continued as ever, it did so without Corso Donati. He had finally generated enough resentment to cause his own demise. His opponents had managed to have him condemned for attempting to take over the city (which was treason). He tried to flee but was caught by Catalan mercenaries who escorted him back to town. He was by then old and crippled with gout but, impetuous to the last, he let himself fall from his horse and tried to escape again. The Catalans killed him with their lances and left him dead in the street.[5] Although Corso had been a key figure in Florence's descent into violent chaos (not to mention the forcible abduction of his own sister Piccarda) he comes off comparatively lightly in the *Comedy*. The only mention of him is made by his own brother, Forese, to whom Dante speaks in Purgatory. He assures us simply that Corso is scheduled to be dragged down to Hell.

Pope Clement V, the successor to Boniface, died in April 1314. Dante calls him 'the lawless priest from the west' (he came from Gascony in France) and makes it clear that he is next in the furnace after Boniface. He gets two more oblique references: one as the betrayer of Henry VII, having at first encouraged and then opposed Dante's favourite emperor, and second for his complicity in the destruction of the Knights Templar as having 'spread his greedy cloak against the temple'.

Although by this time Pope Boniface VIII himself had been dead for nearly a decade, his old adversary Philip IV pursued him beyond the grave. He attempted a full post-mortem condemnation which included all the traditional crimes – corruption, malpractice, buggery – but paid special attention to heresy, this being uniquely the one that would allow all of Boniface's many proclamations to be annulled. He was also accused of having taken a bribe of 50,000 florins from the Templars to turn a blind eye to their sins. Some historians have suggested that the attack on the Templars was itself related to Philip's continuing campaign against him. Frenchman Pope Clement V, safely installed in his fortified palace in Avignon, was of great assistance in this project. But even he drew the line when Philip suggested that Boniface's remains be disinterred, burned and scattered.

In November 1314 Philip IV himself died. In the *Comedy* he is variously referred to as 'the evil of France' and 'a new Pilate' (who condemned Christ). The talking eagle in Paradise refers to him as 'the debaser of coin' because of his money-making devaluation scheme. The eagle also remarks that 'his death will wear the hide of a boar'. Philip was indeed killed when a wild boar charged his horse. He was succeeded by his son Louis X, known as 'the quarrelsome'.

In 1315 a remarkable thing happened. Florence was once again in danger, this time from a man called Ugucione della Faggiola, a one-time ally of Corso Donati. He, together with his army, was presenting a credible threat to the city. The Black government, as it had done four years earlier, adopted the tactic of neutralising exile opposition by allowing selected White dissidents back into the fold. Amazingly – perhaps because his fame was increasing or maybe because, at 50, he was too old to be a threat – Dante was included on the list this time. He received word that, subject to successful negotiation, condemnation would be rescinded and he would be able to come home.

In the Primum Mobile Dante continues to gaze at Beatrice. Then he senses a light behind him, just as if one were looking at a mirror in the half-light and suddenly became aware that candlelight had entered the room.[6] When he turns round there is indeed a light, or rather ten lights. He sees a bright point, more intense than anything he has seen before, around it circle nine others. This is the universe, but visualised in a different way. It is 'what one sees when one looks deeply into the motion of the whirling spheres'.

God is at the centre of this inverted picture (which looks, to modern minds, strangely like the physicists' model of the atom). The other points are the planets or, more accurately, the orders of angels who guide them.[a] They are now in reverse order: the more holy they are, the closer they are to God. The Primum Mobile, therefore, is next to the central light (God) and orbits fast in a tight circle ('love's fire burns it into motion'). The moon, however, is furthest away, swinging in a long, slow arc. This alternative picture, which is a pure invention of Dante's, is quite satisfying: it does make sense for God, the controlling element of the universe, to be at the centre of things.

Dante asks the obvious question: 'If this is what the universe is really like, how come it looks so different?' Beatrice's reply is that in this model love is what is most important. What she does not say is that this is *only* a picture.

---

a The names of the orders, which derive from what read almost like chance remarks in St Paul's letters (Colossians 1:16 and Ephesians 1:21) are, in ascending order of holiness: Angels, Archangels, Principalities, Powers, Virtues, Dominions, Thrones, Cherubim and Seraphim. These orders developed an enormous significance to medieval theologians and Dante is not alone in associating them with the planets.

From her words it is clear that we are meant to understand that this is another aspect of the same reality, no more real than the universe across which Dante has just travelled and no less.

There is a follow-up question which a modern reader might ask: 'how real was the whole journey of the traveller, then?' At one level, of course, it is obviously entirely fictional. But even within the story, we might wonder how Dante the protagonist is meant to understand his experiences. In the *Comedy* we are given indications that Dante is not being shown a solid, timeless reality. In the sphere of the Moon, for example, Beatrice tells him how much things have to be simplified in order for them to be understood by someone like him.[7] Dante the protagonist is interested in this question too: in Heaven he asks his ancestor, Cacciaguida, why he only seems to be meeting famous people. The reply is that it is because he will learn more from them.

It is possible to conclude that Dante's entire journey was no more than a show put on for his benefit. It would make no more sense, therefore, for Dante the protagonist to ask, 'do these souls really live here?' than it would for us to ask whether Homer Simpson really works in a nuclear power plant. The circles of light are one more example of Dante playing with the idea of fiction.

The reality of the offer from Florence turned out to be different from the picture presented. Dante's return could be bought only at a price. Before his death sentence could be rescinded he (along with any other exiles who took advantage of the offer) would have to undergo a ritual humiliation. When he re-entered the city he would be imprisoned, albeit symbolically, and then required to perform a rite known as oblation. This consisted of dressing in sackcloth covered with ashes, topped off with the conical hat that we associate with dunces. He would then be obliged to walk through the streets of Florence to the baptistery. Once inside, Dante would have to prostrate himself and offer his unworthy soul to John the Baptist. Some historians think that political prisoners would have been excused the fancy dress, but counterbalancing this possibility was the fact that the Florentines were also considering imposing a fine. Since Dante had lost his house and all his possessions in the Black takeover twelve years earlier, this did not seem fair.

'Is this the reward for fifteen years of exile? ... Is this the reward for innocence and the sweat and labour of ceaseless study?' He wrote to the signoria: 'I can look upon the face of the sun and the stars anywhere. I can contemplate the most precious truths under any sky without needing to return to Florence and be disgraced in the eyes of my fellow citizens. Rest assured, I will not want for bread.'[8]

Even while adopting this defiant tone, he left the door slightly ajar: earlier on in the letter he mentions that he would come back 'if some other path can be found'.

In 1318 Dante left Verona. Cangrande della Scala had, in recent years, become increasingly autocratic and belligerent. He had pursued a series of military campaigns in northern Italy. When he had virtually eliminated all Guelf opposition the Pope stepped in to defend his own party and threatened Cangrande with excommunication, which he ignored. It may be that Dante felt that his patron had strayed too far from the balanced doctrine of the two suns of empire and papacy. Most accounts of Cangrande portray him as a very strong-willed aristocrat, not the sort of person to whom the balanced sharing of power would come naturally.

Dante's growing fame made it easier for him to find a new home. He moved to the coastal city of Ravenna, famous for its heavenly Byzantine mosaics of, among others, the Emperor Justinian (who speaks about justice in Heaven). It was, and still is, a pleasant place. Dante describes the gentle breeze which blows in the Garden of Eden as being like the wind in the pines near the city. According to Boccaccio, who may have spoken to people who knew, 'Dante lived in Ravenna, having lost all hope of a return to Florence, for some years, under the protection of a kind and benevolent patron'.

His host and patron was the ruler, Guido da Polenta. He was a poet himself. Some of his poems, which are thought to have been written while Dante was in Ravenna, survive. Critics detect the influence of the *Vita Nuova* so it may be that he had known of Dante since his early work. Guido was the nephew of Francesca da Rimini, with whose naked soul Dante has a revealing conversation in Hell. She describes Ravenna, the town of her birth, as 'the place where the Po flows down to find peace'. Guido may not have liked being reminded of the story of adultery and double murder associated with Francesca. On the other hand, he might have been pleased that his sexy aunt had been given such a sympathetic part in the *Comedy*, even if details were a little painful to the family.

In Ravenna Dante was also to meet young poets who would remember him with admiration in their own old age, including one, Bernardo Canacci, who was to write his epitaph. He entered into a correspondence with a professor at the University of Bologna, Giovanni del Virgilio. We know that by then the *Comedy* had been widely circulated because Giovanni was obviously a fan, even though, as a professor, he criticises Dante for not writing it in Latin. Another letter refers to Dante sending him ten new cantos of *Paradiso*, but we do not know which ones they were.

Dante was becoming famous. He was even being recognised in the street. Boccaccio tells the story of a lady who noticed that he had some sort of rash on his face and remarked out loud that 'he has the marks of Hell on him'. Whether it tells us that some simple folk actually believed that Dante had been to Hell or whether she was just one of those people who thinks it is amusing to call out witty remarks to celebrities in the street is impossible to tell.

With the circles of the angelic orders still visible, Beatrice takes a moment to set Dante straight about some of the technical matters. She is exasperated by the mistakes that are caused by mankind's desire to appear clever: 'You mortals do not follow the true path of philosophy because you are so eager to put on a display of wits … Christ did not say to his disciples, "Go forth and preach rubbish to the world".'[9]

The worst mistake concerns angels. Contrary to what some people are saying, they do not have memories. They are in constant touch with the mind of God so they do not need their own memories. They are, as it were, permanently online to the all-knowing deity and therefore have no need to store information on their own account. Even angels, however, cannot know God's mind completely. Having finished her digression, Beatrice reminds Dante of the timeless order of the vision he has just seen: 'You see the height and breadth of the Eternal Goodness: one light, which divides itself through many mirrors yet reflects itself as One.'[10]

The circles of light fade and Dante turns once more to Beatrice, 'if all I have said of her up to now were condensed into a single poem it would be slight compared to what is due'.[11]

Not only is Beatrice now beyond description but, in this spiritually intense place, description itself is becoming impossible. Dante is about to enter a place where everything is beyond description, where even the logic of space and time fail.

Beatrice's beauty now transports him to the final sphere, known as the Empyrean, 'the Heaven of pure light' which is outside the universe. At first Dante is blinded, as if by a flash of lightning, but then he finds his senses have, against expectation, been strangely enhanced and he is able to withstand the intense brilliance. Now, as he looks, he sees in a new way. It feels like the moment at the end of a masquerade ball when all the dancers finally take off their masks.

What he sees is like a vast glowing stadium, crammed with the souls of all who have ever achieved grace. It was to this assembly that the souls were rising when he saw them floating upwards like glowing snowflakes. The vast bowl in which they sit is formed when the beam of God's light strikes the outer surface of the universe and some of it is reflected back spreading out to form a kind of container. Dante calls it the Rose but it is so large that it could enclose the sphere of the sun. Yet he is able to see each soul equally clearly. In this place outside the universe the laws of perspective, touchstone of the early modern mind, have broken down, 'near and far neither add nor take away: where God rules directly natural laws have no effect'.[12]

Beatrice points out the vacant space which is reserved for Emperor Henry VII. When she is speaking, of course, his descent into Italy and his untimely death are all at least a decade in the future. She also foretells that the Pope of that time (Clement V whom Dante considered responsible for Henry's downfall) will be a deceiver who 'does not travel the same road by day as by night'. There is, of course, one pope to whom in time all heavenly conversations must return. And sure enough, Beatrice finishes by confirming in almost vulgar terms that when Clement dies, Boniface, 'the man from Anagni', will find himself shoved further down into his furnace.

Dante sees angels flying across the Rose. They are dipping into it like bees collecting nectar. Even in all the lower heavens, he has never seen anything like this before. He feels, he says, like a barbarian who has just arrived in Rome. The contrasts with all his previous experiences are overwhelming. He lists three of them and in doing so produces the best comedy line in the *Comedy*. To paraphrase:

> The contrasts were enormous. I was witnessing divine splendour, having once lived in the world of mortal men; I was face to face with eternity, having once been constrained by earthly time and I was amongst sane and reasonable people, having once lived in Florence.

> (*Paradiso*, 31:37)

As he always does in moments of overwhelming awe, Dante turns back to Beatrice. But she is not there. Where she was standing there is now a fatherly old man with white hair. It is St Bernard of Clairvaux, one of the major figures in European Christianity who lived about a hundred years earlier. He was a dedicated aesthetic, borderline fanatic and founder of the hugely successful Cistercian order of monks. Although he was a very spiritual man and influential at many levels nobody would ever have described him as fun. He used, for example, to rail against the current fashion of putting gargoyles and other imaginative sculptures on the outside of churches. His opposition to the creative arts seems to make him an odd choice, but he cannot be faulted for his theological credentials or for his courtesy to Dante.

Beatrice meanwhile has taken her seat far up in the Celestial Rose, two places away from the Virgin Mary herself. Because of the suspension of the laws of perspective, Dante can see her clearly and he voices his thanks: 'you led me from bondage to freedom by all paths and by every means you had. Keep your generosity alive in me so that my soul, which you have healed, may please you when it leaves my body.' Up in the Rose, Beatrice does not smile, she does not wave. Her final words to Dante have already been spoken. They were the ones about shoving Boniface VIII deeper into the furnace.

In preparation for the final revelation, St Bernard prays on Dante's behalf to the Virgin Mary. There are echoes of Ulysses in his words. Like him, Dante is an ordinary man, neither a saint nor a king, who has reached his goal as much by determination as by merit. 'This man who, from the deepest pit of the universe up to these heights, has seen the spirits of the dead now begs you, by your grace, to grant him power so that, by lifting up his eyes, he may rise to his ultimate salvation.'[13] What Dante is about to see cannot be described. All theologians and mystics are agreed about that. 'The way that can be spoken is not the true way'[14] is how the Chinese philosopher Lao Zi neatly put it. Dante is going to see the 'Universal Form', the underlying nature of all things, 'the single book of which creation is the scattered pages'.

By now, not being able to describe what he is seeing has become the main dramatic thread of this canto. He tells us the memory is like a dream. It is fading even as he writes, like footprints in the melting snow. We are drawn in by the drama of inexpressibility: the more he says that he can't describe, the more we will him on to do so.

As he looks into the light he feels that if he looks away at this point he will lose his mind. Dante struggles to tell us what he sees but his words 'have no more strength than a baby wetting its tongue at his mother's breast'. His vision does strengthen until, in the middle of the light, he sees three great interlocking luminous circles, 'the first seemed to reflect the next like rainbow on a rainbow and the third was like a flame breathed out by the other two'.[15] Within the circles he makes out the image of a man, not superimposed but integral to them. He is seeing the great Christian mystery of the Trinity: a single god who is composed of three aspects. The nature of the Trinity had already occupied theologians for centuries and Dante, who can see it in front of him, says that he puzzled over it too, like a mathematician working on a difficult problem of geometry. Then, as if struck by a bolt of lightning, he understands.

Dante uses a strange phrase to describe what happened next: *l'alta fantasia mancò possa*, literally 'the great fantasy lost power'. It means that even *his* ability to interpret images (*fantasia*) has failed. In the face of this kind of understanding there can be no more poetry: what he says next is real. The subsequent line begins with the word 'but' – there are only three lines of the *Comedy* to go: '… but my will and my desire were turning, like a wheel in balanced motion, with the love that moves the sun in Heaven and the stars.'

> *Ma già volgeva il mio disio e 'l velle,*
> *sì come rota ch'igualmente è mossa,*
> *l'amor che move il sole e l'altre stelle.*

(Paradiso, 33:143–5)

The *Comedy* ends with the word 'stars'. We leave Dante swept up by the motive force of all creation which is – as should surprise nobody – love.

Dante the writer has brought us to this point, as Virgil brought him to the summit of Purgatory, 'with skill and intellect'. He has told his tale of Heaven without sentimentality, he has faced the toughest intellectual challenges in the history of ideas and, most importantly, he has made it interesting. The drama continues to the last line. *Paradiso* is great fiction.

21

THE OCEAN
AND THE LAND

occaccio tells a story in his biography about the last thirteen cantos of *Paradiso*. When Dante died, he says, the final cantos were missing. His sons Pietro and Jacopo were distraught that their father's great work should remain incomplete and even contemplated finishing it themselves. A little later Jacopo was visited by the figure of Dante in spotless clothes with a strange light in his face. Jacopo asked him if he was alive and he said that he was, but in the true life not in this one. Jacopo asked if he had completed the *Comedy*. By way of answer the figure led him to the bedroom where Dante used to sleep and pointed to a place on the wall. Then Jacopo woke up. While it was still dark he went with a servant to Dante's old bedroom. When they examined the part of the wall which the figure had indicated they did indeed find the last cantos safely hidden. Boccaccio claims the veracity of this tale because he had spoken to the servant in question. It is a fitting tribute to his hero, Dante the storyteller, that he should choose to use his skill as a writer to dramatise the essentially unexciting process of finishing a book.

The *Comedy* was, in fact, not Dante's final work. That distinction belongs to a short essay called *Questio de Aqua et Terra*, 'A Question about Water and Land', written a year before his death. Its subject is the motion of the four elements as described by Aristotle. This question of the title is: 'If, as Aristotle says, the four elements (Fire, Air, Water and Earth) are constrained to move so that they sort themselves out in order of "nobility", with fire at the top and earth at the bottom, why hasn't all the land sunk through the water leaving the surface of the globe one vast ocean?' This is a similar question to the one which crops up at the beginning of *Paradiso* concerning the dark patches on the moon. It is another instance of a theory predicting a homogeneous world with no interesting details when the world we see is actually full of them.

Dante's answer, which involves an argument about the perturbation due to the stars, is technical and not entirely convincing. But it is interesting that, at the very end of his life, he should return to this type of question (which has its modern analogy in the issue of the formation of stars and planets after the big bang). Perhaps the reason is that divine justice is also a theory which sorts souls into layers, according to good and bad. We might naively expect to have more sympathy for souls at the top and progressively less as we go further down. But Dante the novelist knew that this was not the case. Despite the theory, there are souls in the depths who turn out to be sympathetic and therefore interesting. They also are anomalies in the grand order of things and without them the *Comedy* would be a much poorer book.

Dante died at 57, a good age for the time. Filippo Villani, nephew of the more famous chronicler Giovanni, tells the story in a brief monograph. Dante's patron, Guido da Polenta, obviously had great faith in Dante because he chose him to be part of a diplomatic team sent to Venice to reduce tension after a regrettable incident in which a Venetian ship had been attacked by a ship from Ravenna. He seems to have succeeded in brokering a truce. When Dante returned, however, instead of travelling by ship, as he had done on the outward journey, he went overland, following the north-eastern coast of Italy across the estuary of the Po. Filippo Villani does not have a good opinion of the Venetians: he says they lacked culture and did not appreciate quite whom they were dealing with. He also claims that they had refused to give Dante a ship because they were afraid that this articulate, over-educated foreigner would use his rhetorical skills to persuade the crew to defect and betray the Venetian Republic. Filippo tells this story in order to persuade us that Venetian paranoia was responsible for Dante's death, because on the journey through the swampy land he caught malaria.

Dante died in Ravenna on 13 September 1321 'to the great sorrow of Guido da Polenta and all the citizens'. He was buried in the church of St Francis and Guido himself, says Boccaccio, spoke at the funeral. The respectful sadness with which his death was greeted was marred only when one Cardinal

Beltrando, who objected strongly to the ideas about the papacy which Dante had expressed in *Monarchia*, attempted to have his bones burned. He was prevented from doing so by combined resistance from Ravenna and Florence.

Florence has, over the years, made regular requests for the return of the body of its greatest poet. It has always been refused. The city has had to content itself with a monument inside the church of Santa Croce (where Michelangelo, Galileo and Machiavelli are buried) and a statue of him on the steps outside. The poet is shown with a rather haunted face. He is wrapped in classical drapery and an eagle, standing at his feet, looks up at him admiringly. The process of transforming the exile into a cultural superstar was set on the road by Boccaccio, who instituted an annual lecture on the subject of the *Comedy*. Boccaccio himself gave the first *Lectura Dantis* which continue to be delivered to this day. We should give him the last word on the role of Florence in the story of Dante: 'Oh ungrateful city! What insanity and negligence possessed you when, with exceptional cruelty, you put to flight your finest citizen?'[1]

Naturally, we have no information about whether Dante was joined in his final days in Ravenna by his wife Gemma, although we have Boccaccio's opinion that his sons Jacopo and Pietro were there. We do know that she and the children, Jacopo, Pietro and Antonia all survived him, because they are mentioned in later documents. Dante's second biographer, Leonardo Bruni, says that Pietro studied law, made a fortune and settled in Verona (perhaps he had been there with his father). Bruni tells us that Pietro had a son called Dante who in turn had a son called Lionardo whom Bruni met when he visited Florence. He took the young man on a tour. Bruni is interested that this incident shows how mobile families have become in the modern, urbanised age of the fourteenth century. 'And so does fortune roll this world around and shift its inhabitants as she turns her wheels', he remarks and chooses to end his book with that line.

We also know, of course, that his daughter Antonia did come to Ravenna where, as a nun, she took the name 'Sister Beatrice'. Accounts confirm that she was a kind woman so we can guess that she would not have chosen that name if she thought it was going to cause anybody pain. Thus Antonia gives us the only insight we will ever have into how the family regarded Dante's all-embracing theological love.

As for the leading lady herself, we have watched Beatrice in scene after scene in Heaven. She has been a guide, a teacher, a nanny, a comforter, a mother and an object of adoration. She has spoken wisdom; demonstrated scientific principles; prayed and railed against the citizens of Florence in inappropriate language. We ought by now to feel we know her, but we do not. Somehow none of it has quite added up to a real person. At crucial moments of human interaction, such as meeting and parting, there is nothing to be seen of her at all. She is credited with infinite kindness yet when we meet her as a character Dante seems unwilling or unable to endow her with any emotion other than anger. At the end of the *Comedy* we are no wiser about Beatrice than we were at the end of the *Vita Nuova*. It could be argued that she is Dante's least successful invention.

Beatrice withdraws at the end of the *Comedy* to make room for the final vision. It is the culmination of the entire work. Dante the writer has used all his dramatic skill to carry his audience to a world beyond the limits of reason and the journey was worth it. Every human being should have the privilege, at least once, of seeing, if only for an instant, if only second hand, a glimpse of the insight that he describes.

But visions fade and, in the afterglow of the final canto, what is actually left of the *Comedy* is the memory of an assembly of incidents and characters. Together they add up to a great drama but only because they have intrinsic interest, lives of their own. They are the islands in the ocean of theory and they remain in spirit when the show is over, like a group of circus performers after the big top has been taken down. There is an ancient Roman poet, Virgil, who was the writer's best friend but theory would not allow him into Heaven; an elderly gay scholar who inspired him but whom theory consigns to Hell; a woman who lost herself in passion and was murdered along with her lover; a mad, fictional, silver-tongued sailor who was his evil twin. If we admit into the group characters from the writer's life, we can include a wife whom he never mentions and a remarkable young woman whose name may possibly have been Beatrice. Perhaps we can also add to this sparse crowd a member of the audience who has tried to do justice to a writer who was able to hold the entire universe in his head. And finally we must include our central character: a poet who, despite being able to hold the universe in his head, managed to find some sympathy for all of them.

CHRONOLOGY OF THE MAJOR EVENTS OF DANTE'S LIFE

1260	**4 September**: Battle of Montaperti: Ghibellines beat Florence due to the treachery of Bocca degli Abati.
1265	Dante Alighieri born, under the sign of Gemini (probably 29 May) in Florence.
1266	**26 February**: Battle of Benevento: Ghibelline defeat results in effective withdrawal of the empire from Italy and an end to Ghibelline rule of Florence. Houses of the Uberti family razed to the ground.
1267	Dante's Beatrice (possibly Bice Portinari) born.
1270	Dante's mother dies. Dante's father remarries.
1274	**May**: Dante, aged 9, sees Beatrice for the first time.
1277	**9 January**: Dante betrothed to Gemma Donati.
1280–3	Dante's father dies.
1283	Dante writes his first sonnets.
1284	Dante's vision of the Lord of Love, Beatrice and the flaming heart.
1285	Philip IV, the fair, becomes king of France.
1289	**11 June**: Dante takes part in the battle of Campaldino. Florence's victory ensures its dominance and prosperity.

1290	**8 June**: Beatrice dies.
1291	**June**: Dante meets the *Donna Gentile*.
1293	Institution of the Ordinances of Justice by Giano della Bella. Excludes noble families from government.
1294	Dante meets Charles Martel during his visit to Florence. *Vita Nuova* completed (conjectural date). **5 July**: Accession of Pope Celestine V. **13 December**: Resignation of Pope Celestine V. **24 December**: Pope Boniface VIII elected. Work begins on Florence cathedral supervised by Arnolfo di Cambio. Work begins on Franciscan church of Santa Croce supervised by Arnolfo di Cambio. Brunetto Latini dies.
1295	**5 March**: Riots end with the expulsion of Giano della Bella. **6 July**: Dante enrols in the Guild of Doctors and Apothecaries as a perquisite to entering Florentine political life. **December**: Dante is elected to the council of the Heads of the Guilds.
1296	**February**: Boniface VIII issues *Clericos Laicos* forbidding clergy to pay temporal taxes.
1298	Palace of the Priors (*Palazzo Vecchio*) built. Marco Polo's travels written.
1300	Boniface VIII declares a Jubilee. Giotto works on St Francis frescoes in Assisi. **7 April**: Fictional date of Dante's descent into Hell in the *Comedy*. **1 May**: Ricoverino Cerchi's nose is cut off by Donati youths. Conflict between the families heightens. **7 May**: Dante is sent as ambassador to San Gimignano. **15 June – 14 August**: Dante is elected a prior, one of the six highest magistrates in Florence. **23 June**: Incident at St John's Day parade results in summary exile of faction leaders, including Dante's friend Guido Cavalcanti.
1301	**19 June**: Dante takes the floor in the Council of One Hundred to oppose military aid for Pope Boniface VIII. **October**: Dante is sent to Rome as an ambassador to Boniface VIII (probably). **1 November**: Charles de Valois arrives in Florence as the Pope's 'peace envoy'. **4 November**: Corso Donati re-enters Florence and unleashes three days of destructive vengeance on the White party.
1302	**27 January**: Dante is accused *in absentia* of corruption and fined 5,000 florins and banishment for two years. **February**: White exiles meet in Gargonza. **10 March**: Dante's sentence increased to death. **8 June**: Dante is mentioned as being with

	other White exiles in San Godenzo. **October**: Pietro Petrarch (Francesco Petrarch's father) is exiled from Florence.
1303	Spring defeats of White alliance at Mugello. French states general support for king against the Pope. **June**: Boniface VIII indicted by King Philip IV of France on twenty-nine counts. **7 September**: At Anagni Boniface VIII is captured by French forces in his palace. Later released. Florentine decree condemning Dante's sons to exile when they reach the age of 14. **12 October**: Boniface VIII dies. **October 22**: Benedict XI elected.
1304	**17 March**: Cardinal Niccolò da Prato sent by Pope to Florence to heal divisions. **May**: Dante arrives at Arrezzo. **June**: Cardinal Niccolò da Prato leaves Florence, his mission having failed. **10 June**: Riots and fire in Florence. Cavalcanti houses destroyed. **20 July**: Abortive attack on Florence by White exiles. **July**: Benedict XI dies leaving a vacancy for eleven months. Dante writes *De Vulgari Eloquentia*, his history of language.
1305	**June**: Pope Clement V elected.
1307	**13 October**: Arrest of Knights Templar by Philip the Fair.
1308	Corso Donati killed by Florence. **November**: Henry VII (of Luxembourg) elected Holy Roman Emperor.
1309	Dante writes *de Monarchia*, an explanation of the roles of Church and Empire.
1310	Emperor Henry VII arrives in Italy; Dante writes a letter in praise.
1311	**6 January**: Henry VII is crowned king of Italy in Milan; Dante probably present. **31 March**: Dante writes to 'wicked Florentines' (Letter 6).
1312	Dante living in Verona as part of court of Cangrande della Scala. **29 June**: Henry VII is crowned in Rome at church of St John Lateran. **19 September**: Henry VII 'besieges' Florence.
1313	**24 August**: Henry VII leaves Florence and dies on the way to Naples. Birth of Giovanni Boccaccio.
1314	**20 April**: Pope Clement V dies; John XXII elected August 1316. **29 November**: Philip IV (the Fair), king of France, dies; his son Louis X ('the quarrelsome') king.
1315	**19 May**: Proposed pardon for political offenders from Florence; Dante responds with Letter 9. **15 October**: Renewal of death sentence on Dante.

1318	Dante is in Ravenna as the guest of Guido Novello da Polenta; conducts correspondence with the humanist Giovanni del Virgilio.
1320	**20 January**: Dante reads his paper, *Questio de Aqua et Terra*, in Verona.
1321	**August**: Dante travels to Venice on a diplomatic mission for Guido Novello; he catches fever on the way back to Ravenna. **13 August**: Dante dies; Guido Novello da Polenta has him buried with full honours in the church of St Francis, Ravenna.

APPENDIX

THE BEGINNING
OF CANTO 1

Even for a reader who does not speak Italian, it is worth looking at some lines of the *Comedy* in the original. It is easy to note the aba bcb cdc triplet pattern of rhymes. The lines are also noticeably short, much shorter than the Latin verse of Virgil that Dante so admired. Dante's language too is direct and simple, even when he is talking about very abstract things. If you know some French, Spanish or Latin it is possible to make your way through the text relatively easily. This translation is by Longfellow and it helpfully follows the lines quite accurately, even though the language is sometimes a little old fashioned. Dante, of course, did not sound old fashioned to his contemporaries, even though they might have sometimes described the verse as 'poetic'.

Nel mezzo del camin di nostra vita
ni ritrovai per una selva oscura,
hé la diritta via era smarrita.

  Ah quanto a dir qual era è cosa dura
sta selva selvaggia e aspra e forte
he nel pensier rinova la paura!

  Tant' è amara che poco è piu morte;
na per trattar del ben ch'i' vi trovai,
lirò de l'altre cose ch'i' v'ho scorte.

  Io non so ben ridir com' i' v'entrai,
ant' era pieno di sonno a quel punto

Midway upon the journey of our life
I found myself within a forest dark,
For the straightforward pathway had been lost.

  Ah me! how hard a thing it is to say
What was this forest savage, rough, and stern,
Which in the very thought renews the fear.

  So bitter is it, death is little more;
But of the good to treat, which there I found,
Speak will I of the other things I saw there.

  I cannot well repeat how there I entered,
So full was I of slumber at the moment

che la verace via abbandonai.

Ma poi ch'i' fui al piè d'un colle giunto,
là dove terminava quella valle
che m'avea di paura il cor compunto,

guardai in alto e vidi le sue spalle
vestite già de' raggi del pianeta
che mena dritto altrui per ogne calle.

Allor fu la paura un poco queta,
che nel lago del cor m'era durata
la notte ch'i' passai con tanta pieta.

E come quei che con lena affannata,
uscito fuor del pelago a la riva,
si volge all'acqua perigliosa e guata,

così l'animo mio, ch'ancor fuggiva,
si volse a retro a rimirar lo passo
che non lasciò già mai persona viva.

Poi ch'èi posato un poco il corpo lasso,
ripresi via per la piaggia diserta,
sì che 'l piè fermo sempre era 'l più basso.

Ed ecco, quasi al cominciar de l'erta,
una lonza leggiera e presta molto,
che di pel macolato era coverta;

e non mi si partia dinanzi al volto,
anzi 'mpediva tanto il mio cammino,
ch'i' fui per ritornar più volte vòlto.

In which I had abandoned the true way.

But after I had reached a mountain's foot,
At that point where the valley terminated,
Which had with consternation pierced my hea[r]

Upward I looked, and I beheld its shoulders,
Vested already with that planet's rays
Which leadeth others right by every road.

Then was the fear a little quieted
That in my heart's lake had endured throughou[t]
The night, which I had passed so piteously.

And even as he, who, with distressful breath,
Forth issued from the sea upon the shore,
Turns to the water perilous and gazes;

So did my soul, that still was fleeing onward,
Turn itself back to re-behold the pass
Which never yet a living person left.

After my weary body I had rested,
The way resumed I on the desert slope,
So that the firm foot ever was the lower.

And lo! almost where the ascent began,
A panther light and swift exceedingly,
Which with a spotted skin was covered o'er!

And never moved she from before my face,
Nay, rather did impede so much my way,
That many times I to return had turned.

NOTES

1. Vision

1 *Vita Nuova*, II.
2 www.vps.it.
3 'Dante and Beatrice', Walker Art Gallery, Liverpool.
4 *Vita Nuova*, III.
5 Ibid., IV.
6 Ibid.
7 Ibid.
8 Ibid.

3. The Glorious Lady of My Mind

1 *Vita Nuova*, I.
2 Ibid., II.
3 Ibid.

4. The Road to Campaldino

1 *Vita Nuova*, IV.

5. The Followers of Love

1   J.G. Nichols (trans.), *The New Life*, Hesperus, 2003.
2   All Cavalcanti translations are by Lowrie Nelson. *The Poems of Guido Cavalcanti*, Garland Publishing, 1986.

6. 'You, However, Are Not'

1   *Vita Nuova*, XII.
2   Ibid.
3   Ibid.
4   Ibid., XII, *Piangete, amanti, poi che piange.*

7. The Name of Beatrice

1   From Asin Palacios, *Dakhair*, 21–85.
2   *Maria*, West Side Story, lyric by Stephen Sondheim.

8. Lamentations

1   Boccaccio, Biography of Dante, III.
2   *Convivio*, III, 1–3.
3   Ibid., III, iv 19.

9. Ordinances of Justice

1   Dino Compagni, Chronicle, p. 15.
2   *Convivio*, II, *Voi, che 'ntendendo il terzo ciel movete.*
3   *Paradiso*, 8:55.
4   Dino Compagni, Chronicle, p. 18.
5   *Convivio*, I xi.
6   *Paradiso*, 18:92.

10. Two Suns ──────────────────────────

1 *Purgatorio*, 16:97.
2 Régistres de Boniface VIII, in Boase, p. 11.
3 Ibid.
4 *Inferno*, 19:90–114.

11. Invention ──────────────────────────

1 Psalms 90:10.
2 For details see Boyde, *Philomythos*, p. 163.
3 *Annales Casenates*, RR II. SS, in Boase, p. 164.
4 Acts 8:20.
5 *Unam Sanctam.*
6 Ibid.
7 Pope Boniface VIII, Letter to the Florentine Signoria, 1299.
8 *Vita Nuova*, XXXVIII, *Contra questo avversario de la ragione.*

12. Exterior. A Dark Wood – Day ──────────────

1 *Inferno*, 32:6.
2 *Paradiso*, 10:43.
3 *Inferno*, 25:46.
4 Ibid., 1:79.
5 Ibid., 1:112.
6 Ibid., 1:136.
7 Ibid., 2:53.
8 Ibid., 2:62.
9 Ibid., 2:127–9.
10 Ibid., 2:142.
11 See Reynolds.

13. The Black, the White and the Neutral ──────────

1 *Inferno*, 3:57, most famously quoted in Eliot's *The Wasteland*.
2 *Inferno*, 3:64–7.

3   Ibid., 4:46.
4   Ephesians 4:8.
5   *Inferno*, 4:104.
6   Ibid., 5:121.
7   Ibid., 6:7.
8   Boccaccio, *Decameron*, ix, 8.

14.   The Fight for Peace

1   *Inferno*, 8:45.
2   Ibid., 8:93.
3   Ibid., 9:4–6.
4   Ibid., 9:27.
5   Ibid., 10:22–7.
6   Ibid., 10:5.
7   Ibid., 10:61.
8   Ibid., 10:67.
9   Dino Compagni, Chronicle, I, p. 24.

15.   Natural Justice

1   *Inferno*, 13:40.
2   Ibid., 15:81.
3   Ibid., 15:55.
4   Hollander, Reynolds.
5   *Inferno*, 15:124.
6   Ibid., 17:3.
7   Ibid., 19:10.
8   Dino Compagni, Chronicle, p. 38.
9   Ibid., p. 39.

16.   The Place Where Forces Meet

1   *Purgatorio*, 20:43.
2   Dino Compagni, Chronicle, p. 43.
3   *Inferno*, 34:25.

4   Ibid., 33:43–9.
5   Ibid., 33:73–5.
6   Dino Compagni, Chronicle, p. 45.
7   *Inferno*, 34:68.
8   Ibid., 34:136–9.

17.   I Am Beatrice

1   *Purgatorio*, 27:18.
2   Ibid., 30:51.
3   Ibid., 33:142–5.
4   *Convivio*, 1.3.4–5.
5   Boccaccio, Biography of Dante, Ch. 5.
6   Ibid.

18.   A Party of One

1   Dino Compagni, p. 66.
2   Villani, Chronicle, p. 71.
3   *Inferno*, 10:79–81.
4   *Paradiso*, 14:25.
5   Ibid., 14:67.
6   The ninth-century astronomer known as Alfraganus in the West.
7   *Paradiso*, 14:79–84.
8   Ibid., 16:1.
9   Ibid., 17:61–6.

19.   Things Can Only Get Better

1   *Purgatorio*, 20:93.
2   *Paradiso*, 17:85–90.
3   Ibid., 19:7.
4   Dante, Letter 7.
5   Quoted in Havely, *Dante*.
6   *Paradiso*, 21:86.
7   Ibid., 25:6.

8   Ibid., 26:64.
9   Ibid., 26:58.

20. The Starry Dynamo in the Machinery of Night ⸺⸺⸺

1   *Paradiso*, 27:106–8.
2   Ibid., 27:109–11.
3   Ibid., 27:112–4.
4   *Vita Nuova*, XLI.
5   Villani, Chronicle, VIII.
6   *Paradiso*, 28:4.
7   Ibid., 4:40–8.
8   Dante, Letter 12.
9   *Paradiso*, 29:85.
10   Ibid., 29:142.
11   Ibid., 30:16.
12   Ibid., 30:121.
13   Ibid., 33:22–7.
14   Lao Zi, Dao De Jing, traditional paraphrase.
15   *Paradiso*, 33:118.

21.   The Ocean and the Land ⸺⸺⸺⸺⸺

1   Boccaccio, Biography of Dante, Ch. 7.

BIBLIOGRAPHY

Primary Sources

Works by Dante

There is, of course, no such thing as a perfect translation, especially of poetry, but there are numerous very good translations of the *Comedy* into English which can open the door to Dante's world almost completely. I have listed some useful ones here for anybody who wishes to explore his works further.

Divine Comedy

Musa, Mark (trans.), *The Divine Comedy*, 3 vols, Penguin, 1984.
Sinclair, John D., *The Divine Comedy*, 3 vols, Oxford University Press, 1961.

Vita Nuova

Anderson, William (trans.), *Vita Nuova*, Penguin, 1964.
Nichols, J.G. (trans.), *The New Life*, London, Hesperus, 2003.

Lyric Poetry

Foster, K. & Boyde, P. (trans.), *Dante's Lyric Poetry*, Oxford, 1967.

Convivio

Lansing, Richard H., *Dante's Il Convivio (The Banquet)*, New York, London, 1990.

De Vulgari Eloquentia

Botterill, Steven (ed.), *De Vulgari Eloquentia*, Cambridge, 1996.

Letters

Toynbee, Paget (trans. & ed.), *Dantis Aligherii Epistolae. The Letters of Dante*, Oxford, Clarendon Press, 1920.

Monarchia

Shaw, Prue (trans. & ed.), *Monarchia*, Cambridge University Press, 1995.
Wicksteed, P.H. (trans.), *The De Monarchia*, Oxford University Press, 1896.

Eclogues

Brewer, Wilmon (trans.), *Dante's Eclogues*, Francestown (New Hampshire), Marshall Jones Company, 1961.

Questio de Aqua et Terra

Shadwell, Charles Lancelot (trans.), *Questio de Aqua et Terra*, Oxford, Clarendon Press, 1909.

The Princeton Dante Project website at http://etcweb.princeton.edu/dante/index.html contains English translations of all Dante's works, including Robert Hollander's excellent rendering of the *Comedy*, as well as Italian and Latin texts.

Other Works

This list gives English translations where possible.

Alighieri, Pietro, *Comentum Super Poema Comedie Dantis: A Critical Edition of Pietro Alighieri's Commentary on Dante's the Divine Comedy*, ed. Massimiliano Chiamenti, Arizona Center for Medieval and Renaissance Studies, July 2003.

Boccaccio, Giovanni, *Life of Dante*, trans. J.G. Nichols, London, Hesperus, 2002.

Bruni, Leonardo, *History of the Florentine People*, trans. & ed. James Haskins, Harvard University Press, 2001.

———, *Life of Dante, see* Wicksteed.

Cavalcanti, Guido, *Poems*, trans. Lowry Nelson, Garland Publishing, 1986.

Compagni, Dino, *Chronicle of Florence*, trans. Daniel E. Bornstein, University of Pennsylvania Press, 1986.

da Imola, Benvenuto, *Comentum super Dantis Aldighierii Comoediam*, ed. Lacaita, Florence, 1887.

Latini, Brunetto, *Livres de Trésor*, ed. R.A. Nicholson, London, 1911.

Smith, Robinson (trans.), *The Earliest Lives of Dante in English*, New York, Holt, 1901.

Villani, Filippo, *Life of Dante*, *see* Wicksteed.

Villani, Giovanni, *Chronicle: Selections from the first nine books of the Croniche Fiorentine of Giovanni Villani*, trans. Rose E. Selfe, Archibald Constable, 1896.

Vitalis, Oderic, *Ecclesiastical History*, trans. Marjorie Chibnall, Oxford, Clarendon Press, 1969.

Wicksteed, P.H., *The Early Lives of Dante*, London, Moring, 1904.

Select Secondary Sources

Alta, Macadam, *Florence (Blue Guide)*, Adam & Charles Black, 2001.

Anderson, William, *Dante the Maker*, Ebury Press, 1989.

Aroux, Eugene, *Dante, Hérétique, Révolutionnaire et Socialiste: Révélations d'un Catholique sur le Moyen Age*, Paris, 1854.

Auerbach, Erich, *Dante, Poet of the Secular World*, trans. R. Manheim, Chicago, 1961.

Barber, Malcolm, *The Trial of the Templars*, Cambridge University Press, 1978.

Barbi, M., *Vita de Dante*, trans. P. Ruggiers as *Life of Dante*, Notre Dame, Notre Dame University Press, 1997.

Becker, Marvin B., *Florence in Transition*, Baltimore, 1967.

Bemrose, Stephen, *A New Life of Dante*, University of Exeter, 1988.

———, *Dante's Angelic Intelligences*, Rome, Edizione di Storia e Letturatura, 1983.

Borsook, Eve, *The Companion Guide to Florence*, Companion Guides, 2001.

Bosco Umberto (ed.), *Enciclopedia Dantesca*, Rome, Instituto dell'Enciclopedia Italiana, 1970–78.

Boswell, John E., *Dante and the Sodomites*, Dante Studies No 112, 1994, pp. 63–76.

Bowsky, William, *Henry VII in Italy*, Lincoln, Nebraska, 1960.

Boyde, Patrick, *Human Vices and Human Worth in Dante's Comedy*, Cambridge University Press, 2000.

————, *Dante Philomythes and Philosopher: Man in the Cosmos*, Cambridge University Press, 1983.

————, *Perception and Passion in Dante's Comedy*, Cambridge University Press, 2006.

Brucker, Gene Adam, *Florence (1138–1737)*, London, Sidgewick & Jackson, 1984.

Burge, James, *Heloise and Abelard*, Profile, 2003.

Catholic Encyclopaedia, www.newadvent.org/cathen/.

Chittick, William C., *Ibn 'Arabi*, Oxford, Oneworld Publications, 2005.

Copleston, Frank, *A History of Medieval Philosophy*, London, Methuen, 1972.

————, *Aquinas*, Penguin, 1991.

Davidsohn, Robert, *Geschichte von Florenz*, Berlin, Mittler und Sohn, 1896–1927.

Dronke, Peter, *Dante and Medieval Latin Traditions*, Cambridge University Press, 1986.

————, *Dante's Second Love*, Exeter, Society for Italian Studies, 1997.

————, *Francesca and Heloise, Comparative Literature*, Vol. 27, No 2, 1975, pp. 113–35.

Dunbabin, Jean, 'Treason Sodomy and the fate of Adenolfo IV Count of Acerra' in *Journal of Medieval History* 34, 2008, pp. 417–37.

Fergusson, Francis, *Dante*, London, Collier-Macmillan, 1966.

Gombrich, E.H., 'Giotto's Portrait of Dante?' in *The Burlington Magazine*, Vol. 121, No 917, Aug. 1979, pp. 471–83.

Harrison, Robert Pogue, *The Body of Beatrice*, Johns Hopkins, 1988.

Havely, Nick, *Dante*, Blackwell, 2007.

Holbrook, Richard Thayer, *Dante and the Animal Kingdom*, New York, Columbia University Press, 1902.

Hollander, Robert, *Dante: A Life in Works*, Yale University Press, 2001.

————, 'Dante's Harmonious Homosexuals', Electronic Bulletin of the Dante Society of America, June 1996.

Holloway, Julia Bolton, *Brunetto Latini: An Analytic Bibliography*, London, Grant and Cutler, 1986.

Holmes, George, *Dante*, Oxford University Press, 1980.

Jacoff, Rachel (ed.), *The Cambridge Companion to Dante*, Cambridge University Press, 1993.

Lansing, Richard, *The Dante Encyclopaedia*, New York, Garland, 2000.

Lindberg, David, *The Beginnings of Western Science*, Chicago University Press, 1992.

Martines, Lauro, *Lawyers and Statecraft in Renaissance Florence*, Princeton University Press, 1968.

Moore, Edward, *Time References in the Divina Comedia*, London, David Nutt, 1887.

———, 'The Astronomy of Dante', in *Studies in Dante*, Oxford, Clarendon Press, 1896–1917.

Preyer, Brenda, 'Two Cerchi Palaces in Florence', in *Studies in Honor of Craig Hugh Smyth*, ed. A. Morrogh, Florence, 1985.

Oerter, Herbert L., *Campaldino 1289, Speculum 43*, 1968, pp. 429–50.

Ohler, Norbert, *The Medieval Traveller*, Woodbridge, Boydell, 1989.

Palacios, Miguel Asin, *Islam and the Divine Comedy*, trans. Sutherland, Frank Cass and Company, 1968.

Petrocchi, Giorgio, *Vita di Dante*, Roma, Laterza, 1983.

Piattoli, Renato (ed.), *Codice diplomatico dantesco*, Florence, 1950.

Reynolds, Barbara, *Dante: The Poet, the Political Thinker, the Man*, I.B. Tauris, 2007.

Shaw, James Eustace, *The Lady 'Philosophy' in the Convivio*, Cambridge, 1938.

Toynbee, Paget, revised Singleton, *A Dictionary of Proper Names and Notable Matters in the Works of Dante*, Oxford, 1968.

Tuchman, Barbara, *A Distant Mirror*, Penguin, 1978.

Villari, Pasquale, *The First Two Centuries of Florentine History*, trans. Linda Villari, London, T Fisher Unwin, 1908.

LIST OF ILLUSTRATIONS

INDEX

ACKNOWLEDGEMENTS

Thanks must go first of all to the many friends and family members who gave support and encouragement during the long gestation period of this book. For specific discussions about the content of the book I must mention Professor Patrick Boyde, of Saint John's College, Cambridge, and Alexander Murray of University College Oxford, both of whom were generous enough to attempt to pass on some of their wisdom. Professor Sir Christopher Frayling, William Anderson, Tim Cawston and Crispin Dawes all have my gratitude for their invaluable help in understanding this story and for preventing me from making a fool of myself. My thanks to J.G. Nichols for permission to use his excellent translations of the *Vita Nuova* poems and to Janet Nelson Friedell for permission to use the Cavalcanti translations of her brother Lowry Nelson. Thanks also to Stuart Biles, Simon Hamlet, Ross Britton and Mark Beynon of The History Press, to Richard Foreman and his angelic host for their tireless efforts and, of course, to my wife Kate for all her support. Finally I am indebted, as ever, to my friend and agent, Sheila Ableman, who never abandoned hope.